For my family, Martin, Ena, Mary,
Catriona, Helena
and for Donal
Loves old and new.

With admiration, love and appreciation
for my first and best teacher, Mary Cregan Kieran,
and for John, John óg, Brigid, Patrick, Michael and Meabh
who continually make learning an adventure.

C⊙NTENTS

ABBREVIATIONS

References to Church Documents will be by the following abbreviations, often based on the Latin title.

AN: *Aetatis Novae*: Dawning of a New Era (Pontifical Council for Social Communications, 1992).

AG: *Ad Gentes Divinitus*: The Decree on the Church's Missionary Activity (Vatican II, 1965).

CA: *Centesimus Annus* (John Paul II, 1991).

CCC: Catechism of the Catholic Church (John Paul II, 1992).

CPMS: Consecrated Persons and their Mission in Schools (Congregation for Catholic Education, 2002).

CS: The Catholic School (Congregation for Catholic Education, 1977).

CSTTM: The Catholic School on the Threshold of the Third Millennium (Congregation for Catholic Education, 1997).

CT: *Catechesi Tradendae*; On Catechesis in our Time (John Paul II, 1979).

DES: The Department of Education and Science.

DH: *Dignitatis Humanae*: The Declaration on Religious Liberty (Vatican II, 1965).

DV: *Dei Verbum*: The Dogmatic Constitution on Divine Revelation (Vatican II, 1965).

EN: *Evangelii Nuntiandi:* On Evangelisation in the Modern World (Paul VI, 1975).

FR: *Fides et Ratio:* Faith and Reason (John Paul II, 1998).

GE: *Gravissimum Educationis:* The Declaration on Christian Education (Vatican II, 1965).

GDC: General Directory for Catechesis (1997).

GS: *Gaudium et Spes:* The Pastoral Constitution on the Church in the Modern World (Vatican II, 1965).

LCS Lay Catholics in Schools: Witnesses to Faith (Congregation for Catholic Education, 1982).

LE: *Laborem Exercens: On* Human Work (John Paul II, 1981).

LG: *Lumen Gentium;* The Dogmatic Constitution on the Church (Vatican II, 1964).

NA: *Nostra Aetate:* The Declaration on the Church's Relations with non-Christian Religions (Vatican II, 1965).

RDECS: The Religious Dimension of Education in the Catholic School (Congregation for Catholic Education, 1988).

RBOC: Rite of Baptism for One Child (Sacred Congregation for Divine Worship, 1969).

SRS: *Sollicitudo Rei Socialis* (John Paul II, 1987).

UR: *Unitatis Redintegratio:* The Decree on Ecumenism (Vatican II, 1964).

PREFACE

● ●

*Those who teach others unto justice shall shine like the
stars for ever
(Daniel 12:3).*

The university education of primary school teachers is a
privileged responsibility and an exciting challenge. This task is
even more stimulating in light of the growing recognition of
the importance of high quality religious education in an era
characterised by globalisation, pluralism, and the growth of
fundamentalist religion in general. The book had its genesis in
a conversation between two lecturers in religious education at
the two largest colleges of education in Ireland: St. Patrick's
College, Dublin and Mary Immaculate College, Limerick. Out
of that conversation a mutual dissatisfaction at the lack of
suitable material on the topic of religious education at the
primary level, for students and professionals in the field,
emerged.

There is clearly a deficit of serious and sustained academic
literature and research into the history, context, nature,
theoretical foundations of, and contemporary issues in
religious education at the primary level. This book aims to

respond to this deficit by giving an overview and critical analysis of some major aspects of Catholic religious education in Irish primary schools. Each chapter is dedicated to a central and highly relevant foundational or contemporary issue in primary religious education.

Children, Catholicism and Primary Religious Education is intended mainly for student teachers who are studying religious education at undergraduate or postgraduate level in the Catholic colleges of education. It provides these university students with a perspective on primary religious education that fits with the Irish context and takes account of Irish educational history. The book should also appeal to professionals involved with or interested in religious education. This would include primary and post-primary diocesan advisors; primary school teachers, and post- primary religion teachers; professionals involved in parish-based catechesis; postgraduate students engaging in research in education at primary level; Catholic primary school managers; parents; bishops; priests and last but by no means least, academics involved in teaching and researching the subject area of religious education and catechesis in the Irish primary school.

There is increasing recognition of the need for curriculum change in the area of primary religious education. The development of a new syllabus for religious education in Catholic primary schools (2006) is one attempt to respond to this need. This book should be of benefit to all those who wish to contribute to the debate on the future of primary religious education in general in the years ahead.

In this book we have written from our own perspectives as individual scholars. While we have read and responded to one another's chapters, each reflects the author's own particular point of view. In this sense each of these chapters represents one attempt to outline research in the field of primary religious education and to articulate some of the challenges faced by primary teachers at present. The book is a contribution to the sort of pluralistic conversation which we believe is the only way forward in this field.

Throughout the project, we have had the support and help of many people.

Anne: My friend and head of department, Raymond Topley was a constant source of encouragement and support throughout. His fine judgement and editorial skill were of tremendous help in the completion of the project and for this I offer my deepest thanks. I also wish to express my gratitude to Rev. Joseph McCann and to Rev. Fachtna McCarthy who gave direct feedback on draft chapters. I thank my sister Helena, my friend Piaras, and my colleagues Aida, Carol, Paula and Seán, who were encouraging companions throughout the writing process. Finally, I thank my co-writer Patricia for convincing me to take on this project! It has been a new and challenging process for me and it would not have happened without her wisdom, infectious enthusiasm and considerable theological and educational expertise. I was blessed by her companionship in writing this book together.

Patricia: I would like to thank my wise conversation partner and co-writer Anne for her patient, encouraging, critical scholarship. I wish to thank my colleagues at Mary Immaculate College who provided a lively forum for debate and a high standard of scholarship around so many of the issues that were voiced in this book. My sincere thanks go to my esteemed colleagues and friends in religious education, especially to Eileen Lenihan who, as always, gave graciously of her time and expertise. I also wish to thank Eleanor Gormally for her pioneering work as well as Anne O' Leary, Nessa Ni Argadain and Fiona McSorley for their support, clear observations and helpful comments. Huge thanks go to my colleagues in the Education Department at Mary Immaculate College in particular to Tony Lyons whose high standard of scholarship is matched by his kindness, to Jim Deegan whose valuable research challenged my assumptions about religion and education, to Teresa O'Doherty who is an inspirational leader and to Delia O' Connor for just being Delia. I would also like to thank Dermot Lane who set me out on a theological trail many years ago and to Joseph Laishley who journeyed with me. Finally nothing I say could express a scintilla of my thanks to John Mc Donagh whose razor sharp mind, sense of fun and appetite for life made writing this book a positive adventure.

We thank Helen Carr and Daragh Reddin who have been not only wonderful editors but also encouraging friends throughout the writing process. Finally we thank Veritas Publications and in particular its director, Maura Hyland for agreeing to bring this book to publication.

Anne Hession
Patricia Kieran

FOREWORD

Thomas Groome

● ●

Almost forty years ago, I stumbled into my own life vocation as a religious educator and catechist. My first time on the teacher's side of the desk was in a boys' secondary school in the town of Carlow, in about 1967. I experienced it as a most demanding assignment, but I also loved it and began to wonder if it might not be what I should do with my life. And I did, one way or another, ever since.

To be a religious educator or catechist in the Ireland of those bygone days now seems much less challenging than in the Ireland of today. As I view it from the outside, but know it from the inside as well, Ireland is likely going through one of the most far reaching social transitions in its history; I can think of no social context that is more in flux at this time. The stakes are high for the future of its identity and whether or not it will reclaim and renew its spiritual roots or leave them behind – to its great impoverishment.

So, this is a most strategic and vital time to be a religious educator in Ireland. And, with the tree being in the seed, primary religious education is likely the most crucial arena of all. What daunting work, but I can't think of a more worthwhile one to be doing.

If I might summarise the challenge and how best to meet it, I'd say – in brief – that Christian religious education in Ireland today must lend young people a particular identity in Christian faith, but do so in ways that open them to diversity and appreciation, not just toleration, of 'the other'. As Jesus explained to disciples, within God's one family, there are many homes (see John 14: 2). We need to claim our own home but not in a hegemonic way as if no one else has a home except ourselves, or, as if people must belong to ours to be of God's family.

Indeed, we are eminently capable of forming people in Catholic or Protestant identity that is tragically sectarian. In this regard, our future absolutely cannot repeat our past. And yet, instead of the other extreme – falling into a paralysing relativism – we must ground people in the particular in ways that open them to the universal, to the universality of God's love (a dogma of Christian faith), of God's self disclosure, and of God's saving intent for all people.

Children, Catholicism and Religious Education by Anne Hession and Patricia Kieran will go a long way toward helping teachers, parents, pastors and anyone else who might have a hand in this good work to do it well. This is a sustained and scholarly reflection on the contemporary situation of Ireland, the history of its primary religious education, the purpose of Christian religious education at this time, and how best to go about it. Such a work could only be written by people steeped within the context and with both the scholarly resources and practical insights demanded to meet the challenge; Hession and Kieran have done it well. This book will go a long way toward helping all those concerned to do well what needs to be done by way of primary education in faith.

Years ago I learned an old *seanfhocal*, 'a quenching coal is easily lit'. May this book set a new fire to Christian religious education in postmodern Ireland. I am honoured to introduce it to you and strongly recommend that you read on.

Thomas H. Groome, Prof. Theology and Religious Education,
Boston College, and Director, BC's Institute of Religious
Education and Pastoral Ministry

CONTRIBUTORS

••••••••••••••••••••••••••••••••••

Anne Hession is a lecturer in religious education at St Patrick's College, Dublin. She wrote the introduction and chapters 1, 4, 5 and 6.

Dr Patricia Kieran is a lecturer in religous education at Mary Immaculate College, Limerick. She wrote chapters 2, 3, 7, 8 and the conclusion.

INTRODUCTION

● ●

Children, Catholicism and Primary Religious Education is a collection of essays on key topics and themes about which primary teachers should have some knowledge if they are to engage effectively in religious education at the primary level. It presents a critical and creative dialogue with the Roman Catholic religious tradition as a rich perspective from which to approach the task of religious education in contemporary Irish society. This introduction will clarify some key terms to be used in the book; it will reflect on the challenges and opportunities of the contemporary social, cultural, and political context of Catholic primary schools; and it will offer a brief overview of the topics to be addressed.

In this book Catholic refers to persons or communities, parishes, families, schools or religion programmes rooted in the Christian tradition of Roman Catholicism. Richard McBrien notes that 'Catholicism is not a reality that stands by itself. The word Catholic is a qualification of Christian, and Christian is a qualification of religious, and religious is a qualification of human.'[1] The Catholic perspective on the human condition is inspired by the revelation of scripture and by Church tradition. Catholics believe that human beings are created by God for a divine purpose and reach full human development in communion with others, with the created world and with the Divine.

Education involves the human development of persons in their own right and not just in their social, cultural or economic roles. Therefore education offers a picture of human nature and of human development in the light of which certain kinds of learning are particularly important. Catholicism proposes a holistic picture of full human development for education, one that embraces the physical, intellectual, affective, aesthetic, spiritual, moral and religious development of the person. Further, Catholic education is based on the conviction that the ultimate foundations of education are spiritual, in so far as all learning inevitably asks questions of ultimate meaning, goodness and truth, and of the human person's stance towards them. Hence Catholics maintain that education has an essential *religious* dimension and they seek to develop a holistic approach to education that enables people to explore this dimension to the full.

Catholic primary schools are set up under the auspices of the Roman Catholic Church in Ireland. The *Management Board Members' Handbook* for primary schools states that:

> A Roman Catholic School (which is established in connection with the Minister) aims at promoting the full and harmonious development of all aspects of the person of the pupil: intellectual, physical, cultural, moral and spiritual, including a living relationship with God and with other people. The school models and promotes a philosophy of life inspired by belief in God and in the life, death and resurrection of Jesus Christ. The

Catholic school provides Religious education for the pupils in accordance with the doctrines, practices and tradition of the Roman Catholic Church and promotes the formation of pupils in the Catholic Faith.[2]

Currently, 92.7 per cent of schools in the Republic of Ireland are denominationally Catholic.[3] However, in the general scheme of things, it can be expected that schools differ widely in the extent to which they could be said to reflect distinctively Catholic values, beliefs and attitudes. Such values are embodied in the interaction and relationships between the people in the school, which creates a particular spirit or ethos, that is, a way of being and acting that becomes the norm for behaviour, reactions, decisions and approaches to people and events. The existence of a Catholic ethos in schools depends largely on the willingness of teachers, parents and management to engage in ongoing conversation about the beliefs, values, attitudes and ways of acting they wish to promote in the school. Out of this shared understanding different embodiments of the values cherished by that particular community emerge, creating a style of education that is faithful to the Catholic tradition at its best. While acknowledging that a wide variety of Catholic schools exist in practice, the authors of this book assume that the Catholic tradition offers an important perspective on the educational task in contemporary Irish society. Moreover the book is written in the belief that Catholicism has a strong contribution to make to the debate on the future of primary religious education in the years ahead.

The family, the school and the local parish share the task of religiously educating believers in the Christian community. To write a book that purports to be about the Catholic approach to religious education is therefore a particularly challenging task. The Catholic school is only *one* agency of the Church's educational mission. Therefore reflections on the religious dimension of education in Catholic schools should always be situated within the wider context of the parish and the family. Furthermore, the development of a clear pastoral plan for evangelisation and catechesis in all contexts, by the Catholic Church in Ireland, would facilitate discussion on the kinds of religious education appropriate to the contemporary school context. This book offers a contribution to much needed debate around this issue.

It is generally accepted that there are many different activities simultaneously occurring in the Catholic primary school under the umbrella term 'religious education'. On the one hand religious education is a distinct subject on the primary school curriculum, one of seven curricular areas. On the other hand it is widely recognised that religious education extends beyond the classroom-centred religious education lesson and is ultimately an expression of the distinctive spirit or ethos of the school. Louis Dupré's plea for religious inspired education explains the Catholic view:

> 'No amount of practical pressure should force us to surrender learning completely to the functional demands of the moment. The Catholic school should remain a preserve of wonder, a place where nothing can be taken for granted, where each subject should become a source of surprise. To state this is not to adopt a tactical position taken for its expected advantages for the implantation of religious beliefs. No, the religious attitude itself begins with an ability to detect the wonder of Being in each encounter with reality. A God who is only a God of religion is no God at all. His real

presence in the educational process is manifest, not primarily, as subject of a particular discipline but in a particular attitude toward learning as a whole. Hence one might consider it one of the main objectives of the Catholic school to dereligionize our faith by extending the religious attitude beyond the limits of sacred doctrine to all areas of existence.'[4]

Notwithstanding the above quotation, this book focuses largely on religious education as a distinct subject in the primary-school curriculum. At the same time it assumes that questions relating to religious education as a curriculum subject cannot be divorced from an understanding of the wider denominational context of the Catholic school. Furthermore, the approach taken recognises that religious education must be addressed from both theological and educational viewpoints: both are needed to develop a pedagogy that honours the integrity both of the Catholic religion and of the education process. Finally, this book assumes that religious education is not homogenous and that the type of educational activity appropriate to contemporary Catholic schools depends on the faith of the teachers, children, parents, and larger school community as well as on the educational principles being followed.

There is no doubt that the religious, socio-cultural and political context within which Catholic primary religious education is carried out is in a period of transition. This finds expression in increasing pluralism, new management structures for Catholic schools, changing patterns of religious commitment among pupils, parents and school staff, a new primary school curriculum (1999), a new national catechetical programme

(*Alive-O*: 1996-2005), a new syllabus for Catholic primary religious education (2006-7) and a National Catechetical Directory (2006). Furthermore, the Irish Roman Catholic Church is undergoing an enormously painful process of reconstruction at the present time. Catholics are becoming acutely aware of the ways in which Catholic communities have failed in the past to live up to their best ideals and traditions of faith. Clearly, a recognition and repentance of sins, personal and communal, is needed for the integrity of Christian faith at this time.

Ireland is fast becoming a culturally, ethnically and religiously diverse society with the attendant enrichment and challenges that such swift cultural and social change brings. Pluralism describes a situation in which there is a variety of different beliefs and meaning systems (interpretations of reality), cultures, and religions. This new cultural situation calls for approaches to religious education that show greater sensitivity to the way in which religious identities are formed. The question is whether it is possible to forge a religious identity that is distinct and yet open to transformation in dialogue with worldviews and traditions different from one's own. The temptation of a conservative, even fundamentalist retrenchment into an idealised notion of 'Catholic' faith must be avoided, as must a naïve understanding that religious and cultural harmony can be achieved by a withdrawal from or a diminishment of the richness and complexity of different religious traditions and beliefs.

What is needed today more than ever is a strong sense of what one's tradition is. Children need a deep but open and flexible grounding in their own tradition if they are truly to appreciate other traditions and worldviews. It is difficult to have an appreciation for the complexity of someone else's tradition if one's own is unknown. Honouring the particularity of one's own religion is not opposed to valuing pluralism. Indeed pluralism depends on diverse communities enriching and building up their own unique identity. Education for responsible diversity involves celebrating difference so that one is able to engage in a genuine encounter with people whose worldview differs from one's own.

The biggest shift in primary religious education over the past thirty years has been a shift from an emphasis on teaching children to think *about* God to entering into the language or experience of God. The focus has moved from what was essentially theology for children to a focus on the process through which children learn the art of Christian religious knowing as a means to most effectively engage with and explore human existence and the presence of God within it. Viewed in this way the biggest challenge facing religious educators is finding ways to teach the creative potential of religious symbols and religious language to children. This requires that teachers reject neither the experience nor the content of religious faith as the starting point of religious education. They do however have to pay more attention to the ways in which children are interpreting the Christian story so as to make meaning for their lives and to how they relate the gospel to the understanding of human life presumed by media and by popular culture.

The Second Vatican Council (1962-65) brought about a significant change in the self-understanding of Catholicism and hence of Catholic education. The Church called, in its decree on ecumenism, for dialogue between the Christian Churches, declaring that division among Christian Churches 'openly contradicts the will of Christ, provides a stumbling-block to the world and inflicts damage on... the case of proclaiming the good news'.[5] Furthermore, the Church encourages its members to enter into dialogue with members of non-

Christian religious communities, recognising that world religions such as Islam, Hinduism, Buddhism and Judaism 'often reflect a ray of that truth which enlightens all'.[6] The Church, we are told, 'rejects nothing which is true and holy in these religions.'[7] These declarations, endorsed in subsequent Church statements have far-reaching implications for the forms of religious education carried out in Catholic primary schools. Clearly the Vatican II vision of Catholic education remains to be implemented on the ground. The task is to build into the curriculum of religious education a clear educational philosophy in respect of diverse religious faiths. This philosophy and its ensuing approach should enable students to mature toward a dialectical faith stance whereby they are enabled to understand and respect the faiths of others while simultaneously deepening their understanding of and commitment to their own.

Clearly the socio-cultural context in which Catholic schooling is carried out today is quite complex. The nature of family life is changing and many children now encounter religious, cultural, and socio-economic diversity on a daily basis. In such a context it is important to articulate a vision of Catholic identity and of a Catholic approach to religious education that can serve as a guiding principle for teachers in Catholic schools. The extent to which this vision can be translated into the lived practice of education will differ greatly from place to place. Our main aim however is to offer one distinctive perspective on primary religious education. By presenting a Catholic vision for religious education we hope to contribute to the process whereby teachers, parents and school managers make informed choices about the form and future of religious education in Irish primary schools.

Structurally the book is in three parts. The first part outlines some of the background knowledge required by teachers engaged in religious education in Catholic primary schools. Chapter One aims to clarify some of the language used by teachers to describe the work of religious education. Ireland has been significantly influenced by the British and the American meanings of religious education, neither of which adequately describes the unique forms of religious education carried out in Irish Catholic primary schools. By introducing and defining terms such as religious education, religious instruction, catechesis, formation, and critical education, it is hoped that teachers will develop a language with which to engage in reflective debate and dialogue about the forms of religious education appropriate to primary schools today. The chapter closes with a brief outline of some of the tensions inherent to the task of religious education in contemporary Catholic primary schools. The aim here is not to rush to a premature resolution of these tensions, but rather to introduce the reader to the complexity of the debate on this issue.

The second chapter offers a summary of the Catholic Church's theological and philosophical vision for the religious dimension of education in Catholic schools. The chapter focuses in particular on Church documents since the Second Vatican Council (1962-65), which either inform Catholic education or which explicitly address it. A Catholic theology of education proposes that all education has a religious dimension. Seven 'defining principles' are identified as constituting this religious dimension: christocentricity, a distinct Catholic anthropology, the dialogue with contemporary culture, a mission to evangelise, a catechetical orientation, academic integrity and religious freedom. These aspects are explored as positive resources for a Catholic style of education in primary schools. The chapter also alerts the reader to the significant issues raised by these principles for teachers, pupils, parents and managers in primary schools. The issue of the kind of religious education most appropriate in the present cultural context is raised again as a question that needs urgent attention at this time.

The final chapter in this section outlines the main developments impacting upon religious education in the Irish national school system over the last two hundred years. The chapter begins by tracing the development of the mixed system of education in the nineteenth century. This is followed by an account of the gradual denominalisation and clericalisation of the teaching of religion in national schools, and of the way in which this denominational system was placed on a strong legal footing in the Irish Constitution of 1937. The chapter also outlines the various religious and secular authorities who are responsible for religious and ethical education curricula in contemporary Irish primary schools. Finally there follows an exploration of the catechetical methodologies used in Catholic national schools from the inception of the national school system in Ireland up to the twenty-first century. Catechisms were the dominant catechetical tool used until the late 1960s. The attempt to replace this doctrinal, transmissive mode of religious instruction was a strong impetus behind developments in catechesis over the past fifty years.

The second part of the book looks at some foundational themes and topics that constitute the professional knowledge base for primary teachers in Catholic schools. Normally teachers develop an informed theory of religious education in tandem with the ethos and best insights of their own religious traditions. In other words, teachers, as 'reflective practitioners', engage in critical reflection upon the commitments (educational, theological, philosophical) supporting their approach to religious education. Ideally, they will revise these commitments and theoretical understandings in the ongoing dialogue between theory and practice, throughout their teaching career.

The first chapter in this section outlines some foundational theory for Christian religious education, as this is the type of religious education carried out in Catholic primary schools. It examines some of the assumptions about knowledge, action and the nature of the educated individual that crucially affect the form that the Christian religion curriculum and its assessment take.

This is followed by a chapter on children as the subjects of Christian religious education in the primary school. Up until recent times children were largely regarded as empty vessels into which adult religious knowledge was poured. This approach ignored the unique and rich texture of children's spiritual and moral lives. This chapter summarises what the fields of theology, philosophy, psychology and sociology can bring to teachers' understanding of the cognitive, moral, social and spiritual capacities of children. At the heart of the chapter is a brief introduction to four contemporary approaches to the religious and spiritual education of children. The chapter as a whole demonstrates the extent to which Christian religious education aims to fulfil the potential of the whole child.

The final, third part of the book critically explores selective major challenges for Catholic primary religious education. Not least of these is the challenge of educating for a particular religious identity in a religiously diverse and increasingly secular society. Chapter Six sets the scene by exploring the nature of Catholic identity and what it means to educate for Catholic religious identity in a diverse, multi-religious society. Then, a number of contemporary challenges for religious educators are examined. These are globalisation, cultural change, media and communication technologies, educational disadvantage, and special education. The theory that Catholicism has within its own tradition some key resources and perspectives with which to address these challenges is proposed. This is not to say that these are the only challenges currently facing Catholic primary teachers, but the issues raised here do highlight areas of critical importance for the integrity of Catholic identity and hence of Catholic religious education today.

Perhaps the most urgent contemporary challenge to primary education is the issue of diversity. Chapter Seven explores diversity under three headings: (1) religious diversity, (2) diversity of school types and (3) ethnic and cultural diversity. First, Irish cultural and religious diversity both in the past and in the present is celebrated and explored. Then, the current approach to religious diversity in Catholic primary schools is examined and principles for inter-religious education in Catholic schools are outlined. 'Learning for inter-religious awareness' is proposed as an educational imperative for all children in primary schools. With regard to diversity of school types, the current structure of Irish primary education is examined in light of the principles of diversity of values and belief espoused in recent government legislation on education. Finally, the chapter focuses on Ireland's minority ethnic group, the Travelling people, and examines their spirituality and distinctive religious practices, as an example of how the Catholic religious tradition interacts with a distinct ethnic and cultural group to the mutual enhancement of both. Intercultural education is a particularly important aspect of religious education as it challenges racism and discrimination and celebrates cultural diversity in a context where children learn to cherish their own culture while simultaneously valuing and respecting that of others.

The final chapter examines gender issues and religious education. Topics examined here include gender theory, the dynamics of religious socialisation, the influence of patriarchy on the Christian religious tradition, and development in feminist theology and biblical studies which inform the work of religious educators. Particular attention is paid to the religous language and imagery introduced to children, and suggestions for a critical and creative feminist approach to religious education in the primary school are outlined.

To be called to educate is to bring something bigger than ourselves to the centre of our attention. If this book supports you in doing this it will have served its purpose well.

Anne Hession
Feast of St Anne
26 July 2005

NOTES

1   McBrien, Richard P., *Catholicism*, Revised Edition, San Francisco: HarperSanFrancisco, 1994, p. 1187.

2   Catholic Primary School Managers' Association, revised 2000, p. 16.

3   'INTO Survey on Teaching Religion in National Schools, 2002' in *Teaching Religion in the Primary School*, Dublin: Irish National Teachers' Organisation, 2003, p. 44.

4   Louis Dupré, 'Catholic Education and the Predicament of Modern Culture', *The Living Light*, (March 1988), pp. 302-303.

5   UR no. 3.

6   NA no. 2; GS no. 92.

7   NA, no. 2

CHAPTER ONE

Clearing the Ground: Religious Education in Catholic Primary Schools

• •

In all walks of life it is good to examine carefully what one is about. Similarly, primary teachers need to think about the kind of religious education that can be carried out in primary schools. This chapter attempts to 'clear the ground' for such reflection, by suggesting an educational language for primary religious education today. The chapter closes with some suggestions for the curriculum of religious education in Catholic primary schools. However, before we outline forms of religious education found in Catholic primary schools, we need to clarify what education is and what difference it makes to put the word 'religious' in front of the word 'education'.

DEFINING THE TERMS

Education

Education is the human practice of teaching and learning which seeks to sustain and enhance people's capacity to discover the meaning and significance of life and to develop as persons in community. Education fosters peoples' capacity to answer the questions: What is the truth? How do I know it is true? What does the truth mean? How should I live? What kind of person can I become? What kind of society should I help create? To what shall I commit myself? In other words, education enables students to decide what is true and what kind of human life it is good to lead. It does so by helping them to acquire intellectual, moral and religious virtues that enhance their own lives and those of their friends and communities.[1] Education fosters the maturity of pupils in a way that embraces their physical, intellectual, affective, aesthetic, spiritual, moral and religious development throughout their lives.

Religion

Education fosters the personal development of students. The realisation of the human spirit – spirituality – is an integral part of this process. Spirituality describes the way in which we pursue truth and goodness by relating to the reality of ourselves, other people, the universe and some source of value beyond and bigger than ourselves (for example, God). This source of ultimate value is often referred to as 'the Transcendent'. Spiritual development involves the ability to go beyond the conscious self in a movement towards other people, towards the world and towards this transcendent source. Religions enhance spiritual development by directing people's attention to an ultimate source of transcendence for their lives and by inviting them to explore different ways of knowing and being. Religions offer a particular vision of human life and of the goals of human development. They aim to bring human beings to the fullness of humanity by opening them up to the Transcendent.[2]

Religions challenge and invite people to adopt a certain vision of reality as that which is truly true or really real. They address the issue of human significance through challenging people with questions of meaning. In addition, religions offer an ideal of conduct and character to which people may aspire. They redefine what counts as human flourishing or development, often inviting adherents to engage in practices such as fasting, self-sacrifice, reflection and prayer as an integral part of human living. For instance, the Christian follower of Jesus is invited to live in a way that may not lead to the kind of success which the world espouses. It will however lead to true happiness and fulfilment with God, both in this world and in the next. The ultimate goal of Christian spiritual development is an ever-deepening relationship with God such that God's ways become one's own.

Religious education

Religious education brings religion and education together. It is the educational process by which people are invited to explore the human religious traditions that protect and illuminate the transcendent dimension of their lives.[3] Though the foundation of religious education is religion, it is linked to and dependent on education as a discipline. Religious education is a lifelong process and can occur in many different contexts such as the family, the community and the school. Religious education can be examined from two perspectives, which are outlined below.

First, religious education invites people to acquire the knowledge, forms of knowing, attitudes, values, skills and sensibilities that being religious involves. This is an integral part of human development. The goal is a heightened awareness of the presence of the Transcendent in human life. Religious education enables students to develop religious modes of thinking, feeling and doing which touch on the transcendent dimension of their lives through the resources and practices of religious traditions. This process should lead to both personal and social transformation. From this first perspective, the study of religion involves helping students to respond to transcendence by becoming that which religious ways of thinking, feeling and doing enable them to become, namely fully human.

The second perspective from which one can examine religious education concerns the need to teach people to think critically about religion. This need stems from the fact that people ought to be free to accept or reject what is taught in religion. Human beings are fundamentally free; they are invited to explore religion, but cannot be coerced into it. Critical religious education enables people to liberate themselves from the conditioning that prevents them from making choices in religion which are both free and consistent. Critical religious education also teaches people to study religion objectively from a distance, examining their own religion in relation to other religious and non-religious options. The capacity to reflect critically in this way develops as the person matures.

Critical religious education also allows people to discern whether their quest for the true and the good is enhanced or impeded by religion as it manifests itself in their particular time and place. John Hull argues that the critique of religion is necessary because of the highly ambiguous nature of religion. By this he means that religions can become corrupt and false, encouraging a diminished and degrading kind of human development. They can become focused on themselves rather than on the goal of religion, which is spiritual development in the context of transcendence. Hence there is need to help people both to appreciate the richness of religion, its liberating and life-enhancing aspects, *and* to discern when religion becomes oppressive and detrimental to their integral human development.[4]

Theology is one mode of understanding religion. Religion can also be studied by means of disciplines such as anthropology, history, psychology, philosophy and sociology.

These disciplines enable religious educators to understand the processes by which people acquire religion. Such processes include the ability to think religiously, to participate in ritual, to engage in religious practices and so on. There need not be any conflict between having a strong commitment to a revealed religion (for example, Christianity) whilst asserting that the human context within which people become religious can and must be the subject of scientific investigation and philosophical reflection. Religious educators draw upon the best educational research and social–scientific theories available to them as they discern how to educate religiously in different settings.

Religious education need not be undertaken with the assumption that people will commit to *one* particular religious way of life. It may, for example, happen in a context in which people explore religious questions and issues, drawing from the resources of many different religions. Nevertheless, religious education should be carried out in such a way that students are invited to align what they know, who they become and how they live. Those who learn from a religion in religious education should be expected to adopt some elements of that religion's spirituality leading to 'human development', 'healing', 'meaning', 'purpose,' 'faith', or 'salvation'.[5] In sum, while the degree of emphasis placed on different religions varies according to the context in which religious education takes place, all religious education is formative in nature: it should enable students to become aware of and respond to the transcendent dimension of their lives.

Christian religious education

Christian religious education occurs when the Christian religious community draws on its specific tradition to sponsor religious education. Christian religious education denotes the educational process of teaching and learning the Christian religion.[6] It enables students to acquire the knowledge, beliefs, skills, values, attitudes and sensibilities that being Christian involves. The central aim of Christian religious education is to bring students to the knowledge of God the Father, through Jesus, in the Spirit. Therefore, all decisions concerning curriculum, religion programmes and methodology in Christian religious education serve the goal of inviting students to become disciples of Jesus in loving God and serving humanity.

The work of Christian religious education is informed by *education*, thus enabling teachers to decide which forms of Christian religious education (for example, community, prayer, social justice activities, instruction) are appropriate to different educational contexts.[7] Christian religious education is lifelong and is realised in many different settings, including Christian schools. Finally, Christian religious education carried out within contemporary multicultural and multi-faith societies may include the study of the other great spiritual traditions of humanity in ways that promote understanding, dialogue and community with people of other religious traditions and none.

Christian religious education in a Roman Catholic context[8]

In the Catholic religious community, Christian religious education is carried out in accordance with the doctrines, practices and traditions of the Roman Catholic Church. Catholicism presents its own particular perspective on the task of Christian religious education although religious education in the Catholic tradition has much in common with other forms of Christian religious education (Anglican, Presbyterian, Methodist, Baptist). Catholic religious education should not be a sectarian or narrowly denominational enterprise, but should aim to promote genuine movement towards the one, holy, catholic and apostolic Church. While teaching from within the particularity of the Catholic educational tradition, religious educators should have a genuine openness to all other religious educators, Christian and non-Christian alike.

Schooling

Religious education takes place in many different settings including the home, the religious faith community and the school. The school provides an institutional context for educational activity and the structure of contemporary schools determines the range of educational activities that can be legitimately carried out there. The main focus of religious education in the school is the classroom-centered religious education lesson. This kind of religious education is often called religious instruction and is based on a set curriculum which is integrated with other subject curricula in the school.

In addition, religious education can be understood within the wider religious, cultural and institutional framework of the school. In denominational schools, for example, there is a clear link between the kind of religious education undertaken and the requirement to uphold and enhance the school's specific religious ethos. In this context religious education extends beyond the classroom-centered lesson to encompass various activities going on in the school; for example, participation in community worship and involvement in action for social justice.[9]

THE PRACTICE OF RELIGIOUS EDUCATION

What kind of religious education is practised within a denominational primary school setting? The intention of the following reflections is to name the different forms and processes of religious education which might be found in Catholic primary schools. It is expected that there will be differences in the extent to which the various dimensions of religious education outlined will occur in any particular school. The aim is to offer some clear *educational* distinctions for teachers about the different dimensions of their work rather than be excessively prescriptive.

Gabriel Moran, the eminent American religious education theorist, argues that the practice of religious education has two aspects, or 'faces'. These aspects correspond to the two perspectives on religious education explored at the beginning of this chapter. Religious education involves two types of learning: one focused on learning how to live a religious life, the other on learning for the sake of understanding. Both aims are required for intelligent religious life in contemporary pluralist, multi-religious societies. Indeed, Moran claims, it is in the tension between these two aspects of religious education that the logic of religion emerges. He explains that the 'paradoxical logic of religion' is that 'the universal is approached not by abstracting from the particular but by going more deeply into it'. Pluralism in religion emerges from the manner in which the universal and the particular are held in tension. Therefore, every human being should have an opportunity to learn how to practice a particular religious way of life *and* have an appreciative understanding of the religions of others.[10]

Religious education in most Catholic primary schools incorporates both of these dimensions of religious education that Moran outlines. For the purposes of conceptual clarity we will call them the 'faith formation dimension' and the 'critical educational dimension'.[11] The former is strongly informed by the relationship between religion and religious education; the latter draws its language mainly from the philosophical and educational domains. There should be a creative and interdependent relationship between these two aspects of religious education in Irish Catholic primary schools.

In the reflections that follow, each of the dimensions of religious education will first be described in general terms. Then the specific Catholic interpretation and manifestation of these dimensions will be examined. Finally, there will follow a reflection on how these dimensions influence the shape of religious education in Catholic primary schools.

Religious education as formation

The first aspect of religious education outlined by Moran describes the way in which experienced and devoted members of a religious group try to form new members who will carry on the practices and mission of the group. The root metaphors describing this process are formation, socialisation, enculturation, induction, and initiation. Formation refers to personal development: the process whereby a person's way of being, knowing and doing are shaped and transformed by religious education. All education is formative whether or not educators consciously engage in formation. Socialisation refers to the reality that all formation involves the learning of roles and how to negotiate interpersonal relationships within a particular religious group. Likewise, enculturation is the process whereby a person learns a religion's cultural symbols, rituals, rites and values. This process can be conscious or unconscious.

Induction describes an entry process – the journey or path towards full and mature membership of a particular religious group. Initiation is about entry into a particular religious practice or course of action. It often involves a trial and some form of introductory rite which marks the change in the person's life brought about by this new life course. Initiation is something undertaken by choice by those who wish to adopt and live a distinct religious identity, for example, those who freely choose to become Christians. The intention is that the person who is initiated becomes part of the religious group and engages in the practices of that religion. The assumption is that both teacher and learner in the situation of initiation are adherents of the same religious faith.

Religious formation often involves providing opportunities for students to immerse themselves in the practices – ritual, aesthetic, ethical – of a religious community.[12] Becoming religious in this way means adopting the ways of thinking, feeling and acting characteristic of adherents of that particular religion. According to commentators, it is only when one approaches a religion from within – by engaging in religious practices, learning its forms of religious knowing, imitating models of that particular religious way of life – that one truly experiences what it means to be religious. Furthermore, it appears that people who have acquired a strong religious identity in this way are capable of genuine dialogue with adherents of other religions.[13]

Religious formation in a Catholic context

Catechesis

Within Catholic circles, one often refers to this aspect of religious education by using the language of catechetics (with its associated words catechesis, catechist, catechise and catechism).[14] Catechesis describes the educational process whereby the good news of the gospel is announced and the faith of the Church is handed on to believers in the Church community. It takes place in the local Church community over the whole of a person's lifetime. The educational agent and the process whereby catechesis occurs is the lived life of the Christian community or congregation. Hence, while catechesis is primarily the responsibility of bishops, as recognised leaders of the local community, all members of the Church have a responsibility for catechesis.[15]

Catechesis is an option chosen by those who wish to become Christians or by parents who choose at baptism to nurture their child in Christian faith.[16] The heart of catechesis is initiation into the way of Jesus and it 'presupposes that the hearer is receiving the Christian message as a salvific reality.'[17] Its process is therefore one of evangelisation and conversion to Jesus Christ. Catechesis presumes an initial conversion and openness to ongoing conversion. Furthermore, there is a clear linkage in catechesis between instruction, and sacramental ritual. Catechesis is grounded in the bible and takes place in the context of worship. Through the experience of learning about the faith, liturgy, morality and prayer, 'catechesis prepares the Christian to live in community and to participate actively in the life and mission of the Church' (GDC 86). For this aspect of religious education, catechists draw on contemporary literature such as *Catechesis in our Time* (1979), *The General Directory for Catechesis* (1997), *The Catechism of the Catholic Church* (1994) and the documents of the Second Vatican Council.[18]

Religious instruction

Religious instruction also aims to form students in the Christian religion. It involves the academic study of religion in the classroom context. Church documents clearly distinguish this form of religious education from catechesis. For example, *The General Directory for Catechesis* states that catechesis should be seen as distinct from and yet complementary to religious instruction in Catholic schools, and that '...religious instruction in schools should appear as a scholastic discipline with the same rigour as other disciplines' (#73). The aim of such religious instruction is the learning of forms of religious knowing and the acquisition of knowledge of religious beliefs and practices, neither of which require a faith commitment in principle. This instruction fosters an understanding of the Christian way of religious knowing, of the teachings of the gospel, and of the call to discipleship. Religious instruction aims to promote genuine understanding of the Christian religion and of Christian forms of religious knowing, among baptised and non-baptised students alike.

Religious education as formation in the Catholic primary school

The overarching perspective for teaching and learning in religion in Catholic primary schools is the Roman Catholic tradition, its beliefs and practices. This is so because Catholic primary schools support the educational value of being grounded in a particular faith tradition to the extent that it informs one's worldview and lived commitments. The distinguishing characteristic of the Catholic school is its religious dimension, which creates a climate in the school which is permeated by the gospel spirit of freedom and love.

The Catholic approach to religious education is both theological and confessional.[19] It involves, where appropriate, the intentional nurturing of a religious commitment to Jesus Christ through various educational practices. The Catholic school ideally forms part of a network of interlocking and mutually supportive institutions and people who welcome, nurture, educate and motivate the child to identify with the Church and its mission. In this context, the Catholic school is an agency of religious formation for the Church. Appropriately, therefore some of the work of religious formation is carried on in such a school.

Parents who have chosen at baptism that their child be Christian welcome the support of Catholic schools as they carry out their responsibilities to offer their child a Christian formation. In other words, there is an understanding that these children have come to the Catholic school to be formed in their faith. In these situations, school-based catechetical activities such as liturgies and prayer, retreats and reflection days, outreach and social justice activities provide a connection between the school and the larger faith community which nurtures the growing child. These activities are carried on in the name of, with the approval of, and under the guidance of the bishop in each diocese, and contribute to the formative process by which students become part of the local Church community.

The more particular contribution of the Catholic school (as opposed to other educational agencies in the Church) to the formative aspect of religious education is that it enables the students to become religiously literate in the Christian religious tradition as their ability to do so develops. To this end, Catholic beliefs, narratives and practices are taught in a systematic, comprehensive, and age-appropriate fashion through classroom-based religious education programs. For Catholic students, religious instruction in school complements the work of catechesis carried out in the home, the school and in the parish community. The *General Directory for Catechesis* states that 'when given in the context of the Catholic school, religious instruction is part of and completed by other forms of the ministry of the word (catechesis, homilies, liturgical celebration, etc.)' (GDC no.74). The vision of the *Directory* is that religious education in the Catholic school includes some elements of catechesis as well as the teaching of Catholic beliefs and practices in programmes of classroom–based religious instruction. In summary, current Church thinking seems to accept that elements of both catechesis and religious instruction can contribute to the formative dimension of religious education in the Catholic primary school.

Religious education as critical education

The second aspect of religious education – learning to understand religion – involves critical understanding of and debate about religion, both one's own and that of others. Critical religious education is largely an academic endeavour and fosters an open, critical consciousness in the learner. According to Moran, this dimension of religious education aims to enable students to understand and appreciate the place of religious experience, beliefs and practices in human life, and to learn to explore issues of religion in a critical and unbiased way.[20] Here religion is examined as a sphere of human thought and action and students are invited to reflect critically on religious tradition(s) in their own terms.

This critical dimension of religious education might be sponsored for instance by a single religious community, by several different religious bodies or by a nonreligious organisation such as the State.[21] Critical religious education does not require either teacher or learner to be a person of faith. It only invites the student to *imagine* what it would be like to be a person of faith, or (in a situation where a pupil is being educated in his or her own faith) critical education invites the pupil to step back from that faith to critically examine it.[22]

The word 'critical' means 'careful judgement and decision'. It is used here to describe a kind of education that enables students to engage in the kind of search for truth that is animated by ultimate questions such as 'Is this true?', 'How should I live?' and 'Who should I become?'; inviting them to use the resources of religious tradition to make decisions for their lives. Critical openness in religious education should be informed by analysis and rational judgment which tends towards decision and commitment. In this way, critical education should lead to moral and personal transformation as well as the intellectual criticism of religious traditions. It should enable students to discover, judge and decide how religious experience and insight impacts upon their way of living in the world. This kind of discovery becomes possible when people are taught to reflect critically on their own religious traditions and those of others.[23]

Understanding and evaluating one's own religion
The student of Christian religious education is introduced to a religious tradition of beliefs, values and practices. A critical approach to this tradition is an indispensable part of the process whereby people adopt a religious way of life as their own. Critical religious education enables students to reflect critically on their own religious tradition and self-understanding. For example, students can be taught to grasp the process by which this tradition legitimately evolves and develops with the passing of time. This type of reflection becomes possible as students' capacities for critical reflection develop.

The ability to evaluate one's own religion includes critically assessing that which is taught in the light of one's own experiences and that of others, both in the past in the present. Religious faith must stand up under the test of the truth of lived experience – of self, others, and world. Ultimately, critical religious education provides a context for students to make a decision for or against their experiences of the religion into which they have been initiated. Religious education that does not allow this free decision will be open to the charge of indoctrination.[24]

44

Students will be both challenged and enriched by their engagement with their own religious tradition. For example, they can be invited to examine the myriad ways in which people of faith down through the ages lived their lives in response to the experience of God in their midst. Often this response was forged in situations of difficulty and these people of faith may have had to resist the prevailing culture of their time. Such stories become a source of challenge, insight and wisdom for the present generation. A rich exploration and interpretation of the Christian story and symbols can transform the belief, values and actions of students today.

Critical education in one's own religious tradition also involves examining the way in which that tradition has become distorted through human failure and sin. The aim of this study is to enable students to discern when their religious tradition is or has been used in ways which are detrimental to human flourishing. In this way, the religious tradition is recreated, reshaped and transformed through the educational process. In summary, critical religious education serves the goals of fidelity to and reform of the religious tradition such that it becomes a source of genuine personal and social transformation in peoples' lives.

Inter-religious education
A primary task for religious education is teaching people to live with 'otherness' in a multi-cultural, multi-religious society while maintaining a purposeful life in the midst of pluralism and diversity. To this end, critical religious education fosters the ability to learn *about* and *from* other religious and non-religious interpretations of life.[25] Moreover, as Michael Grimmitt notes, when students study religions in conjunction with each other rather than in isolation, they develop some 'appreciation of how religion as a generic concept provides a unique means of

critiquing secular, materialistic, mechanistic and pragmatist approaches to values and the human condition and offers an alternative way of formulating the goals to which human consciousness may aspire'.[26]

Inter-religious education includes teaching students how to engage in inter-subjective dialogue with adherents of other religions. Such dialogue fosters deeper understanding of the religions of others as well as a heightened appreciation of one's own religious life. Inter-religious education involves such skills as developing an empathic understanding of other religions, exploring forms of religious knowing practiced by adherents of those religions, and the critical examination and evaluation of the truth-claims of various religions and their derivative moral values.[27]

An ability to evaluate the contribution of religion to human life and society is an essential pre-requisite for intelligent religious living in the contemporary world. The place of religions in political struggles all over the world is but one example of their immense importance in the public life of nations. One aspect of this evaluation is the ideological critique of religions and their power to transform and impede human flourishing. The ways in which religions interact with popular culture is another important area to study in this regard. Students can also be taught the place of religions in civil society. Religious adherents need to learn a public religious language so that they can bring a religious perspective to public debates on economic, political and social forces affecting people's lives.[28]

Critical religious education in a Catholic context

Support for the critical aspect of religious education in a Catholic context is to be found in some contemporary expressions of a philosophy of Catholic education. This philosophy can be described as a humanising philosophy which understands that education has an inherent value of its own, namely the promotion of integral human development. Hence, while the literature of catechesis emphasises the task of fostering maturity in Christian faith, the literature of Catholic education recognises a distinction between the intention to bring up one's children as Christians within the Church and the desire to educate them socially, intellectually, ethically and spiritually for life in the world.

Catholicism has a number of defining features. Two of these will serve to illustrate the possible strengths of a Catholic approach to the critical dimension of religious education. First, a defining characteristic of Catholicism is its commitment to rationality, to the partnership between reason and revelation, understanding and faith. Catholicism's commitment to rationality suggests that if faith is to have a public role in pluralist, multicultural societies, Christians must be enabled to defend the reasonableness and rationality of the substantive truth claims of Christianity in the public domain. Therefore, Catholic religious education should equip students with an understanding of the nature of religion and the nature of religious knowing. It should also enable them to distinguish and relate to different religious ways of life. These skills will enable Catholics to engage with others in the public conversations about religious and ethical issues, such as racism, violence, world poverty, the effects of globalisation and inter-religious strife.

Second, a tradition marked by catholicity embraces the totality of human experience. This attempt to integrate all of life implies a commitment to 'wholeness, comprehensiveness and inclusivity' and a 'radical openness to every truth and value'.[29] Hence, Catholic education will always search for unifying perspectives, seeking for real harmony within the real differences that exist between Catholicism and other religious and nonreligious interpretations of life. As Fayette Veverka argues, 'Catholic education's claim to comprehensiveness in a postmodern world entails an embrace of irreducible pluralism in the search for meaning and truth'. Catholic religious education seeks to respect this pluralism and diversity by helping students to acknowledge the limits of their own particularity and explore the 'boundaries' that differentiate them from others. The goal of such religious education is 'mutual transformation through a genuine encounter with the other who is both a source of affirmation and a challenge to the limits of my own particular standpoint.'[30] In summary a Catholic philosophy of education strongly promotes a form of being religious that is reasonable, critical and open to a variety of viewpoints.

Critical religious education in the Catholic primary school

In the primary school the skills of critical openness can be fostered through methods that emphasise discovery, exploration, and the child's own construction of meaning. Young children can be encouraged to engage in critical reflection about their own experiences and about the religious tradition, thus laying the foundations for many of the skills of critical religious education mentioned above which are more fully developed in adolescence and adulthood.

There are a number of ways in which children's capacity for critical reflection can be nurtured through religious education in the primary school. First, students can be taught to critically assess societal values, events and structures in light of the Catholic religious tradition. For example, when teaching the story of the ten lepers, students might be invited to dramatise the story 'as it might happen today'. This challenges them to reflect upon people who find themselves on the margins of contemporary Irish society, and on the kinds of transformation necessary to eliminate injustice and suffering in Ireland today.

Second, students need to be taught how to bring a critical openness to the tradition itself. For example, teachers should be very circumspect in the language they use for God, thus conveying to children that we can never fully exhaust all the possible descriptions of God. In addition, children can be taught to make use of many different descriptions and names for God. The tradition can be seriously in error when it leads children to imagine that God is male. This approach to religious language teaches children how to remain flexible theological thinkers and helps to mitigate against a fundamentalist approach to religious tradition.

Third, religious education can introduce older children to the concepts that will enable them to engage in the ideological critique of religion. For example children can be helped to see how religion and the market can combine at Christmas time to turn them into consumers.[31] They can also be helped to see how religious identity can be a powerfully positive and also a very destructive force in the world. This can be done through any activity that helps children see the link between spiritual insights, religious beliefs and the political and social implications that flow from them.

Fourth, it is never too early to help students develop an awareness of the religious pluralism of their society. As Moran notes 'a religion can be "transmitted" today only in the context of a continuing conversation with other religions'.[32] The primary aim of this kind of inter-religious learning is empathy, tolerance and mutual understanding, but goes beyond these to genuine enrichment of one's own perspective and worldview. In the primary school students should be helped to develop powers of empathy and sensitivity to adherents of other religions and none. They can be taught to distinguish between different religious 'ways' and to celebrate this diversity as a gift from God. A concrete method such as 'The Gift to the Child Approach' is particularly suitable for this task, as it does not require children to generalise about religion. Instead, it enables children both to approach and stand back from different religions, all of which are viewed as possible sources of enrichment and understanding.[33] Similarly, Tom Groome suggests that students be taught to approach other religious traditions as spiritual resources from which to learn life-giving wisdom. He notes that 'expecting to find spiritual wisdom can encourage appreciation for 'the other' without falling into a naïve relativism.'[34] This is an approach that encourages children to remain faithful to their unique Christian religious identity while remaining open to learning from the religious identities of others.

THE FUTURE OF RELIGIOUS EDUCATION IN CATHOLIC PRIMARY SCHOOLS

In this chapter an outline has been given of the forms of religious education that one might find in Catholic primary schools. It is important that the distinctions between these various forms as well as their complementarities are properly understood. When this does not occur two common errors can emerge. For instance, some people equate religious education with catechesis. They assume that all of the processes and activities of catechesis are appropriate for the primary school. These people do not pay adequate attention to the various contexts in which catechesis takes place, nor to the kinds of religious education appropriate to the formal school context. On the other hand there are people who argue that religious education should be sharply distinguished from catechesis and that catechetical activity has no place in the Catholic school. They emphasise the freedom of conscience of non-baptised students in Catholic schools and sharply distinguish catechesis from school-based religious education. That neither of these viewpoints is adequate becomes clear when one examines the philosophy of the Catholic school and the current reality of Irish primary schools. Reflecting on such issues will help to clarify and point up the future direction and expression of the Catholic Church's commitment to religious education in Catholic primary schools.

A Catholic philosophy of education

The raison d'être of the Catholic school is to promote integral human formation and to proclaim the gospel of Jesus Christ. It is important to recall these purposes as one considers the kinds of religious education appropriate to Catholic schools. All education is based on a certain understanding of the human person and of her development. Catholicism proposes for education a holistic understanding of full human development of the person. Such an understanding is open to the spiritual and religious dimension of being human. In other words, Catholic educators believe that the task of religious formation and human development are inseparable because to become fully human requires that one respond to a loving and compassionate God who is to be found at the heart of human life. For Catholics becoming a disciple of Jesus Christ, and developing as a human being are two facets of a single reality. This is the basis of the kind of education carried out in Catholic primary schools.

Formation in Christian faith pervades the whole curriculum of the Catholic school. The Second Vatican Council's *Declaration on Christian Education* speaks of the Catholic school as striving 'to relate all human culture eventually to the news of salvation so that the light of faith will illumine the knowledge which students gradually gain of the world, of life and of mankind', and it speaks also of the need 'to create for the school community an atmosphere enlivened by the gospel spirit of freedom and love.'[35] The Catholic school is thus understood to be one agent of the Church's mission of evangelisation in Irish society. *The General Directory for Catechesis* describes evangelisation as 'the process by which the Church, moved by the Spirit proclaims and spreads the gospel throughout the entire world' (no. 48). Through its schools the Church seeks to implement the injunction of Christ at the close of Matthew's gospel:

> All authority in heaven and on earth have been given to me. Go therefore, make disciples of all nations: baptising them in the name of the Father and of the Son and of the Holy Spirit, and teach them to obey everything that I have commanded you. (Mt 28: 18-19).

In other words, the school is one place where the Church continues to invite people to embrace the revelation of Christ which it has continually reinterpreted through its history. However, this evangelising mission needs to be carried out in ways which take account of changes in the Irish Catholic Church, in Catholic schools and in Irish society and culture generally which have occurred over the past twenty years.

The way the Church understands its mission of evangelisation has developed considerably in recent times. For instance, while Catholics traditionally thought of evangelisation as bringing non-Christians into the Church, contemporary theologies of evangelisation emphasise the importance of Christians living their discipleship in the world, serving the poor, and respecting the personal response of faith to God's invitation. The essence of the Church's evangelising mission is the proclamation of Jesus Christ and not a desire for self-preservation as a society through, for instance, the imposition of its creed and teaching. Its mission is revealed rather in the goals towards which it strives. For instance, it is revealed in its stance regarding the struggle between rich and poor, between oppressors and oppressed. In this sense the Church continually strives to serve the wider community in which it finds itself. Catholic schools participate in this service to humanity and to the world.

Dilemma for teachers

This new understanding of the Church's mission of evangelisation, coupled with the new cultural reality in Ireland, has led to confusion among teachers about the nature of their role as religious educators in the Catholic primary school. On the one hand teachers are asked to accept the duty and responsibility of contributing to the process whereby baptised children are formed and initiated in the Christian faith; on the other, teachers are conscious of their duty to educate and hence serve those children who have not come to the Catholic school to be formed in Christian faith. Furthermore, teachers are faced with the reality that many Catholic children are receiving little if any faith formation outside of the school context, so they try to accomplish the tasks of evangelisation and catechesis without the supports which catechesis requires and assumes.

This difficulty is especially heightened by the understanding of the integral character of the curriculum in Catholic primary schools. The fact that catechesis is integrated into the whole curriculum of the Catholic school poses a severe difficulty for non-baptised children. This is a difficulty that cannot easily be resolved given that most Irish primary schools are Catholic Church schools. However the evolving situation urgently requires reflection on the forms of religious education appropriate to the present context of Catholic schools and on the structures within which a believing community's religious education mission is exercised.

The traditional Catholic school: a model under strain

Traditionally Catholic schools transmitted religious values to children from committed families residing in strong Catholic communities. Within such a context, the staff, students and parents of the schools were Catholic, with a strong level of affiliation to their Church. The role of the Catholic school in transmitting essential doctrines and traditional devotions of Catholicism was generally accepted by all concerned. Not surprisingly, in this context religious education was decidedly catechetical, with sacramental preparation as a central goal. The programme served to promote children's affiliation to the Church as an institution and as a community nurturing the faith commitment of its members.

This model of the Catholic School is increasingly under strain in view of the decline of Catholic religious culture and practice in Irish society in general. This shift in culture now faced by Catholic schools is described well by Kevin Treston:

> The massive decline in affiliation to the liturgical Church, as well as growing paganism, suggest that increasing numbers of children enrolling in Catholic schools come from homes with little or no religious culture. The collapse of a Catholic sub-culture has diminished opportunities for religious socialisation. Teachers in Catholic schools report a significant increment in 'folk'

Catholics and a veritable wasteland of religious knowledge and practice.[36]

The weakening of Catholic culture described above means that there is no real consensus between teachers, parents and school management as to the kind of religious education appropriately carried out in such schools at present.

The Republic of Ireland does not have a dual education system with a clear choice available to parents, pupils and teachers between a Church schooling system and a State schooling system. Ideally, the state should ensure that parents can send their children to schools congruent with their beliefs. Genuine pluralism in Irish education will happen when different religious and non-religious groups are enabled to establish schools that express and realise what is distinctive to each of them. In recent years a growing number of multi-denominational and inter-denominational schools have been established. However, almost ninety-three per cent of Irish primary schools are Catholic Church schools. This means that the majority of Irish parents have no choice but to send their children to a Catholic school. Consequently, Catholic schools continue to cater for the children of parents who have no commitment to a Catholic ethos or form of education. For many of these parents the principal purpose of the school is education for citizenship. For them this does not include the promotion of a Catholic faith commitment. Similarly, some teachers employed in these schools may have little or no commitment to the evangelising mission of the Church and may, in turn, be reluctant to view their profession in Church terms. Nevertheless, they are currently charged with the responsibility of nurturing children's affiliation to an ecclesial community which they themselves may not be sufficiently or fully committed to.

The Vatican document *The Religious Dimension of Education in a Catholic School* (no. 67) refers to the fact that 'the student body in a Catholic school includes increasing numbers of young people from different faiths and different ideological backgrounds'. It acknowledges that in these situations, 'evangelisation is not easy—it may not even be possible'. Catholic boards of management and teachers must face the ethical question of whether catechising can take place in the school in a way that respects 'the religious freedom and personal conscience of students and their families'. While the school has a right and duty to proclaim the gospel to those who are open to receiving it, 'the imposition' of the gospel or Christian formation 'is strictly forbidden, both by the gospel and by Church law.'[37] The Church's position is echoed in Article 14.1 of the *National Convention of the Rights of the Child* (ratified by Ireland in 1992). It outlines that 'states parties shall respect the right of the child to freedom of thought, conscience and religion'. The challenge for Catholic school managers is to respond to the rights of all children attending Catholic schools while simultaneously upholding the rights of Catholic children to receive a holistic religious education in the context of a school which upholds a distinct religious ethos.

In summary, the obligation to work out the implications for school-based religious education of the fact that freedom is a necessary condition of catechesis is imperative for Catholic schools at this time.[38] Given that a percentage of Irish parents will have no choice for the foreseeable future but to send their children to Catholic primary schools, the challenge is to develop an approach to religious education that respects the right of the Catholic Church to pursue its educational mission and which takes account of the rights of all the children attending primary schools.[39] Equally, the situation of teachers who neither profess nor practise the religion of their particular school and yet who must find employment in an almost exclusively denominational school system needs to be addressed. Teachers should not be expected to compromise themselves, their personal beliefs and convictions and act as catechists in Catholic schools. To do so can all too easily give rise to deception and avoidance.

Looking to the Future

As already indicated, the new understanding of the Church's evangelising mission and the new cultural situation in Ireland suggests the need for a fresh approach to primary religious education. Clearly, Irish society continues to need Catholic schools where children can be religiously educated from the perspective of the Christian religious tradition. Consequently, Christian religious education, both in its formative and critical dimensions, will continue to be taught in Catholic primary schools. Equally however, a new approach will have to take account of the differing faith stances and levels of commitment of an increasing cohort of parents, students and teachers presently associated with Catholic primary schools. The duty of the Church to foster the faith of its committed members will have to be balanced with the responsibility to religiously educate all children in a manner that is appropriate to their real capacities for engagement with and commitment to the gospel of Jesus Christ.

One way of addressing this task would be to create a distinction between the kinds of catechesis appropriate to the home and parish context and the kinds of catechesis appropriate to contemporary Catholic schools. Recent Catholic thinking has emphasised that the key carrier and hence educator in Christian faith is the local community. The primary locus of catechesis is the family, and by extension the local parish Church. The school cannot be expected to provide the full range of formation necessary for a full initiation into the Church community. Many of the goals and outcomes of catechesis simply cannot be met by the school.

There are aspects of catechesis that are best exercised within the parish, rather than the school context, for example sacramental preparation. With regard to the sacraments the task is to discover what educational practice will best safeguard the integrity of the sacraments themselves while at the same time developing the faith life of the participants. The lack of structures facilitating adequate sacramental preparation outside the school setting in some Church communities is a real problem which requires urgent attention. Clearly, sacramental integrity is in jeopardy when all baptised children receive the sacraments by virtue of being in the Catholic school, regardless of the level of commitment in the home and in the wider Christian community towards children's religious initiation.

Another important task is to outline the educational contribution of the study of religion to all children in Catholic primary schools, some of whom are not and may never be adherents of Christianity, but who nevertheless, deserve to be educated *religiously*. Christian religious education can be carried out in such a way that all children are affirmed in their own religious faith and that all are invited to grow in their understanding of the place of religion in human life. Furthermore, when carried out within a school context, Christian religious education should have an educational rationale quite independent of an explicit faith rationale. For example, education in Christian symbols has a place in the school, because the ability to engage with religious symbol is an integral part of religious education in any context. Similarly, rituals that enable students to learn how to participate in ritual (engaging with symbol and metaphor, learning ritual gestures, praying with other people, and so on) should be distinguished from ritual activities that require a high level of piety from students. In other words there are sound educational reasons for teaching all children in the Catholic school how to participate in religious ritual as this is an important aspect of what it means to be religious. In summary, the articulation of a strong educational rationale for religious education in the formal school curriculum is urgently needed and highly desirable, as it would enable teachers to decide what forms of religious education are appropriate to children who have not come to the Catholic school to be initiated in Christian faith. The development of a national core syllabus for primary religious education would be extremely helpful in this regard, as it would outline the kind of religious education appropriate to all primary schools regardless of the denominational affiliation involved.[40]

CONCLUSION

This chapter provides readers with an educational language with which to engage in reflective debate and dialogue on this issue. The current dominance of the denominational school system throughout the country creates a unique challenge for the Catholic Christian community to live up to the best of its own tradition of openness and inclusivity, mission and outreach, evangelisation and education. The Catholic faith community will continue to educate its members to the extent that its religious traditions are embodied and enacted in the structures and practices of Catholic community life and the Catholic primary school will continue to play an important role in this process. This commitment, however, must be balanced by its wider responsibility to all the students and teachers involved in Catholic schools, both adherents and non-adherents alike.

NOTES

1   Joseph Dunne, 'Arguing for Teaching as a Practice', *Journal of Philosophy of Education*, 37: 2 (2003), p. 368.

2   John M. Hull, 'Spirituality, Religion, Faith: Mapping the Territory', p. 6. www.johnmhull.biz/ accessed 16/02/04.

3   This is an adaptation of Dwayne Huebner's definition of religious education in 'Education in the Church', *Andover-Newton Quarterly*, Vol. 12, January 1972, p.125.

4   Hull, 'Spirituality, Religion, Faith', p.6. Hull defines religious education as a discipline within the critical social sciences whose goal is human freedom. Religious education incorporates activities of both affirmation and critique, enabling people to enter religion in a way which truly serves their integral human development. John M. Hull, 'Religion and Education in a Pluralist Society', pp.3-4. Article on John M Hull's website www.johnmhull.biz/.

5   The British educator Michael Grimmitt proposes that pupils in secular schools may learn *from* religions as they are exposed to religious questions and are enabled to explore how these questions impact their own developing sense of identity. Grimmitt distinguishes between learning religion in the mode of transmissive models of education, learning *about* religion in an objective manner, and learning *from* religion. The value of this last point is that it suggests an educational perspective which asks 'what is the educational advantage to be gained by the study of religion?' Michael Grimmitt, *Religious Education and Human Development*, Great Wakering, Essex: England, McCrimmon Publishing Co. LTD, 1987, p. 225.

     On religions of salvation and liberation see John Hick, *An Interpretation of Religion*, New Haven: Yale University Press; London: Macmillan, 1989, chap., 3 and passim.

6   Jeff Astley, *The Philosophy of Christian Religious Education*, Birmingham, Ala.: Religious Education Press, 1994, pp. 9, 14.

7   See chapter four in this volume where some of the forms of religious education appropriate to the primary school are outlined.

8   The Catholic Church's distinct theological and philosophical vision for the religious dimension of education is outlined in chapter three of this book.

9   In Ireland a religion has a constitutional right to administer schools with its own ethos. A parent has a constitutional right to have his or her child educated religiously, with the assistance of the state. If non-Catholics want their children to attend a Catholic school, they attend it freely accepting the Catholic school as it is. The child withdraws from the religious instruction, but accepts the Catholic ethos in general.

10   Gabriel Moran, 'The Aims of Religious Education' in Maria Harris and Gabriel Moran, *Reshaping Religious Education: Conversations on Contemporary Practice*, Louisville, Kentucky: Westminster/ John Knox Press, 1998, p.30, 39-41.

11   This distinction was suggested to me by Astley's description of formative education and critical education. Astley, *Philosophy*, p.78. The value of these categories is that they enable us to recognise that Christian nurture/ socialisation is legitimately described as education as opposed to training or indoctrination. The language of education must be used for each aspect of religious education as both depend on the science of education (and thus to the many other sciences which inform education) for their effectiveness. On the importance of educational language see Thomas H. Groome, *Christian Religious Education*, San Francisco: Harper & Row, 1980, pp. 23-27; Gabriel Moran, 'Religious Education after Vatican II' in David Efroymson and John Raines (eds), *Open Catholicism: The Tradition at its Best*, Collegeville, Minn: Liturgical Press, 1997, pp. 156-7; and Astley, *Philosophy*, pp. 24-29.

12   Moran, 'Religious Education after Vatican II' , p.153.

13   See Hobson and Edwards, *Religious Education in a Pluralist Society*, p. 39, for the idea that children need to begin with a 'primary paradigm.'

14   The word *catechesis* comes from the Greek verb *katéchein*, which means 'to resound, 'to echo,' or 'to hand down'. The etymology of the word implies an oral instruction and this is the meaning that has prevailed through much of Church history. The Fathers of the Second Vatican Council speak of catechesis as instruction and place it within the 'ministry of the word'. In recent years catechesis has been understood as a sub-category within evangelisation the function of which is to 'promote and mature initial conversion, educate the convert in

the faith and incorporate him(sic) into the Christian community' (GDC, no. 61). This rearranges the pattern of the early Church in that the first Christian communities recognised evangelisation and catechesis as two distinct functions in the Church's mission.

15   Kieran Scott, 'A Middle Way: The Road not travelled', *The Living Light*, 37:4, (2001), p. 41. The ecclesial nature of catechesis is emphasized again and again in the GDC nos 77, 78, 87, 105, 106, 141. 'The Catholic School' considers that 'the proper place for catechesis is the family helped by other Christian communities, especially the local parish.' CS 51. The catechetical duty of all Church members is noted in GDC nos 220, 224, 231, 233.

16   RBOC, nos 77, 93,

17   RDECS, nos. 68, 69.

18   It is important to note that Church catechetical documents generally provide principles of pastoral theology rather than educational theory as such.

19   Theological approaches to the study of religious education cover conceptual and doctrinal issues from an insider's descriptive point of view. Other approaches that look at religion from an empirical, descriptive position include the phenomenological, sociological, and historical approaches. Hobson and Edwards, *Religious Education in a Pluralist Society*, p. 22.

20   Gabriel Moran, 'Two Languages of Religious Education', in J. Astley & L. J. Francis (eds), *Critical Perspectives on Christian Education*, Leominster, Herfordshire: Gracewing, 1994, p. 45.

21   In Britain and most of Europe school-based religious education is carried out mainly in non-denominational state schools. Many of these countries possess specific legislation for religious education as a curriculum subject for all pupils regardless of religious affiliation. Religious education in British secular schools focuses on the academic study of religions and teachers are precluded from teaching in a confessional manner. This kind of religious education often involves developing an objective and empathic understanding of the phenomena of different religions.

22   John M. Hull et al, 'Critical Openness in Christian Nurture' in Astley and Francis (eds), *Critical Perspectives*, p. 274. See also

John M. Hull, *Studies in Religion and Education*, Lewes, England: Falmer, 1984, chap., 19. And Leslie J. Francis, 'The Logic of Education, Theology and the Church School', *Oxford Review of Education*, 9: 2 (1983).

23   Jeff Astley explains how critical study of religion includes aspects of critical pedagogy in that it aims to maximise the intellectual autonomy, responsibility and accountability of learners, but it is not confined to it. Critical reason must be combined with developing capacities for positive insight and openness to the possibility of nonsensory knowledge. Therefore, it is a form of critical openness that leads to the decision to act for the good, rather than autonomous speculation, that is the mark of the kind of education proposed here. See Astley's arguments for a 'qualified critical approach' to religious education in *Philosophy*, p. 83 and pp. 94-99.

24   The need for a critical dimension to religious education in religiously-sponsored schools has been defended on both educational and theological grounds. The educational argument relates to the need in modern pluralist societies for people who are capable of being critically reflective in the midst of competing claims about the value and meaning of human life. The theological reasons stem from the nature of Christian revelation and the nature of God. See John M. Hull et al, 'Critical Openness in Christian Nurture' in Astley and Francis (eds), *Critical Perspectives*, pp. 251-275. For the Catholic emphasis on the partnership between reason and revelation see Thomas H. Groome, 'Religious education and Catechesis: no divorce for the children's sake' *The Furrow*, (November 2002), pp. 590-591. See also Elmer J. Thiessen, *Teaching for Commitment*. London: McGill, 1993.

25   See footnote five for these distinctions. 'The Gift to the Child Approach' developed at the university of Birmingham is an example of how children can be taught to learn *from* religious phenomena. The problems with a merely descriptive approach to other religions are that it requires children to generalise and it is false to the ideological nature of religion. John M. Hull, 'A Gift to the Child: A New Pedagogy For Teaching Religion to Young Children', *Religious Education*, 91:2 (Spring 1996), p. 81.

26   Michael Grimmitt (ed), *Pedagogies of Religious Education*, Great

Wakering, Essex, McCrimmons, 2000, p. 12.

27   Brian V. Hill. 'Will and Should religious studies appropriate to schools in a pluralistic society foster religious relativism?', in Astley and Francis (eds), *Critical Perspectives*, p.149. This kind of work is most appropriate to secondary and tertiary levels. I would not advocate much comparison of religions at primary level as there is a strong possibility of misleading comparisons.

28   Charles R. Foster, 'Religious Education at the Edge of History', *Religious Education*, 99:1 (Winter 2004), pp.75-76.

29   Fayette Breaux Veverka, 'Re-imagining Catholic Identity: Toward an Analogical Paradigm', *Religious Education* 88:2 (1993), p. 245. Richard McBrien, *Catholicism*, Minneapolis: Winston Press, 1980, p.1174.

30   Veverka, 'Re-imagining Catholic Identity', p.247. See chapter six for a fuller explanation of catholicity.

31   This example and the idea that the concepts central to the ideological critique of religion can be interpreted pedagogically for very young children come from John M. Hull. See Hull, ' Religion and Education in a Pluralist Society,' p. 5. and 'Religion in the Service of the Child Project: The Gift Approach to Religious Education', in Michael Grimmitt (ed), *Pedagogies of Religious Education*, pp. 112-129.

32   Gabriel Moran, *Interplay: a theory of Religion and Education*. Winona: St Mary's Press, 1981, p. 17.

33   See John M. Hull, 'A Gift to the Child: a New Pedagogy for Teaching Religion to Young Children', *Religious Education* 9:2 (1996). 'The Gift to the Child Approach' is discussed in more detail in chapter five.

34   Thomas H. Groome, 'Religious Education and Catechesis', *The Furrow* (November 2002), p. 595.

35   GE no. 8.

36   Kevin Treston, 'The School as an Agent in Evangelisation', in Feheney (ed), *From Ideal to Action*, p. 64.

37   RDECS, nos 6 and 108.

38   On freedom as a principle of education see Joseph Dunne, 'The Catholic School and Civil Society', p. 29. On the centrality of freedom and choice in catechesis, see Michael Warren, 'Catechesis and Religious Education: Respecting the Differences', *Rea 4* (2003), pp. 88-105.

39   GE par 3 and 6.

40   The Irish National Teacher's Organisation has called for the development of a religious education programme for all primary schools in the State which would reflect the diversity of religious faiths in our primary schools today. The INTO adopted this resolution at its Annual Congress in April 2003.

CHAPTER TWO

A Brief History of Religious Education in the Irish Primary School

• •

This chapter provides a brief overview of the main developments impacting upon religious education in the Irish elementary or national school system over the last two hundred years. The topic is vast and therefore only some of the major themes can be identified. Religion and Irish primary education are inextricably linked. This chapter sketches their interrelationship in broad outline and is divided into two parts. Part One provides a survey of the educational context at the beginning of the nineteenth century followed by an account of the establishment of the national interdenominational system of education in 1831. In the nineteenth century an increasing dissatisfaction with interdenominational education occurred within certain circles, and this resulted in the gradual denominationalisation and clericalisation of the control of teaching of religion in national schools in the twentieth century.[1] This section concentrates largely on the nineteenth century as it set the foundation and framework for the subsequent development of primary education in the twentieth century. Part One ends with an exploration of the diverse types of schools which have been established in the twentieth century to cater for the religious needs of children. Part Two provides a brief general outline of Catholic catechetical methodologies operative in national schools from 1831 to 1995. This chapter does not outline the forms of religious instruction provided by the Established (Anglican) and Presbyterian churches nor does it focus on all seven school types which existed at the end of the nineteenth century.[2]

Part 1: The Educational Context From 1800 Onwards

The story of Catholic religious education cannot be told without mentioning the role played by the 'hedge schools' of the eighteeenth century. The penal laws were a series of laws designed to suppress all religious, cultural, political and economic activity by those who were not members of the Established Church.[3] Under the penal laws:

> No popish person could send his child abroad to receive an education (1695). No person was permitted to act in the capacity of a tutor to a Catholic family. Trinity College (the only university in Ireland) was closed to Catholics. Catholic schools were forbidden (1704) and licensed schools became saturated with Protestantism.[4]

Virtually from the reign of Henry VIII (1491-1547) until the abolition of the penal laws in the 1782 and 1793,[5] those who were not members of the Established Church, including Catholics and Presbyterians, were unable to promote or teach their faith. Amid this religious repression 'hedge' or 'pay' schools gained popularity. They were so called because classes, for which the pupils paid a small fee, were held outdoors in the summer months and whenever weather permitted. During the worst times of penal repression Catholic and dissenting

Protestant (for example, Presbyterian) children were separately and secretly educated among the hedgerows, or in any available hut, by freelance denominational teachers who were under pain of death if they were caught. In one sense 'hedge' school is a misnomer because by the end of the eighteenth century practically all schools were located in some type of building. However, as a consequence of a Window Tax[6] levied on the number of windows contained in a building it was not uncommon for windows to be bricked up to avoid tax. Ensuing problems with light meant that whenever possible classes were held outdoors giving rise to the term 'hedge' school. In 1782 with the abolition of the penal laws it became legally possible for Catholics and Presbyterians to have their own schools where children were educated for a modest fee.[7] By 1829 up to 300,000 Catholic pupils paid for an unregulated education of variable quality delivered by Catholic teachers.[8]

After the Act of Union in 1800 Ireland was ruled directly by parliament at Westminster. In the late eighteenth century there was an almost complete lack of formal educational opportunities for a large number of children in Ireland and Westminster wavered between a policy of *laissez faire* indifference to the education of the Irish to paradoxically using Ireland as a laboratory for social and educational experimentation. 'Ireland, as a colony, could be used as an experimental milieu for social legislation which might not be tolerated in England.'[9] From 1831 onwards Westminster funded an innovative national system of primary education in Ireland almost four decades prior to the 1870 Education Act which introduced a similar national system of education in England.[10] The motives behind such an enterprise are complex. Education was undoubtedly seen as a vehicle of cultural, linguistic, social, religious and political assimilation and could be used as a reinforcement of colonisation. The national schools, which focused mainly on literacy and numeracy, used the colonial language, English, as their *lingua franca*, and so were vehicles of anglicisation.

In the eighteenth century the official schools that did exist in Ireland tended to be privately funded denominational, proselytising schools.[11] The *Association for Discountenancing Vice and Promoting the Knowledge and Practice of the Christian Religion*, which was founded in 1792, was viewed by Catholics as a centre for proselytising, de-nationalising and anglicising Irish Catholics. Catholic parents strongly resisted sending their children to Protestant run denominational institutions, and while many of these schools were free, they were ultimately seen as jeopardising the Catholic faith and tradition. In this climate Catholic Religious Orders set about establishing their own denominational schools and teaching Orders such as the Presentation sisters (1775); The Presentation Brothers (1802); the Christian Brothers (1802); the Sisters of Loreto (1822) and the Sisters of Mercy (1827), among others, were founded with an explicit emphasis on providing Catholic education for the poor. Catholics who could afford to pay for an education provided by these Religious Orders did so.

The *Society for Promoting the Education of the Poor of Ireland* was a voluntary charitable Protestant Society, which aimed at providing a basic, undenominational education for all children, regardless of religious belief. While it did prohibit the teaching of denominational religious doctrine in its schools, it also provided compulsory Bible reading 'without note or comment'.[12] In many ways the 1831 national system of education in Ireland emulated the Society's approach with very minor differences. This partly government-funded charitable Society did ground breaking work during the early decades of the nineteenth century. Its innovative approach to education involved publishing cheap and affordable spelling, arithmetic and reading schoolbooks for use in its schools. It gained government grants for the establishment of over 1,600 schools and it systematically trained almost 2,500 teachers. Its very real legacy to the subsequent development of education in Ireland is visibly and geographically embodied by the fact that its headquarters were in Kildare Place in Dublin, on the site of the current headquarters for the Department of Education and Science.

However religion was the rock upon which this Society ultimately perished. The rule that mandated compulsory Bible reading in each of the Society's schools, while being non-sectarian and inclusive of all Christian denominations in intent, was effectively viewed with suspicion by many Catholics as a covert proselytising device. The Society welcomed 'children of all religious persuasions' without interfering 'with the peculiar tenets of any' yet it insisted on compulsory Bible reading from what was viewed as a 'Protestant' King James Version of the Bible.[13] In 1820 Daniel O'Connell addressed the Annual General Meeting of the Society and stressed that its emphasis on compulsory Bible reading placed Catholics at a disadvantage and despite the Society's explicit non-sectarian intent this rule effectively constituted a method of proselytising. O'Connell argued that for Catholics the Bible could not be viewed as a school-book to be read without note or comment. He stressed that in the Roman Catholic Church the Bible had to be located in the context of the Catholic tradition. As a text, it must be authoritatively interpreted by the Catholic authorities.

> The Bible never can be received without note of comment by the Catholic persuasion….we believe that a portion has been preserved in the church which preserved that writing… you cannot expect to have the Catholic clergy submit, when their

attention is roused, to have the Bible used without note or comment, because they must have tradition, which we also call the word of God.[14]

As a consequence of the objections raised by O'Connell and other Irish parliamentary members,[15] the 1824 Commission on Education in Ireland was established to survey, the work of bodies involved in Irish education, including the Society. The Commission recommended the cessation of the practice of funnelling English parliamentary funding for education through voluntary agencies with a proselytising agenda.

'The commissioners said that the Roman Catholic clergy did not rest their opposition to the Society on the ground that proselytism had actually been effected, but on an allegation that such was the object of the Society; that such was the tendency of the schools; and that such might be the effect of the system if it were allowed to continue.'[16]

The 1824-5 Commission on Education recommended that two teachers, one Roman Catholic and one Protestant, be appointed to each school whose primary role would be to supervise the separate religious education of pupils in the school and to agree a mutually acceptable schedule of readings from scripture. However it was increasingly evident that a satisfactory system of education could not be built on the remains of a Society whose work was already viewed as a form of proselytism. On 31 October 1831, the Chief Secretary of Ireland, Edward G. Stanley (1799-1869)[17] wrote his famous letter to the Duke of Leinster, outlining the principles upon which a new National Education Board would be established. It is important to note that even though the Irish national system of education was funded by parliament it was not founded by an act of parliament. Indeed there was no statutory basis to Irish Education until the 1998 Education Act came into operation in the year 2000. In 1831 Stanley wished to rid the Irish educational system of any hint of proselytism or inequitable funding and so his letter established a National Board composed of seven commissioners,[18] who were nominated by different religious denominations in Ireland, with a task of running the national system of schools. The principles which Stanley outlined in his letter exercised a lasting influence on the Irish educational system and were hugely influential on the subsequent development of religious instruction and religious education in Ireland. Therefore it is worthwhile to look in some detail at the principles contained within the Stanley letter.[19]

The Stanley Letter and Religious Education

The Stanley letter was used as a basis from which the first seven[20] commissioners of the National Board drew up the code of rules governing the national school system. The Stanley letter outlined the constitution of the Board of Education, the function and role of the Commissioners, as well as the role allocated to religion within the new national school system. The greater part of the Stanley letter focused on accommodations necessary to ensure that Christians of all denominations, while united in one system of 'mixed' education, maintain a right to separate denominational religious instruction. Stanley's original national school system was mixed, in other words Protestants, Presbyterians and Catholics were jointly educated, and the government authorities worked to ensure that 'the religious denominations in the country should co-operate with one another in conducting national schools.'[21] The Stanley letter makes it clear that joint Roman Catholic and Protestant applications for funding would 'probably' be given preferential treatment over applications from one single denomination. The principle of mixed education was politically motivated as it was envisaged that after the Irish Rebellion of 1798, a non-sectarian system of education could help neutralise radical political leanings. The interdenominational system was based on the principle of integrated secular lessons in 'moral and literary education', with separate and distinct religious instruction as appropriate to the denominational needs of the children. However the Board stated that a written general moral and religious lesson exhorting tolerance and understanding should be displayed prominently in every classroom. A sample form of this *General Lesson* which hung on the wall of every classroom stated:

> Christians should endeavour, as the Apostle Paul commands them, to 'live peaceably with all men; (Rom. Ch. XII. V. 17); even with those of a different religious persuasion.
>
> Our Saviour, Christ, commanded his disciples to 'love one another.' He taught them to love even their enemies, to bless those that cursed them, and to pray for those who persecuted them. He himself prayed for his murderers.
>
> Many men hold erroneous doctrines, but we ought not to hate or persecute them; We ought to seek for the truth, and to hold fast what we are convinced is the truth; but not to treat harshly those who are in error. Jesus Christ did not intend his religion to be forced on men by violent means. He would not allow his disciples to fight for him.
>
> …
>
> Quarrelling with our neighbours and abusing them is not the way to convince them that we are in the right and they in the wrong. It is more likely to convince them that we have not a Christian spirit.[22]

These principles of tolerance and respect underlying this mixed system of education may be interpreted, from a twenty-first century vantage point, as representing quite a liberal and tolerant approach to religious diversity. However admirable the principles of interdenominational education were in theory, in practice the separate religious denominations were mutually suspicious. Among Catholics there was a fear of those who 'scatter the deadly seeds of bad doctrines' that disable humans from discerning between good and evil and lead them to damnation.[23] Such perceptions inhibited any large-scale interdenominational activity including joint funding applications or joint school management projects. Mixed Catholic and Protestant education was seen as a potentially perilous enterprise. It is unsurprising that in this climate the *General Lesson* was viewed as an attempt to chastise the religious denominations for their 'erroneous doctrines'. The fact that the Protestant Archbishop Richard Whately (1787-1863), was the author of a work entitled *On the Errors of Romanism traced to their origin in Human Nature*, as well as the General Lesson, did little to allay the fears of those who saw this Lesson as an attack on Catholicism.[24] Since the composition of the board was originally five sevenths Protestant, many Catholics feared that the national school system would become a proselytising instrument for the Protestant Churches. Despite the fact that in 1841 Pope Gregory XVI exhorted Catholics to support national systems of education, some members of the Irish Catholic hierarchy were hesitant to support the national school system. Catholic children in schools controlled by Protestant landlords were occasionally encouraged to attend Protestant religious instruction[25] and Catholics, with recent memories of the harsh repressions of the Penal Laws, were fearful of proselytism. Protestants, who were just coming to terms with the implications of Catholic emancipation in 1829, feared that a mixed educational environment would be exploited by Catholics as a mechanism for proselytising Protestant children. Some Presbyterians objected to Catholics being given a seat on the Board and refused to submit joint applications for funding with other denominations.[26] Some Protestants also argued that a greater emphasis on teaching the Bible should be made in the national schools.

The efficacy of the interdenominational national school project was questionable from its very origin since the children were only jointly taught for secular aspects of the curriculum – moral and literary education. The Stanley letter outlined the principle that schools were to be kept open for a set number of days, either four or five days each week, for secular education so that for the remaining days of the week, the religious clergy of the relevant denominations could provide separate religious instruction as appropriate. The Board also permitted the clergy to give religious instruction to the children of their respective persuasions, either before or after ordinary school hours, on the other days of the week.[27]

As early as 1838 the guiding principles established by the Stanley letter were by-passed and denominational religious instruction was allowed during the official school day.[28] The teachers did not normally engage in religious instruction, and the programme for training teachers did not include any element of religious instruction. In effect the teaching of religious instruction in national schools was placed in the hands of the relevant clergy. This had already begun at a local level in the 'hedge school' era where the priest and teacher were closely connected. The clergy gained increasing control of the system and in 1840, on the eve of the famine that reduced the Irish population by almost 2 million, a series of proposals was introduced to placate fears that national schools were being used as instruments of proselytism. A local bishop or clergyman from each denomination could apply to become a patron of a mixed interdenominational school. The patron appointed a manager and the manager appointed, or dismissed, the teacher in the relevant school. The religious authorities were powerfully positioned at the heart of the national system of education. If the religious authorities undertook to provide the site upon which the school was built, to maintain the school and pay the teachers' salaries, as well as one third of the original cost of building the school, the Board of Commissioners would provide the remaining two thirds of the building cost. In many cases the denominational 'pay' or 'chapel' schools, which pre-existed the 1831 national school system, applied to the Board of Education to have their situation regularised and to be funded by the Board. In some cases the one third of funding which the local community were supposed to contribute was not forthcoming.[29] The vast majority of schools were built on grounds owned by religious denominations and the denominationalisation and clericalisation of the educational system gained momentum. Today this legacy is visibly manifested in the close physical proximity of many schools and churches.

Stanley's interdenominational project seems never to have gained universal support among the Christian denominations and was blighted by continuous squabbling. The children became the real casualties as school managers expended their energy on issues of denominational difference as opposed to the quality of educational provision or the state of the school buildings. In 1835 it was intended that the national system of education would be spearheaded by thirty-two 'model' or 'flagship' interdenominational schools, which would be staffed by high achieving teachers, who would exemplify the best principles of teaching and pupil attainment in an interdenominational context. This vision was never realised and as the nineteenth century drew to a close, the attendance of Catholic children at model schools became the exception rather than the rule. Catholic clergy objected to model schools because they were centres for training teachers in an interdenominational context. Even as early as 1826 the Catholic bishops had made it abundantly clear that no Catholic teacher should be trained by those professing a different faith.[30] The Catholic Archbishop, Dr Paul Cullen (1803-1878),[31] spearheaded Catholic resistance to the system of national schools because he saw its interdenominationalism as inherently dangerous for the faith of Catholic children and as a proselytising and anglicising mechanism. The Synod of Thurles (1850) condemned the state system of mixed education and warned that 'the separate education of Catholic youth is, in every way, to be preferred to it'.[32] In the 1850s and 1860s as the Catholic Church gained increasing power within the national system of education it called for state funded education for Catholics. In 1859 ten of the now twenty commissioners on the Board of Education were Catholic. By 1860 the Catholic bishops banned all Catholic children and teachers from attending interdenominational model schools and training colleges.[33]

Successive arguments over what constituted secular and religious instruction, over text books and methodologies, over the training and appointment of teachers, as well as the funding and management of schools, meant that the interdenominational project was showing signs of terminal illness by the middle of the nineteenth century. The decline of this denominationally mixed system appears to have been constant and irreversible. The national system had become, *de facto*, denominational by the end of the nineteenth century. The Government, who recognised the denominational training colleges from 1883 onwards, displayed an outward sign of having conceded to the demands for denominational education. As there was no legislation governing the national system, since it was never established by an act of parliament, it is impossible to say when the system became *de jure* denominational and so the recognition and award of funding to the denominational training colleges, both Protestant and Catholic, in 1883, is a landmark date. St Patrick's Training College for men was founded in 1875 under the direct auspices of the Archbishop of Dublin, but its recognition and funding by the Government in 1883, as well as the recognition and funding of Our Lady of Mercy Training College for women teachers, Baggot Street (1883), subsequently known as Carysfort College, and the Church of Ireland Training College in Kildare Place, Dublin, indicated an almost total and irreversible disintegration of the interdenominational project. At the turn of the century more denominational training colleges were opened by the De La Salle Brothers in Waterford (1891), the Mercy Sisters in Limerick (1898), and the Dominican Sisters in Belfast (1900).[34] The disintegration of the denominational system was also aided by the 1878 Intermediate Education Act which established a secondary system of education and funded denominational schools on a payments by examination results basis. The 1878 Act prohibited examinations in religion at secondary level. It also included a conscience clause which governed all schools and gave parents the right to withdraw children from denominational religious instruction of which they did not approve.

By the early 1880s just over 55 per cent of national schools were attended by both Catholic and Protestant children whereas this figure was reduced to nearly 28 per cent by 1912.

'In 1899, out of a total of 8,670 national schools, 3,993 were under Roman Catholic teachers exclusively, and attended solely by Roman Catholic children; 1,393 schools were under Protestant teachers exclusively and attended solely by Protestant children.'[35]

By the end of the nineteenth century the Education Board governed seven types of schools – ordinary national schools, model schools, jail schools, workhouse schools, industrial schools, model agricultural schools and evening schools. When surveying the whole elementary or national school sector in the nineteenth century one can observe that the system of education was formal and academic and 'the three R's' figured prominently. The movement from an interdenominational to a denominational national school system in the nineteenth century left the Catholic Church in a very strong position. At the beginning of the nineteenth century the Catholic Church was recovering from the wounds of penal legislation and persecution. As the century advanced, the Catholic Church's power increased dramatically and its influence in the educational system augmented so that by 1900, it was 'rich, enormously influential, and superbly organised.'[36]

The Twentieth Century Onwards

In 1900 a new Revised Programme for National Schools was adopted. Schools began to focus more on the education of infants and greater attention was paid to creating a pleasant learning environment in the school. With the celtic revival bi-lingual programmes were adopted for schools in gaeltacht areas and discovery methods of teaching meant that children explored their local environments and engaged in nature and local studies.[37]

The Treaty was signed on December 6, 1921 and the Free State came into being on December 6, 1922.[38] The system of education operative after the founding of the Irish Free State largely involved maintaining the same British imperial structure that had prevailed in the nineteenth century. Between 1922 and 1924 there was no Department of Education. In 1924 the Department of Education was established to co-ordinate primary, secondary and technical education under the one Minister for Education. The Free State did not engage in a radical revision of the educational system as it simply accepted the colonial structures and management systems, which had given rise to the national school system. It did however adjust aspects of the system relating to the position of Irish language, culture, music, tradition and history that it found dissatisfactory. From St Patrick's day 1922, Irish became an obligatory subject in all national schools and children were obliged to study it for at least one hour each day. Indeed Irish became the sole medium for teaching in some national schools and just as the schools had been used as tools for anglicisation under colonial rule they now became tools for gaelicisation and nationalism under the Free State. After 1922 the situation with regard to religious instruction was not greatly changed with the exception that in this post-colonial era the huge emphasis on all things Irish, including language, sport, music, dance, literature and history, meant a greater emphasis on Catholicism as the religion of nationalism.[39] In 1929 a voluntary Primary Certificate examination was introduced to assess primary children's competence in a range of subject areas. By 1943 this examination, which focused on 'the three R's', became compulsory for all children in sixth standard (equivalent to today's sixth class in primary school).

In the twentieth century the Catholic Church occupied a central position in the formation of primary teachers and in the patronage, management and ownership of primary schools.

'Practically all of the national schools were managed by boards which are chaired *ex officio* by clergymen and whose other membership was determined partly by church decision; in addition the legal trustees of the school property also came from the ranks of senior diocesan clergymen and church parochial officers.'[40]

Some have argued that since independence the state has benefited financially from the involvement of the Churches in education. Religious or parish owned schools contribute financially to the building cost and maintenance of the school. For their part the Churches have benefited significantly from their involvement in education and they have been granted a huge degree of autonomy in the management of schools, in the formation and appointment of teachers, and in the design, delivery and assessment of the syllabus for religious education in primary schools.[41] This relationship was placed on a strong legal foothold in the Irish Constitution of 1937 which outlined the basic rights of all Irish citizens. Article 42 concerns education and identifies the family as the primary educator of the child and guarantees to respect the right of parents to provide for the religious and moral, intellectual, physical and social education of their children. Article 44 concerns religion and originally the Constitution gave privileged status to the Catholic Church. Article 44.2 originally stated that 'the State recognises the special position of the Holy Catholic Apostolic and Roman Church as the guardian of the Faith professed by the great majority of the citizens.'[42] This special relationship between the Catholic Church and the state was applauded as a 'rebirth and a fine flowering of Irish education, hindered only on the material side by the very limited economic development of the country.'[43] However the special relationship changed when Article 44.2 was subsequently repealed so that the Constitution now reads 'The State guarantees not to endow any religion.'

While there were many significant twentieth and twenty-first century developments within primary education in general, this chapter's particular focus on the history of religious education mandates that only certain aspects of some important events and debates can be touched upon. Key developments in Irish primary education in the latter half of the twentieth century such as the introduction of the 1971 curriculum, the 1998 Education Act and the 1999 curriculum will be explored more fully in chapter seven. At this juncture it is sufficient to note that neither curricula (1971, 1999) provided a radical alteration of the status of what was termed religious instruction (1971) or religious education (1999) within the Irish national school system. For now it is important to stress that the 1998 Education Act recognised 'the rights of the different Church authorities to design curricula in religious education at primary level and to supervise their teaching and implementation'.[44] Thus the various Church or religious authorities, and not the Department of Education and Science, are responsible for the religious education curriculum in the primary school. Both curricula recognised the parents' right to withdraw the child from religious education. The 1999 curriculum stresses the individual's right to religious freedom as well as the school's duty to be 'flexible in making alternative organisational arrangements for those who do not wish to avail of the particular religious education it offers.'[45]

Diversity of School Types to Cater for Specific Religious Needs

One major recent historical development of great significance for religious education in Ireland is the provision of diverse types of primary schools to cater for the religious and educational needs of children. The Dublin Talmud Torah is part of an international Jewish educational movement which was originally established to promote Jewish religious education and which subsequently broadened to include all areas of education. In 1934 Zion National School was founded in Bloomfield Avenue, Dublin, under the management of The Dublin Talmud Torah to provide children with a national school education within a Jewish ethos. In 1980 the school relocated to its present day site at Stratford College, Rathgar and simultaneously changed its name to Stratford National School or as it is officially known Scoil Náisiúnta Stratford. The School's Official Handbook states that 'Stratford National School is Ireland's only Jewish primary school and (it) provides a primary education within a Jewish ethos, as defined by The Chief Rabbi of Ireland. However, we are very proud that our enrolment consists of pupils from a wide range of religious and cultural backgrounds and we cherish the valuable contribution all our families make to the school.' In the same text The Chief Rabbi states that 'The goal of Stratford National School is to educate our students in an inclusive, exemplary academic environment that promotes the ethics and values of the Jewish people, while simultaneously teaching our Irish heritage. We produce young people who have a keen sense of compassion, of commitment to lifelong learning, of respect for diversity and of service to the community.'

At Stratford National School religious education for Jewish children is structured around six subjects, comprising General Jewish Knowledge, Study of the Five Books of Moses, Prayers, Hebrew Writing, Hebrew Reading and Hebrew Grammar. This Jewish Study programme aims to enable Jewish children to cultivate a love for Jewish learning, to nurture a pride in being part of the Jewish people and to attain a proficiency in Jewish learning and practice by promoting and developing Jewish study skills. Many pupils at Stratford National School come from a wide range of religious and cultural backgrounds. A full programme of Catholic sacramental preparation and Catholic religious education is available at Stratford National School for Catholic children from junior infants up to sixth class. Each day in the national school the Jewish Studies programme is available for Jewish children and the Catholic religious education programme is available for Catholic children from 8.40 a.m. before secular classes commence at 10.05 a.m.

The founding of the Dalkey School Project in 1978 marks the beginning of Ireland's multi-denominational primary school sector. This rapidly expanding multi-denominational sector has had a considerable impact on Irish primary education and it revised and challenged perceived notions of the role of religious education in the primary educational system. The recognition by the recent 1998 Act of the rights of 'the different Church authorities' to design curricula excludes a reference to a non-religious body designing a curriculum for religious education in primary schools. Chapter Seven engages in an analysis of the philosophy of Educate Together schools as well as the positive contribution which *Learn Together* (2004), the Ethical Education Curriculum for Educate Together schools, has made to the debate on religious education and inclusivity.

Another major development occurred in Dublin on 1 September 1990 when the first Muslim national school in Ireland opened its doors. This multi-cultural and multi-racial school is confessional and denominational in nature and has a distinct Muslim ethos that is reflected in its uniform (in accordance with Islamic code of dress), Islamic resources and practices. Many children are multilingual and while English is the common linguistic medium, children learn Irish and Arabic. Holidays coincide with major Islamic festivals (Ramadan, Eid-ul-Fitr, Eid-al-Adha) and from Third Class onwards children perform daily midday prayer (Dhuhr) and attend weekly Jummah (Friday prayers). At the official opening of the school in April 1993, the then president, Mary Robinson, said that the Irish Muslim children who welcomed her to the school 'help to broaden our sense of Irishness, they enrich us with their strong and symbolic sense of culture and ideals.'[46]

The teaching of Religious Studies, Qur'an and Arabic is carried out by specialist Muslim teachers. As the Irish Muslim community grew in the nineties it became evident that there was a huge need to provide Religious Studies, Qur'an and Arabic for Muslim children who could not attend the State's sole Muslim national school. In 2000 the Weekend Islamic School opened in Dublin to provide regular Islamic education (Arabic, Qur'an and Religious Studies) for children who did not receive Islamic education in their local schools. In 2001 a second Muslim national school opened (North Dublin Muslim School). In 2002 an evening Qur'anic school opened to teach Qur'an to children from four years old upward.

A further increase in the provision of types of national school was brought about by a secular patronal body, An Foras Patrúnachta. An Foras Patrúnachta was founded in 1993 with the aim of establishing Gaelscoileanna. An Foras is patron to catholic (with a small 'c'), interdenominational and multidenominational schools. The existence of a patronal body with involvement in three different school types exemplifies the increasing demand for choice in Irish primary education. In the interdenominational schools Church of Ireland and Catholic faith traditions are fully respected and taught. The confessional religious education programme followed for each denomination (for example, *Follow Me* and *Alive-O*) is set down by the respective bishops. The 'Dunboyne controversy', in which a primary school principal was dismissed in an interdenominational Gaelscoil in 2002, testifies to the difficulty faced by one teacher, in one classroom, simultaneously leading children from two distinct denominations to a mature faith, as that is understood by each of those separate denominations.[47] Teachers have to be conversant with the doctrinal nuances of both traditions, while providing a respectful confessional and (for Catholics) sacramental education which identifies the differences and similarities in both traditions and which is acceptable to the Episcopal authorities of both traditions as well as the patronal body.[48] An Foras sees it as crucial that both the Catholic and Church of Ireland religious education programmes are to be followed, within school hours, in their entirety.

PART 2: THE HISTORY OF RELIGIOUS EDUCATION IN THE NATIONAL SCHOOL SYSTEM

The Catechism as a Catechetical Tool

The catechism was the major catechetical tool used by the Catholic Church from the inception of the national school system in Ireland (1831) until after Vatican II (1962-1965). Indeed Edward Rogan claims that the catechism contributed to the remarkable success of Roman Catholicism in Ireland from the mid-nineteenth to the mid-twentieth century. The catechism was responsible for the fact that in this period 'Irish Catholics in general were instructed in the truths of their religion with a thoroughness previously unseen in Ireland.'[49] The catechism was 'the basis of the primary school catechetical system in Ireland' up until the nineteen seventies.[50] For this reason it is important to examine the catechism's history and influence in the Irish national school system.

The word catechism comes from the Greek *katekhismos*, which means to teach by word of mouth. It refers to a summary of Christian teaching and principles often designed in easily memorised question and answer form. Catechisms, which are found in many Christian denominations,[51] became popular after the Reformation (c.1500–c.1600). In the post-reformation period the Catholic Church was greatly concerned with the preservation of doctrinal and moral truth, and the elimination of error. The Council of Trent (1545-1563) acknowledged the importance of teaching the faith accurately and to this end prescribed what was subsequently known as *The Roman Catechism* (1566), for use in the teaching of clergy. This catechism was initially used to help priests make appropriate links in their homilies at mass between the Gospel text and official Church teaching or doctrine. In 1614 the Provincial Synod of Armagh prescribed the Roman catechism for Irish clergy and in 1660 the Tuam Synod directed that every parish priest should have a copy of *The Roman Catechism*.[52] The Catechism provided a summary of officially sanctioned Church doctrine which covered the major areas of faith and morals. In the immediate aftermath of the Reformation catechisms were clergy-oriented and provided more detailed explanatory accounts of the topics under discussion. Subsequently catechisms were devised by different Religious Orders and dioceses for the instruction of the laity. Two Jesuits, Robert Bellarmine (1542-1621) and Peter Canisius (1520-1597), produced classic catechism texts that exercised great influence on Irish catechisms. For instance 'all the Irish language catechisms of the seventeenth century are rooted, directly or indirectly, in the Jesuit texts.'[53] It should also be noted that *A Catechism of Christian Doctrine*, most commonly referred to as 'the penny catechism' was written by the English Bishop Challoner (1691-1781) and was based on the work of Bellarmine and Canisius. It is estimated that up to 15 million copies of the penny catechism have been sold worldwide and it has undoubtedly had a significant influence on faith formation in Ireland.[54] From the nineteenth to the mid-twentieth century catechisms were designed for use in an Irish classroom context and they condensed doctrine into shorter, more easily memorisable phrases. As the focus of the catechism moved from the pulpit to the classroom the material was simplified to suit the more general needs of the teacher and pupil. The question and answer format was a mnemonic device used to enable Catholics to access and assimilate 'a summary of Catholic theology'.[55] The catechism is still viewed as an important catechetical device designed 'to guard and present better the precious deposit of Christian doctrine in order to make it more accessible to the Christian faithful and to all people of good will.'[56] If one wishes to find out what the official Catholic Church teaching on a subject is, the authorised and logically structured *Catechism of the Catholic Church* (1994), should be a standard reference text. It is also to be noted that there are many contemporary on-line versions of catechisms.[57]

To present the notion that over the last two hundred years one standard version of a catechism was ferverently adhered to at all times by Catholics and clergy is to generalise and caricature the reality. From 1831 onward the religious instruction given to Catholic children in national school was neither uniform in content nor mode of delivery. Multiple accounts testify to its variable quality. One account written just before the famine castigates Irish priests for the poor quality of their sermons and suggests that 'the ignorance of the people in matters of religion was frightful, and, in particular, that the doctrine of the Trinity was rarely known or ever heard of'.[58] There were complaints that clergy failed to visit the national schools and neglected to instruct children.[59] In more recent decades a survey of Ireland's primary Diocesan Inspectors carried out in the 1960s uncovered that regionally varied syllabi, texts and teaching methods were the norm.[60] However from the inception of the national school system up until the nineteen seventies, the catechism methodology, which was interpreted variously from diocese to diocese and which was supported by a whole variety of different catechism texts, dominated the field of Catholic religious instruction.

The format or lay out of the catechisms varies. For instance the *Catechism of the Council of Trent* is broken into four parts dealing with the Creed (Part I); the Sacraments (Part II); the Ten Commandments (Part III) and Prayer (Part IV). A commonly used mid-twentieth century catechism textbook *A Catechism of Catholic Doctrine*[61] followed this standard Creed, Commandments, Prayer and Sacraments presentation of material. This is the 'traditional' order of Catholic Catechisms and it is interesting to note that more recent catechisms generally conform to these four parts.[62]

Although catechisms have the same general structure they vary greatly in how they select and sequence material for presentation. In general, Catholic catechisms tell the story of God's relationship to human beings through the creation, the fall, the incarnation, the sacraments, the commandments and prayer. The advantages of using a catechism text in a school context were obvious. Catechisms enabled teachers to teach a clear, structured, authorised, programme of religious instruction with its own definite question and answer methodology and inbuilt assessment procedure. A teacher knew exactly what he or she had to teach and a child knew exactly what he or she had to learn. The child's capacity to reproduce the exact answer to the question prescribed in the catechism text indicated whether appropriate teaching and learning had taken place. Futhermore, the one inexpensive catechism text was generally used from infants up to senior classes. Consequently children could give a progressive, precise account of official Church teaching on a host of doctrinal, moral and spiritual matters.

In the early eighteenth century there were two Irish traditions of Catechisms which exercised an enormous influence on religious instruction in Irish schools. The first catechism tradition came from the catechisms of Andrew

Donleavy (1680-1746) and Michael O'Reilly (d. 1758).[63] Opinions vary on how the catechisms in the Donleavy–O'Reilly tradition interrelate, and on whether Donleavy's and O'Reilly's catechisms were both dependant on an older unknown source.[64] The second tradition stems from the Butler Catechism, so called because it originated from the Catechism written by the Archbishop of Cashel, Dr James Butler (1774-1791). Butler's catechism which was originally published around 1775,[65] was revised in 1802. It became known as Butler's General[66] because the hierarchy adopted it as a catechism for general use in Ireland. A further revision of Butler's General in 1882 became known as the 'Maynooth Catechism'. Some academics have made a detailed study of the various versions of the catechisms within these two main traditions by examining their composition dates as well as the main influences and merits of each individual text.[67] While an analysis of this detailed research is beyond the scope of this chapter it is important to note that these two catechism traditions were hugely influential on the religious formation of Irish clergy and laity for almost two hundred years. In particular various editions and versions of the Butler and Maynooth catechisms exercised a profound influence on religious instruction in Irish national schools from the 1850s until the 1970s.[68] James Joyce (1882-1941) illustrated how the catechism had permeated the intellectual and social fabric of everyday Irish life as he set the scene for his short story, 'A Painful Case', in his *Dubliners* collection (1914). Joyce describes the contents of James Duffy's room and notes that on a wooden bookcase 'A complete Wordsworth stood at one end of the lowest shelf and a copy of the Maynooth Catechism, sewn into the cloth cover of a notebook, stood at one end of the top shelf.'[69] Joyce's listing of Duffy's physical and intellectual furniture, is a literary testimony to the prevalence of the Maynooth catechism.

The influence of the Catechism in the Nineteenth Century

The hierarchical, clericalised Church and education system of the nineteenth century meant that bishops controlled the diocese and its priests and in turn the priest controlled the parish, including the catechetical activity within the parish school. The priest, either in the church or school, actively initiated catechetical work for a largely passive and recipient laity. For those who attended Sunday mass the religious instruction provided to Catholic children in the national school was complimented by the catechesis or faith formation given by the priest at the homily. There is also some evidence to suggest that some hedge school masters taught catechism in the chapel before mass on Sundays.[70] Lay people were also involved in the religious instruction of Catholic children through religious and devotional societies such as Confraternities and Sodalities which flourished in Ireland from the early nineteenth to the early twentieth century. Confraternity members were lay people who pledged to attend church on a weekly basis, usually on a Sunday, to give moral and catechetical instruction to children. The catechism, which was used as a vehicle for catechesis by some of these confraternities, was sometimes distributed free of charge to confraternity members.[71]

A variety of catechetical materials were used in classrooms, churches and homes in the form of pamphlets, missals, brievaries, editions of the lives of the saints, and pious books which exercised a profound influence on the education of both clergy, lay people and children. In general one can say that as literacy levels improved in the nineteenth and twentieth centuries, the influence of the Catechism on the religious instruction of Catholics was unrivalled. With rising school attendance it is unsurprising that children and adults came under the direct and formal influence of the methodology and content of the catechism in a manner unequalled by any other text or method.[72]

The Catechism in the Twentieth Century

For the first half of the twentieth century the catechism became so identified with religious instruction that the two almost became identical. Many dioceses had their own programme of religious instruction with their own versions of the catechism. These regionally varied catechisms were generally based on the Butler and Maynooth catechism traditions and the Diocesan Inspector of Catholic religious instruction paid an annual visit to the school to assess the children's knowledge of the catechism and the teacher's capacity to teach it.[73] Brendan Behan recounts the nerve-wracking experience of learning the catechism as part of the preparation for the sacrament of Confirmation at the beginning of his famous short story, 'The Confirmation Suit'.

> For weeks it was nothing but simony and sacrilege, and the sins crying to heaven for vengeance, the big green Catechism in our hands, walking home along the brewery wall, with a butt too, to help our wits, what is pure spirit, and don't kill that, Billser has to get a drag out of it yet, what do I mean by apostate, and hell and heaven and despair and presumption and hope.[74]

Behan's presentation of the influence of the catechism on the lives of the children is simultaneously comic and tragic. However learning the catechism was no laughing matter. Once the teacher and child were immersed in the world view of the catechism the logic of its system was flawless. The catechism ressembled a legal document in its clarity of definition,

methodology and logic. Clear concise questions were followed
by short focused answers. In one sense catechisms function like
a memory rap with some part of the question being typically
repeated in the answer. Questions 232 and 297 of the
Explanatory Catechism of Christian Doctrine (1921) ask:

> Q. *Is it a mortal sin to neglect to hear Mass on Sundays*
> *and Holydays of Obligation?*
> A. It is a mortal sin to neglect to hear Mass on
> Sundays and Holydays of Obligation.
> Q. *How many things have we to do in order to prepare*
> *for confession?*
> A. We have four things to do in order to prepare
> for confession: first, we must heartily pray for
> grace to make a good confession; secondly, we
> must carefully examine our conscience; thirdly, we
> must take time and care to make a good act of
> contrition; and fourthly, we must resolve by the
> help of God to renounce our sins, and to begin a
> new life for the future.[75]

In the course of the primary education children were typically
required to memorise more than four hundred catechism
questions of varying degrees of difficulty. By the 1950s real
attempts were made to make the catechism format and text
child friendly. Monsignor Tynan, a leader in the field of Irish
Catechetics, inserted coloured illustrations into his *My First
Catechism* (1953) text so the teachers and children could have
some visual stimulation for their religious imaginations.
However even in the 1960s visual aids were not commonly used
in the text-dependent teaching of religious instruction.[76]
Tynan's catechism made reference to scripture and provided
notes to parents and teachers outlining the system for three
levels of age-appropriate material in the one book. Questions

with a blue dot were intended for six-year-olds, questions with a red dot for seven-year-olds and questions with a black dot for eight-year-olds. From nine years onwards all children were required to learn all of the catechism questions.

The text, *A Catechism of Catholic Doctrine* (1951), contains four hundred and forty three questions as well as the main devotional prayers of the Catholic Church. This catechism could be described as a book of the 'hereafter' with little attention on the now as questions in the section on the commandments focus on Hell and Limbo and present a legalistic, harsh and fearful image of God.[77] The catechism's question and answer format was intended as a summary of a much larger doctrine which the teacher was required to explain to the pupil. In a catechism titled *Doctrine for Seniors*[78] the teacher's introduction states that 'it should be remembered, however, that the question and answer are merely a convenient summary of our Doctrine. The fuller understanding required can be got only by carefully studying the explanation.'[79] The notion of differentiating the material to suit the age of the children was quite commonplace by the 1960s when the catechism was in serious decline as a catechetical tool. For example the Dioceses of Cork and Ross' *Short Catechism* (1962) outlined the programme of religious instruction for children in its primary schools. Junior Infants were given simple instructions on 'God, Creation, Jesus Christ, Our Blessed Lady, Sin, Heaven, Hell, Purgatory.' In Senior Infants these topics were given more 'advanced treatment'. By First Class children who were making their First Communion were introduced to the 'Life of Our Lord, in outline (Incarnation to Ascension); Sacraments of Penance and the Blessed Eucharist; the Joyful mysteries of the Rosary.' Each subsequent year the children were introduced to further and increasingly complex new topics while simultaneously revising previously covered topics. By sixth standard the children were expected to know the whole of the Senior Catechism with additional prayers in Irish or English and Latin and were instructed in a 'Synopsis of the Old Testament; Sacraments of Matrimony and Holy Orders; Vocations; duties of station-in-life; a rule of life'. The cognitive content of this doctrinally laden religious instruction programme was challenging for both teachers and children. While an attempt was made to make the catechism more accessible to the child, the theological concepts and language meant that much of the religious teaching went over the children's heads. For instance the seven-year-old Communion Class child had to learn numerous questions including fouteen questions on the Sacrament of Penance, some of which concerned contrition or sorrow for ones sins.

6. *How many kinds of contrition are there?*
There are two kinds of contrition: perfect contrition and imperfect contrition, which is also called attrition.
7. *Can a person in mortal sin regain the state of grace before receiving the sacrament of Penance?*
A person in mortal sin can regain the state of grace by making an act of perfect contrition, but he must intend to receive the sacrament, and must confess the sin in his next confession.[80]

The dichotomy between the child's lived experience and the cerebral, legalistic language and concepts of the catechism was enormous. While other educators were profiling the psychological and intellectual development of the child and attempting to design child-centred, age-appropriate learning experiences, Catechists continued to rely on the catechism.

The Decline of the Catechism as a Pedagogical Tool in the Twentieth Century

Concern about the efficacy of the catechism's question and answer methodology and reliance on memorisation was raised in the early decades of the twentieth century. In Europe from the nineteen twenties onwards, what was subsequently known as the Munich Method or Catechetical Renewal left the existing catechisms unchallenged but sought a new method to teach them more effectively. This method was influenced by Friedrich Herbart's (1776-1841) educational psychology which proposed that children learn in three stages: (1) through the senses, (2) through their intellect and (3) through putting what they have understood into practice. The Munich method proposed that teaching should provide three corresponding steps: (1) through presentation of visual aids or Bible stories, (2) through explanation of doctrines and (3) through application to the child's life.[81]

While there was no direct correlation of the Catechetical Renewal or Munich method in Irish primary schools, attempts were being made from the nineteen thirties onwards to find better ways of teaching the catechism. Speaking in 1937 at a conference on the teaching of Religion in Dublin, Rev. Dr E. Leen lamented that the poor results obtained from teaching the catechism were disproportionate to the energy put into teaching it. This, he argued, was because the wording of the catechism was too difficult and too theological for children, and the repetitious methods of rote learning and memorisation were not child friendly. Leen concluded that while children who were taught the catechism learned 'a certain amount of doctrinal matter', it had no formative effect on their souls. Consequently children suffered from an excess of information and a paucity of formation.[82]

A series of articles written in the 1940s and 1950s lamented the huge gap which developed between the child's lived experience and their perception of the catechism. A typical illustration of this fissure comes from a woman who tells of her confusion as a seven-year-old child, in a 1920's catechism class, when she had to rote learn that there were 'seven deadly or capital sins, namely: Pride, Covetousness, Lust, Anger, Gluttony, Envy and Sloth.' She was puzzled by this as she counted eight sins, since she was under the impression that 'namely' was a deadly sin! To a child of seven years of age none of these sins made any sense and so the catechism cultivated parrotism where 'namely' was as deadly as covetousness or sloth! The level of the theologically laden content of the catechism was hugely inappropriate for children. Even the very bright children experienced considerable difficulties in memorising the doctrinal content which they failed to understand. One can only conjecture how torturous the catechism must have been for children who experienced difficulties in literacy, comprehension and memorisation. Those children who could recite the catechism off by heart had little or no knowledge of what it meant.[83] It was believed that children were investing in their future as adults when they would come to a full understanding of the catechism's content. However, the methods used to teach the catechism were often counterproductive. It must not be forgotten that at this time memorisation played a large part in the school curriculum for other subject areas and the catechism was taught, through rote learning and memorisation, in a manner that was consistent with many other subject areas.

In his poem 'Catechism' Brendan Kennelly explores the spiritual poverty and savage repercussions of badly taught catechism. Here the catechism's question and answer format becomes a theatre for violence as the omniscient teacher, Mulcahy, savagely fires missile-like questions at his terrified pupils. Mulcahy who 'teaches God' simultaneously brutalises his pupils through actions which directly contradict the material being taught.

> Religion class. Mulcahy taught us God
> While he heated his arse to a winter fire
> Testing with his fingers the supple sallyrod.
> 'Explain the Immaculate Conception, Maguire,
> And tell us then about the Mystical Blood.'
> Maguire failed. Mulcahy covered the boy's head
> With his satchel, shoved him stumbling among the
> desks, lashed his bare legs until they bled.[84]

The most poignant images linking the mystical blood with the blood on Maguire's legs, culminate in the pithy sentence 'Maguire failed'. The catechism becomes a catalyst for the child's failure, a teacher's reign of terror, and the failure of a whole system of religious instruction. Mulcahy asks unrelenting questions 'Who goes to hell, Dineen? Kane, what's a saint? Doolin what constitutes a mortal sin? Flynn, what of the man who calls his brother a fool?'. In Kennelly's poem deep religious questions surrounding Mary's birth, Jesus' death, the Eucharist and evil, became an opportunity for a frustrated teacher's violence and a savage repression of the children's own religious imaginations. Kennelly's poetic device highlights some of the difficulties with the catechism's methodology and content.

The irony of this system of religious instruction is that although it was based on a question and answer methodology it effectively destroyed the child's natural capacity to question any aspect of religion.[85] While the catechism had the positive advantage of providing a definite body of content, a clear logical structure, and a systematic approach to religious instruction, it did not encourage the children to ask their own questions, in their own voice as they spontaneously and idiosyncratically arose. In the catechism's worldview preset questions were allocated preset answers and the passive learner received the wisdom of the tradition through memorisation. In the catechism system the question which many contemporary adults find the most difficult question to answer, that is 'Who is God?', is one of the easiest questions which a six-year-old is called on to answer. In *My First Catechism* 'Who is God?' is the second question asked to Infants after the question 'Who made the world?'[86]

Kerygmatic Approach

The Kerygmatic approach originated with the work of two pioneering Jesuits, Josef Andreas Jungmann and Johannes Hofinger. Jungmann's text *The Good News, Yesterday and Today* (1936) marked a radical initiative in religious education by outlining a three stage catechetical process focusing on (1) 'The Situation', (2) 'Historical Reflections' and (3) 'Our Task'. Jungmann identified the situation as one of crisis because a scholastic theological system (catechism) was superimposed on Catholics when the Church should have been engaging in a pastoral proclamation of the Good News, the gospel of Jesus Christ. Jungmann's historical reflections brought him right back to the early Church's proclamation of faith which was joyously centred on Christ. He was aware that for too long the Catholic Church was involved in a defensive, anti-protestant counter-reformation. He heralded the arrival of the positive reformation where the Church, inspired by the early Christian communities, should joyfully centre her teaching on the person of Jesus Christ.[87] A survey of salvation history convinced him that Christ, the Bible and the sacraments, should be the central 'kerygma' ('Christian message') of all catechesis. Catechesis based on Christ, and not on catechisms or doctrine, are the heart of religious education. The teacher assumes great importance in Jungmann's kerygmatic system and is the herald or joyful messanger of God's word. In this approach the catechism is used by the teacher as a secondary reference text to help compile material for lessons.

There is no direct correspondence between Irish religious instruction and Jungmann's kerygmatic method although its influence on Irish catechesis is evident in the more bible-centred approach from the fifties onwards. In the fifties and sixties attempts were made to make the catechism more child-friendly, more age- and ability- appropriate, and more Christ-centred, but they could not redeem a system that was already under pressure. Ireland was experiencing the crisis that Jungmann had outlined in the 1930s. *Catechism Notes* (1959) disarmingly accepts that 'religious topics are naturally dry' while King notes that catechism class 'is at least a dull business for both teacher and pupil'.[88] The whole catechism methodology tended to rely too heavily on the text, the intellect and doctrine, and it concentrated too little on the pupil and the teacher. Church doctrine replaced Jesus Christ at the heart of religious instruction as teachers presented the catechism text to their pupils and almost said 'take this book and eat it'.[89] This is a world away from Jungmann's joyful proclamation of the Good News and yet many Irish catechists recognised that they were undergoing a crisis and even though they did not generally have the language to describe its cause they knew intuitively that doctrine should be subservient to kerygma. Experts recognised that 'The Catechism will always be of far less importance than the catechist'.[90]

Inevitably there were gifted teachers who taught the catechism creatively and nurtured the children's own religious questions, however a survey of the literature would suggest that these were the exception as opposed to the rule. Despite the fact that gifted teachers did use their skills to bring the doctrine to life, the text more often than not supplanted the teacher while the child as learner was almost forgotten in the whole enterprise.[91] By the 1960s it was readily accepted that catechisms could provide theological information for children but they were not 'life' texts[92] and could not form them spiritually. It became increasingly common for diocesan programmes to exclude catechism texts for infants classes. From the 1930s onwards there had been successive calls for the reform of the doctrinally based catechism system of religious instruction. In the sixties and seventies Tynan argued that where the catechism is concerned 'instruction should mingle with piety' for 'study of the Catechism demands something besides the exercise of intelligence and goodwill. It demands that we should be saying our prayers and participating faithfully in the sacred liturgy.'[93] Kerygmatic influences were discernable in the 1960s which tended to emphasise the teacher's explanation of the catechism more and the children's recitation less. To this end catechisms included more teacher notes, more visual illustrations, and more emphasis on biblical texts. Innovative dioceses such as Ossory and Limerick began to use concrete materials and visual aids in teaching religion. In 1960 a Filmstrip library for catechetical use was founded by the Bishop of Ossory.[94] Attempts to modernise catechisms and to make them more Christ-centred, more liturgical and more pastoral were influenced by the kerygmatic approach.[95] The scriptural and christocentric *On Our Way* series that was used in some primary schools in the 1960s and 1970s bears the hallmark of kerygmatic renewal.

The Anthropological Approach

While the kerygmatic approach placed the Kerygma (Good News) at the heart of catechesis, the anthropological approach which succeeded it placed the human person at the centre of the catechetical process. The anthropological approach was influenced by Vatican II's understanding of revelation as God's personal disclosure to human persons, and not as a set of abstract doctrines and propositions (catechism). Theologians who placed renewed emphasis on the human person stated that God did not by-pass human experience which mediates and manifests the human-divine relationship. Religious Educators were dissatisfied with approaches which placed a body of content (doctrinal) or a message (kerygmatic approach) at the heart of catechesis. By the mid sixties, in what is now known as the 'early anthropological approach', writers such as Gabriel Moran placed the learner – the child – at the heart of catechesis. Later more radical understandings of the anthropological approach looked at the learners' political and social situation and argued that religious education should be a transforming force for social justice. The anthropological approach relied on the disciplines of anthropology and sociology and attempted to make catechesis relevant to the concrete, lived experience of those being catechised.

In the early seventies the Irish Bishops decided to provide a national, standardised programme of religious education in all Catholic Irish primary schools. In 1973 the first National Catechetical Programme, the *Children of God* series, was developed and widely used in Ireland and the United Kingdom.[96] The early anthropological approach is visible in the programme's aims to communicate 'Christian Revelation to children in their concrete situation with a view to fostering faith'. The programme also included elements of the doctrinal (revelation; question & answer; rote learning), kerygmatic (scripture-centred; Christ-centred)[97] and early anthropological (child-centred; experience centred) approaches to catechesis.[98] The series consisted of eight teacher's manuals and eight pupil's books covering the primary cycle from Junior Infants to Sixth Class.[99] Each teacher's book contained a detailed introduction to the programme and an explanation of its rationale. The programme recognised the need to form a partnership between parents, teacher and priests and it located the starting point for religious reflection in the child's concrete situation and experiences.

The syllabus for the *Children of God* series, while unpublished, has changed in the course of its second presentation and representation[100] yet the general methodological approach, the anthropological-experiential approach which has guided the Irish National Catechetical Programme from 1973 to 2005 has remained the same. From 1983 to 1987 Maura Hyland engaged in a *second* presentation of the original *Children of God* series.[101] This bi-lingual second presentation which consisted of eight teacher manuals and eight children's text books, 'used themes based on the life experiences of the children'.[102] The *re*-presentation of the National Catechetical Programme in 1996 resulted in the *Alive-O* series (1996-2004). According to its writers the *Alive-O* programme, titled from St Irenaeus' phrase that 'the glory of God is people fully alive',[103] is profoundly biblical and anthropological and it aims to 'help the children to relate their discovery of themselves, of other people and of their world to God who is the creator of all things, the source of all life, who loves and cares for each of them and is always with them'.[104] The programme is deeply conscious of the need to provide religious education in a manner appropriate to children's ability, age, 'stage of faith development and life experience.'[105] *Alive-O* is a bilingual programme[106] consisting of eight *Alive-O* kits, specifically designed for each class in the primary school. The kits consist of 'the teacher's book, the pupil text, the relevant video tape, music CDs or cassette tapes, a workbook, parent information sheets, liturgical information sheets and other specific materials'.[107] The need to update the programme was inspired by several factors including (i) the need to update and replace worn resources, (ii) the need to accommodate religious and social change in Ireland, (iii) the need to strengthen home, school and parish links, (iv) the need to use inclusive language, (v) the need to accommodate cultural diversity, (vi) the need to reflect more child-centred and discovery approaches to learning, for example, little beings, chatting, my thoughts 'n' things, (vii) the need to present a variety of approaches to prayer, (viii) the need to make use of contemporary ICT in the service of the Gospel, for example, DVDs, websites, (ix) the need to present more activity-based and interdisciplinary approaches to the teaching of religion, for example, pottery, weaving, dance and juggling.

From Junior Infants up to Second Class the programme uses a *Focus* (significant experience is introduced), *Explore* (active reflection on experience) and *Response* (active/prayerful acknowledgement of how the experience has affected the child) format. From Junior Infants up to Fourth Class inclusive each religious education lesson is divided into five parts, one part for each day of the week.[108] For Fifth and Sixth class the programme presents four flexible 'Moments' and 'More!' which the teacher can arrange to suit the needs of their class over five days.[109] The whole programme provides the raw ingredients for religious education in the form of stories, poems, songs, drama and so on. Each lesson offers the teacher the opportunity to select, arrange and present these elements (with the exception of story and prayer which must be covered) in a manner that is appropriate for the children.

One of the programme writers describes its approach as 'eclectic'[110] and it could be argued that this is both its strength and weakness. It has been argued that *Alive-O*'s interdisciplinary experiential approach is lacking in sufficient explicit religious or doctrinal content and could be seen as 'SPHE with a prayer added on'. Others see its methodological fluidity, where the teacher may select content from the menu within the lesson as insufficiently consistent and confusing. However it is important to keep in view that an initial evaluation of the programme shows that children, teachers, parents and priests view it 'very positively'.[111] A detailed evaluation of the entire programme has not been carried out to date although several significant pieces of research on various aspects of the programme have been undertaken.[112] *Alive-O's* 'Thought for the Teacher', its newsletters, liturgical links, publications for priests and parish personnel, as well as encouragement of parental involvement in school and parish based services (enrolement/sacramental/prayer/graduation services), strengthen the sense of religious education as a collaborative enterprise. The programme has been used widely in the UK and adapted for use in Scotland. The Church of Ireland, Methodist and Presbyterian Boards of Education have also based their own *Follow Me* series (2001)[113] on the *Alive-O* programme with the permission of the Irish Episcopal Commission.

Concluding Remarks

Religious education in Ireland has undergone enormous change in the last two hundred years. A radical shift in emphasis has moved religious education from the doctrinally laden catechism to the contemporary anthropological–experiental approach of the National Catechetical Programme. This shift in emphasis almost parallels the seismic change from pay and hedge school accommodation at the end of the eighteenth century to the purpose built, architecturally designed national school buildings of the twenty-first century. Religion has played a major role in the development of the Irish national school system and the rejection of the original interdenominational system established by the Stanley letter gave way to a denominationally-based and -driven educational system. The legacy of this system is seen in the denominational control of national school buildings, the management of the school personnel, control of enrolement policies and control of the design, delivery and assessment of the religious education programme. It is highly unlikely that Stanley envisaged that his mixed system of education would soon become a denominationally based system with Catholic schools accounting for almost 93 per cent of schools.

The diversification of multi-denominational, inter-denominational and confessional school types in the twentieth century marks an emphasis on the need for greater choice of school type for children, parents and teachers. It is ironic that the reintroduction of the interdenominational school sector at the end of the twentieth century was viewed as a new departure when it was, in some sense, a return to basic principles. While educational policy has changed enormously from the Stanley letter in 1831 to the 1998 Education Act, religious education has shown a lack of flexibility in the same time period and tended to become embedded in catechism methodology and texts. The National Catechetical Programme marked a watershed departure from the catechism, yet post-Conciliar religious education in Catholic schools has largely been operating under the one anthroplogical approach, which has been most recently re-presented in the *Alive-O* format. Irish religious education in Catholic schools needs a change of syllabus, programme and direction. In the last two hundred years the pendulum has swung from a doctrinally laden catechism approach to a more biblically based and experiental child-centred approach, by moving from theology to scripture to anthropology, from text to child, from assessment driven programme to a programme where formal assessment is almost entirely absent. At the beginning of the twenty first century it is necessary to move beyond this almost antithetical doctrinal-anthropological motion. Change is necessary so that Catholic religious education programmes with a strong interfaith and ecumenical emphasis can respond to the needs of a religiously diverse society. Furthermore, children's different learning styles and needs require a variety of Catholic religious education programmes, based on a national syllabus, instead of the present situation where there is one nationally agreed programme. A greater emphasis on the cognitive aspect of the faith and on religious ideas appropriate to the age and ability of the child could complement and deepen the experiential approach. Catholic schools in the Irish primary school system need a new syllabus and programme to meet the contemporary challenges which face religious education.

NOTES

1   Edward Rogan, *Irish Catechesis A Juridico-Historical Study of The Five Plenary Synods, 1850-1956*, Pontificia Universitas Gregoriana, Roma, 1987, p.xv.

2   At the end of the nineteenth century seven different types of national schools existed: ordinary national schools; model schools; jail schools; workhouse schools; industrial schools; model agricultural schools and evening schools.

3   Rogan, *Irish Catechesis*, p.6.

4   Rogan, *Irish Catechesis*, p. 7.

5   The last of the Penal Laws disappeared in 1829 with Catholic Emancipation. However as far as education was concerned the Penal Laws disappeared in 1782 with conditions and in 1793 with the Repeal Act.

6   From 1696 a Window Tax had to be paid on a house of more than 6 windows. This number changed to 7-9 windows in 1792 and 8 windows in 1825. The Window Tax ended in 1851.

7   J.D. King, *Religious Education in Ireland*, Fallons, 1970, p.3.

8   King, *Religious Education*, p.4. cf. Thomas Joseph Durcan, *History of Irish Education from 1800*, Dragon Books, 1972, p.6. The number could have been as high as half a million children. The 1826 Report shows that there were 9,000 pay schools in existence.

9   John Coolahan, *Irish Education history and structure*, Dublin: Institute of Public Administration, 1981, p.4.

10   Coolahan, *Irish Education*, p.3. In 1881 a national system of education was introduced in France.

11   In Ireland these official schools were known as English Schools.

12   Durcan, *History*, p.9.

13   King, *Religious Education*, p.5.

14   Áine Hyland & Kenneth Milne Eds. *Irish Educational Documents*, Volume 1., C.I.C.E., 1987, p.90.

15   These included Thomas Spring-Rice and Thomas Wyse.

16   Durcan, *History*, p.11.

17   Edward G. Stanley was sympathetic to Catholic concerns about proselytism and he noted that 'the indiscriminate reading of the Holy Scriptures without note or comment by children' was a defect which 'must be particularly obnoxious to a Church (Roman Catholic) which denies, even to adults, the right of unaided private interpretation of the Sacred Volume with respect to articles of religious belief' cf. Durcan, *History*, p.223.

18   Two Catholics, one Unitarian, one Presbyterian and three members of the Established church including the president of the Board, the Duke of Leinster.

19   In the four decades preceeding the Stanley Letter the blueprint for the 1831 National System of education was laid down in the 1791 Report, The Edgeworth Bill 1799, The 1813 Report and the 1828 Report.

20   Subsequently extended to nine in 1838; to twelve in 1839; to fifteen in 1845 and to twenty in 1861. cf. Durcan, *History*, p.19.

21   Durcan, *History*, p. 15.

22   Durcan, *History*, p.15-16.

23   Cf. Rev. J. Donovan, *Catechism of the Council of Trent*, Dublin: James Duffy & Co. Ltd., 1829. p. 492.

24   Whately was a gifted scholar and a supporter of non-sectarian education as well as the state endowment of Catholic clergy yet he was a complex character who reputedly saw the national

school system as a means of 'weaning the Irish people from popery'. Cf. Durcan, *History*, p.18.

25   King, *Religious Education*, p.6.

26   Durcan, *History*, p.24.

27   Durcan, *History*, p. 225.

28   King, *Religious Education*, p.6.

29   Coolahan, *Irish Education*, p.19.

30   Hyland, *Irish Educational*, p.91.

31   Dr Cullen had distinguished himself as a brilliant academic and scripture scholar in Rome and in 1850 as the newly appointed Archbishop of Armagh he convened the Synod of Thurles, the first national synod to be held in Ireland since the reformation.

32   Coolahan, *Irish Education*, p.18.

33   Coolahan, *Irish Education*, p.6.

34   These two colleges, Mary Immaculate College, Limerick and St Mary's University College, Belfast, continue to be involved in teacher formation, as does St Patrick's College, Drumcondra, a college of Dublin City University, Coláiste Mhuire, Marino, Froebel College, Dublin and The Church of Ireland College of Education, all colleges of TCD.

35   Durcan, *History* , p.21.

36   Rogan, *Irish Catechesis*, p.15.

37   Coolahan, *Irish Education*, p.35.

38   Ireland became a Republic in 1949.

39   See T.A. O'Donoghue, *The Catholic Church and the Secondary School Curriculum in Ireland 1922-62*, New York: Peter Lang, 1999.

40   S. O'Buachalla, *Educational Policy in Twentieth Century Ireland*, Dublin: Wolfhound Press, p.205.

41   S. Drudy & K. Lynch, *Schools and Society in Ireland*, Dublin: Gill and Macmillan, 1993, p.75-6.

42   Cf. John Mescal, *Religion in the Irish System of Education*, Dublin: Clonmore and Reynolds, 1957, p.45. cf. Gerry Whyte's essay in Dermot Lane Ed., *Religion, Education and the Constitution*, Columba Press, 1992, p.84ff.

43   Mescal, *Religion*, p.24.

44   *Primary School Curriculum*, 1999, p.58.

45   This is enshrined in Rule 69 of National Schools.

46   http://www.islaminireland.com/contentsfiles/Contents%20Frame /Education.htm accessed 16/6/05.

47   Patricia Kieran, 'Children, The Eucharist and Interdenominational Schools', *Doctrine & Life*, Vol. 52, No. 8, October 2002, p.459. 'The controversy centred on conflicting interpretations of whether Catholic children should receive sacramental preparation in an interdenominational school context. The principal felt sacramental preparation was inappropriate while the school patron insisted it was necessary. The controversey resulted in the dismissal of the principal.'

48   Kieran, *Children*, p.462.

49   Rogan, *Irish Catechesis*, p.xix.

50   King, *Religious Education in Ireland*, Dublin: Fallons, 1970, p.29.

51   E.g. Jean Calvin, *The Catechisme or Manner to Teache Children the Christian Religion 1556* ,Amsterdam: Da Capo Press, 1968. cf. Martin Luther's *Small Catechism* (1529) and *Large Catechism* (1530) which are still used in Lutheran churches. *The Geneva Catechism, The Heidelberg Catechism* and *The Westminster Catechism* are examples of catechisms used by the Reformed Churches. The Anglican *Book of Common Prayer* includes a small catechism section.

52   Michael Tynan, *Catholic Instruction in Ireland 1720-1950*, Four Courts Press, 1985, p.13.

53   Tynan, *Catholic Instruction*, p.10. cf. Bonaventure O'Hussey's Teagasg Críosdaidhe (1608). For more recent Irish catechism see *Teagasc Críostaí do Leanaí*, Treóraí Luimní Teoranta, 1959.

54   G. Meynell, *Explanation of the Penny Catechism*, Vol. I, Yorkshire: St William Press, 1895.

55   E. Leen, On the Teaching of Catechism and the Teaching of Religion, Reprint from *The Buckle*, The Magazine of Craiglockhart Training College, Edinburgh, 1937, p.4.

56   *Catechism of the Catholic Church*, London: Geoffrey Chapman, 1994, p.2. Originally printed as *Catechismus Catholicae Ecclesiae* (1992).

57   Cf. http://www.catholictradition.org/catechism.htm ; www.memorare.com/catechism/   ; www.memorare.com/catechism/pennycat.txt accessed 26/6/05.

58   Rogan, *Irish Catechesis*, p.81.

59   In 1879 Bishop MacEvilly of Tuam complained that clergy never visited the schools and neglected to instruct children.

60   King, Religious Education, pp.57-78.

61   *A Catechism of Catholic Doctrine*, Dublin: M. H. Gill and Son Ltd., 1951. cf. King, *Religious Education*, p.25f.

62   See *Catechism of the Catholic Church* (1994) which covers the Creed (Part 1); the Sacred Liturgy including the sacraments (Part 11); the Christian way of life including the Ten Commandments (Part 111) and Christian Prayer (Part 1V).

63   Rogan, *Irish Catechesis*, p.41.

64   Tynan, *Catholic Instruction*, also Michael Tynan, *In Search of Butler's Own Catechism*, unpublished manuscript, 1974, p.1.

65   Mgr. Tynan dates it 1777.

66   Rogan, *Irish Catechesis*, p.45-6.

67   Cf. Rev. Patrick Wallace, *Irish Catechesis – the Heritage from James Butler 11, Archbishop of Cashel, 1774-1791*, Doctoral Thesis, Catholic University of America, Washington, 1965. Also Tynan, *Catholic Instruction*, 1985, & Tynan, *In Search*.

68   Rogan, *Irish Catechesis*, p.42f. Tynan, *In Search*, p.1. King, *Religious Education*, p.26ff.

69   James Joyce, *Dubliners*, Penguin, 2000, p.103.

70   cf. The Folklore collections of 1937-8.

71   Rogan, *Irish Catechesis*, p.60f.

72   Rogan, *Irish Catechesis*, p.40, p.50f.

73   Raymond Topley, *Primary School Religius Educaiton A Basic Introduction to the Children of God Programme*, n.d. p.2.

74   Augustine Martin Ed., *An Anthology of Short Stories*, Dublin: Gill and Macmillan, 1987, p. 244.

75   *Explanatory Catechism of Christian Doctrine Chiefly Intended for the Use of Children in Catholic Schools*, Burns, Oates & Washbourne Ltd., 1921, p.41, p.54.

76   King, *Religious Education*, p.55.

77   cf. Questions 176 & 177. cf. Topley, *Primary School*, p.2.

78   *Doctrine For Seniors*, Dublin: Fallon. Interestingly this undated text which is approved by the Catholic Hierarchy of Ghana for use in Middle Schools, was obviously used in a missionary context. It contains colour plates, notes for teachers and differentiated materials for different form pupils and so could be classified as a post 1950's catechism text.

79   *Doctrine for Seniors*, p.5.

80   *Short Catechism*, Cork: Diocese of Cork and Ross, 1962, p.69.

81   Patrick M. Devitt, *That You May Believe*, Dublin: Dominican Publications, 1992, p.71, p.74f.

82   Leen, *Teaching*, p.3.

83   T. McDonnell, The Catechism in Our Schools, *Irish Ecclesiastical Record*, LVI, August 1940, p.169.

84   Brendan Kennelly, *A Time for Voices*, Bloodaxe Books, 1990, p.21.

85   Kennelly states 'Years killed raving questions.'

86   *My First Catechism*, p.4.

87   Josef Andreas Jungmann, *The Good News Yesterday and Today*, W.H. Sadlier, 1968, p.77.

88   *Catechism Notes*, 1959, Preface vi. advises teachers that 'ideas must be expressed in such a way that they can be grasped;..in a manner that is 'suitable to the dullest'. Also King, *Religious Education*, p.29.

89   Cf. James M.Thompson, 'Modern Developments in Teaching Religion', *Irish Ecclesiastical Record*, LIX, Feb. 1942, p.101.

90   Leen, *Teaching*, p.4. Jungmann states 'Dogma must be known; the kerygma must be proclaimed.' Jungmann, *The Good News*, p.34.

91   Kevin Cronin, *Teaching the Religion Lesson*, Paternoster Publications, 1963, p.29f. provides three guiding principles for the teaching of the catechism. 1. The catechism should be produced at the end and not the beginning of a lesson. 2. The order of the catechism need not be adhered to and 3. memorisation should be preceded by explanation and understanding.

92   King, *Religious Education*, p.27.

93   Monsignor Michael Tynan, *Catechism for Catholics*, Four Courts Press, p.8.

94   King, *Religious Education*, p.61.

95   William J. Conway, *The Child and the Catechism*, Maynooth: The Furrow Trust, 1959, p.5ff.

96   Sean Mc Entee, Kathleen Glennon, William Murphy, *The Children of God Series*, Veritas, 1973.

97   Devitt, *That You May*, p.83.

98   Topley, *Primary School*, p.4. Devitt, *That You May*, p.87.

99   Teachers' books in Italics. Children's text in brackets. *The Father Loves You 1, 11*, (Catching Sunshine 1 &2, 3&4) *Show Us the Father* (Come & See), *You are My Friends* (My Friends), *Walk in Love* (Remember me Together), *Grow in Love* (A Time to Grow), *Workers for the Kingdom* (Your Kingdom Come), *Walk in My Presence* (Called to Serve).

100   A syllabus document for the *Children of God* series was produced in 1974 but it has never been published. The nearest published approximation to a contemporary syllabus which exists is

Brendan O'Reilly, *Alive-O 5-8 Overview of the Alive-O Religion Programme for primary schools*, Veritas, n.d.

101 Junior Infants, Primary 1, 1983; Senior Infants Primary 2, 1983; First Class, Primary 3, 1984; Second Class, Primary 4, 1984; Third Class, Primary 5, 1985; Fourth Class, Primary 6, 1985; Fifth Class, Primary 7, 1987; Sixth Class, Primary 8, 1987.

102 See Fr Sean Melody, *Leading Our Children to God: A Guide to the Veritas Religious Education Programme*, Veritas, 1987, p.3.

103 This phrase is found on the title page of each of the *Alive-O* Teacher's Books.

104 *Alive-0 4*, p.xv.

105 See Brendan O'Reilly's essay '*Alive-O* The Irish Church's Response to the Religious Education Needs of Children' in Raymond Topley and Gareth Byrne, *Nurturing Children's Religious Imagination The Challenge of Primary Religious Education Today*, Dublin: Veritas, 2004, p.113.

106 *Beo go Deo*.

107 Topley, *Nurturing*, p.117.

108 *Connecting School and Parish An Alive 0 1-4 Handbook Compiled by Eleanor Gormally*, Dublin: Veritas, 2001, p.15.

109 *Alive-0 7 Teacher's Book*, Veritas, 2003, p.31.

110 Topley, *Nurturing*, p.117.

111 Martin Kennedy, *Islands Apart*, Veritas, 2000, p.3.

112 See Betty Galvin, *Alive-O 7 Religious Education Programme in Primary Schools A Survey of Teacher Perception*, unpublished M.Ed. Thesis, University of Hull, 2005. See also Michael Kilcrann & Brendan O'Reilly's chapters in Topley, *Nurturing Children's Imaginations*, also Martin Kennedy, *Island's Apart*.

113 *Follow Me* Series (2001) edited by Jacqui Wilkinson and developed by the Church of Ireland, Methodist and Presbyterian Boards of Education based on the Alive O series. See the excellent website that supports this programme at www.followmeseries.org/intro/home.htm accessed 24/6/05.

CHAPTER THREE

A Vision of Catholic Education

• •

There is a helpful body of Catholic documentation with which everyone involved in Catholic religious education should be familiar. This documentation consists of a series of official teachings which outline who Catholic educators are and what Catholic education is about. These rich and positive texts contain Church statements on Catholic education, teaching, children and schools. At a time when people experience confusion about what it means to be Catholic and what the characteristic spirit of a Catholic school should be, this documentation provides the teacher with a focused, clear and fundamental vision of Catholic education. This chapter identifies seven key principles which emerge from a close reading of official Church teaching on Catholic education.

Knowledge of the documentation is the first stage in an ongoing process. One must subsequently ask whether this documentation is of contemporary relevance to Irish Catholic primary schools. It is obvious that the existence of a body of positive documentation might feed into wonderful mission statements about Catholic education without translating positively into discernable attitudes and actions in the Catholic school community. Once the seven principles of Catholic

Education are identified they raise the question of whether or not contemporary Irish Catholic primary schools are recognisable in this profile. Furthermore there is a need to ask how a Catholic vision of education can be translated from positive statement into effective action in Catholic schools in the future.

Nothing is to be gained from pretending that this documentation is universally known, accepted or applied in Irish Catholic schools. It is also obvious that Catholic educators can embody the principles of Catholic education without being aware of the official documentation. Most Catholic primary schools are doing outstanding work in providing a very high quality of education for children, in all aspects of the curriculum. Irish Catholic primary schools make a huge and sometimes undervalued contribution to the faith formation of children. Inevitably there are areas of difficulty, where discrepancies arise between the ideal vision of Catholic education which the Church espouses and the real, lived experience of life in Irish Catholic primary schools, Colleges of Education and Catholic institutions. This chapter explores some of these issues and attempts to offer a vision which may guide Catholic educators in the future.

VATICAN II ONWARDS

Vatican II, the second major council in the Catholic Church (1962-1965),[1] signalled a new era in the Church's understanding of education.[2] Since Vatican II the Catholic Church produced a series of documents and statements concerning Catholic education, evangelisation and catechesis which provide a focused and detailed insight into the Church's vision of Catholic education.[3] *Gravissimum Educationis* (1965)[4] succinctly outlines the nature of Christian education, the pivotal role that parents play in the education of their children and the purpose and import of the Catholic school. In a very significant manner *Gravissimum Educationis* gave impetus to, and framed the general terms of reference for, subsequent Church teaching on Catholic education. This chapter attempts to identify *a* Catholic vision of education that emerges from landmark texts which are 'solidly established in Church documents'.[5] It is important to note that the chapter is deliberately titled 'A' as opposed to 'The' Catholic vision of Education. A brief survey of contemporary literature on Catholic education is sufficient to support the viewpoint that there is no one homogenous, universally endorsed vision of Catholic education.[6] When it comes to Catholic schools the same plurality of interpretation can be seen since:

> the Catholic schooling enterprise in Ireland has radical elements within it (often associated with religious orders) as well as conservative elements. In other words, the Irish Catholic school system is not monolithic but is characterised by internal differentiation and by internal ideological struggles.[7]

Given the multivalence of the term 'Catholic' and the diversity of types of Catholic schools this chapter nevertheless argues that official post-Conciliar Church teaching presents an incrementally developed and largely consistent vision of the nature of Catholic education. The key issues which emerge from Church documentation are the nature of evangelisation and catechesis, the purpose and mission of the Catholic school as well as the role of teachers, pupils, parents and clergy in Catholic education. Education is a lifelong process that can occur in different contexts such as the family, the community and the school.[8] Initiating Christians into the faith is the work of the entire Christian community and not just the teacher or priest.[9] While parish based catechesis, for example the Rite of Christian Initiation for Adults (RCIA), provides a model for all catechesis that is highly appropriate for the initiation of Catholics, this chapter focuses specifically on the primary school child, teacher and parent, in the formal educational or school context.[10]

Seven defining principles

At least seven defining principles can be discerned from official post-Conciliar Catholic teaching on education. These are: 1. Religious Freedom: 2. Academic integrity; 3. Christocentricity; 4. Catholic anthropology; 5. Dialogue with contemporary culture; 6. Mission to evangelise and 7. Catechetical orientation. Some exploration of these seven principles is desirable before providing a general response to a Catholic vision of education.[11]

1. A CATHOLIC VISION OF EDUCATION RESPECTS THE UNIVERSAL RIGHT TO RELIGIOUS FREEDOM

In 1965 *Gravissimum Educationis* emphasised the universal right of all human beings 'of whatever race, condition, and age' to education.[12] The Vatican statement echoed the United Nations' 1948 citing of the right to education as one of the fundamental human rights. The Catholic Church respects the rights of religiously diverse communities to an educational system appropriate to their needs and has no desire to coerce the State into providing and imposing a uniform and exclusive Catholic system of education on all people. However it argues that all Christians have a right to a Christian education [13] and that Catholic parents, children and communities have a right to be supported by the State through the provision of Catholic schools. *Gravissimum Educationis* reiterates the Catholic

Church's teaching that parents are the principal educators of their children and civil society should protect their duties and rights to choose a Christian education for their children.[14] The state is obliged 'where the common good demands it' to carry out the wishes of the parents and build schools and institutions which cater for their religious needs.[15] Furthermore the Catholic Church is mindful that the educational system of a country should not be monopolised and that participants within a system should respect the rights of others.

'But it (*the state*) must always keep in mind the principle of subsidiarity so that there is no kind of school monopoly, for this is opposed to the native rights of the human person, to the development and spread of culture, to the peaceful association of citizens and to the pluralism that exists today in ever so many societies.'[16]

This principle of subsidiarity means that different groupings within an organisation or society should recognise and respect their different roles and tasks.[17] The Church constantly emphasises that a high degree of collaboration and participation should exist between the Catholic hierarchy and the various groups who work in the Catholic educational community. Nonetheless it affirms the distinctive tasks and responsibilities given to teachers, children, parents and guardians, school managers and bishops that the principle of subsidiarity emphasises.[18]

Schools are mentioned as a particular aid to Christian education as they foster the intellectual, moral, cultural and religious development not alone of their pupils but of the entire human community.[19] The Catholic Church reaffirms its right 'freely to establish and to run schools of every kind and at every level', from pre-school to university.[20] Furthermore within the Catholic school a Catholic education should lead to the full development of the whole person, which liberates them to live a full human life in response to the Gospel.

This means that Catholic education has a strong social justice agenda. If the aim of the Catholic school is to develop and liberate the whole human person, then Catholic schools are not indifferent to the socio-economic situation of the school community. The Catholic school attempts to create an inclusive, non-discriminatory environment.[21] In order to do this it pays 'special attention to those who are weakest'.[22] The Catholic school has a special mission to aid those who are materially or socially disadvantaged. Sexism, racism, aggression, violence, and indeed any diminishment of the human person have no place in the Catholic school.

Emerging Issues

Now the issue of religious freedom impacts directly on those primary teachers who have either opted out of teaching religion or who teach it unwillingly. A 2002 survey of Irish primary teachers revealed that teachers who failed to inform the school that they were unwilling or unable to teach religious education commonly cited a fear with regard to employment, job mobility and career prospects as the reason for their silence.[23] In a context where the Catholic Church manages the majority of primary schools, the perceived direct relationship between teacher employability and membership of the Catholic Church needs to be addressed. Teachers fear that if they are non-practising Catholics or have major difficulties with aspects of Church doctrine, that their chances of employment or promotion within the school will be considerably decreased. The fact that teachers tend to remain silent about such issues has the capacity to comprise not alone the academic integrity of the subject area of religious education in the school, but also the integrity of the teacher and efficacy of the faith formation of pupils as well as the school's Catholic ethos.

The Catholic Church's respect for the universal and fundamental right to religious freedom also raises the issue of whether or not the Catholic Church, which manages almost 93 per cent of Irish primary schools, has a monopoly on the primary educational system with the inevitable consequence of denial of choice for minority belief groups.[24] In 2005 the Educate Together sector presented a report to the United Nations Committee on the Convention on the Elimination of all Forms of Racial Discrimination. Educate Together argued that the Irish denominational national school system was discriminatory because of the absence of 'a national network of schools that provide legal guarantees to ensure that all children enjoy equality of access and esteem irrespective of their social, racial, ethnic, cultural or religious background.'[25] The United Nations found in favour of Educate Together. While the Catholic Church upholds the rights of parents to choose freely an education which is appropriate to their children's needs, and while it condemns any monopolisation of the educational system, it is part of an Irish primary education system that is viewed as discriminatory. One could argue that the Catholic primary school system is serving the legitimate needs of Catholic communities and that the Catholic Church has no desire to impede the diversification of school types, however there are still uncomfortable questions concerning the Catholic Church's unwitting or undesired majority control of the primary educational system in Ireland.

2. A CATHOLIC VISION OF EDUCATION RESPECTS THE ACADEMIC INTEGRITY OF THE EDUCATIONAL COMMUNITY

The second principle of Catholic education involves the Church's recognition of the integrity of academic disciplines within the educational context as well as the independence and necessity of different methodologies used in the delivery of different subject areas in the school curriculum. *The Catholic School* (1977) reveals a huge respect for the quality of education in Catholic schools and for the integrity of individual disciplines which bring with them their independent methodologies, knowledge, skills and 'intellectual methods and moral and social attitudes.'[26] The Church has no desire to hijack individual disciplines for the purposes of apologetics (the justification of the truth-claims of the Catholic faith) or to present them as mere 'adjuncts to faith'.[27] In terms of the organisation and planning of the Catholic school 'ecclesiastical authority respects the competence of the professionals in teaching and education'.[28] Vatican II holds the career of teaching in very high esteem and it speaks of the 'excellence of the teaching vocation'[29]. It notes that 'young people of special ability who appear suited for teaching and research should be trained with particular care and urged to undertake a teaching career.'[30] In *The Catholic School on the Threshold of the Third Millennium* the Church describes teaching as an activity of 'extraordinary moral depth' which 'is one of man's (*sic.*) most excellent and creative activities, for the teacher does not write on inanimate material, but on the very spirits of human beings'.[31]

The Church wants to enable Catholic educators to identify and select the most age, ability and culturally appropriate methodologies for the subject matter they are teaching.[32] Catechesis should avail of a plurality of methodologies which are a 'sign of life and richness' as well as a necessary demonstration of respect for those to whom catechesis is addressed.[33] The objective of all methodology in catechesis is education in the faith and any educationally sound method which nurtures a maturity of faith is appropriate. The Church does warn about an exclusive over-emphasis on either method or content in catechesis, what it calls a 'content–method dualism' where an unbalanced concern for doctrine (content) or in turn pedagogy (method) displaces the harmony that should exist between both the message and the medium.[34] Content driven or method driven catechesis is not the most educationally appropriate or theologically creative way of nurturing the development of the whole human being. The Church presents both inductive (moving from particular experience to general principle) and deductive (moving from general principle to particular experience) methods of communicating the faith as equally appropriate and complimentary methods in catechesis.[35] *Alive-O* generally uses the inductive method by starting with the child's experience and subsequently exploring its relationship to the religious event or idea on which the lesson focuses. Whether one approaches God by beginning with human experience (the existential condition) or with the Word of God given in sacred texts and doctrines (Bible, Creed, Church teaching) is not important as long as both of these vital aspects of transmitting the faith are incorporated and nurtured in the method and content of catechesis.[36]

Emerging Issues

The second principle of academic integrity raises the issue of whether or not the State should end the anomaly of providing no curriculum content or syllabus outline or assessment procedures for religious education, one of the seven curricular areas of the Irish primary school curriculum. In 2003 the INTO called 'for the initiation of discussion with a view to establishing an appropriate religious education programme for all schools which would reflect this diversity (of religious faiths)'.[36] If the State provided a core syllabus for religious education in the primary school, as it has done in the post-primary sector, this core syllabus could subsequently be adapted and delivered by different denominational, multi-denominational and inter-denominational schools, to address their own situational and confessional needs. Such a State syllabus may well protect the integrity of the primary school teacher whose role, according to Padraig Hogan 'is different from that of the preacher'.[38]

3. ALL CATHOLIC EDUCATION IS CHRISTOCENTRIC

A Catholic vision of education is radically Christocentric, that is, centred on the person of Christ. Effective Catholic schools promote and manifest a common outlook on life,[39] that is, a common Christian vision which is centered on the person and teaching of Jesus Christ.[40] Inspired by the vision of Christ who is the perfect embodiment of what it means to be human, Catholic schools have as their aim the education and development of the whole human person.[41] Catholic schools are literally centres of education where each member of the school community is called to become more Christ-like.

In an educational context being 'Christ-like' means being called to build communities of unconditional love and service modeled on Jesus' spirit of self-sacrifice and other-centredness. John's Gospel provides a simple criterion for evaluating whether or not Christians are legitimate heirs and witnesses to Jesus Christ's message. Jesus said 'If you have love for one another, then everyone will know that you are my disciples' (John 13:35). Catholic educators cannot by-pass this criterion or evade the radical implications of this discipleship. The great commandment calls all Christian educators to make a deliberate pledge not to exploit or diminish the human person, but to cherish and uphold their sacredness through unconditional love.

Catholic schools attempt to break open the Gospel message based on the life, death and resurrection of Jesus Christ and to enflesh it and bring it to life, in contemporary culture. Catholic education is deeply immersed in a sense of social justice and service to humanity based on the example and life, death and resurrection of Jesus Christ. Christ's ministry of service was most acutely visible in his transformative care for those at the periphery of his society. The woman who bled (Mk 8:30); those with contagious diseases (Mt 8:3); the blind (Jn 9:7); the deaf (Mk 7:32); the young (Mk 5:22); the ethnically despised (Lk 10:33) and those suffering from mental anguish (Mt 8:28) were not the objects of Christ's patronising, debilitating pity, but were catalysts for the development of his ministry of justice and peace and for the inauguration of the reign of God. Jesus was a radical thinker whose stance on numerous social issues sprang from the depths of his spirituality. Jesus did not simply heal individuals, he offered healing to the whole community and he empowered the healed individuals to continue this ministry of healing. The lives of people were completely transformed as a consequence of his liberative love. A Christ-centred educational community must work for the healing and transformation of the whole society including those considered to be peripheral or marginal. If any Catholic school is to be considered a legitimate continuation of the life of Jesus Christ, then the marginalised; those with special needs; the minority ethnic group; the socio-economically disadvantaged; the depressed or alienated, must be seen as centrally important within this community. Christ-centredness means that each follower of Christ is called to permeate the world with the spirit of justice and love, devotion to God and example of self-sacrifice and other-centredness, which Christ embodied. Indeed this Christ-centredness is so vital that if Catholic education does not focus on the life, death and resurrection of Jesus Christ one could say that it is not Catholic.

Jesus Christ was keenly identified with education and teaching and the title of 'rabbi' or 'teacher' was applied to him forty-eight times in the four Gospels. Catholic education which is focused on the person of Christ is deeply personal and explores what it means to be a human being.[42] Each member, not alone of the Catholic community, but of the human family, is entitled to be part of the body of Christ, and each is of inestimable, unique value. Christ calls each person to actualise their full human potential, to develop their own capacity as human beings, and to enable others to do so. The imprint of the divine, the incarnation of the Word of God, is present in each human being and the Catholic educator is called to acknowledge and respect the sacredness of all human life.

A balanced Christology or understanding of Jesus Christ integrates and accommodates Christ's full humanity, his incarnation as a full human being, like us in all things but sin, while simultaneously recognising his complete divinity or embodiment and actualisation of God.[43] The *General Directory for Catechesis* (GDC) states that the object of catechesis is 'to promote communion with Jesus Christ'[44] and whether or not Catholic teachers present a high descending Christology (starting with Christ's divinity and subsequently exploring his humanity) or a low ascending Christology (starting with Jesus' humanity and subsequently exploring his divinity) is not at issue as long as both aspects of his divine-human nature are emphasised. In the Christian community Christ is always presented in the context of the Trinitarian God (God the Father, God the Son and God the Spirit). A Christocentric Catholic catechesis is committed to promoting the 'trinitarian experience of life in Christ as the centre of the life of faith'.[45] Catholic education is radically committed to a relational God who is father, son and spirit.

Emerging Issues

The Christocentric focus of Catholic education raises questions about the place of non-Christian children and indeed non-

Christian teachers in Catholic schools. In the post-modern context many Catholic schools experience a tension between explicitly teaching children about Jesus Christ and simultaneously accommodating the diverse religious needs of non-Christian pupils, teachers and parents. While the official Church teaches that Catholic schools are places 'of apprenticeship in a lively dialogue between young people of different religions and social backgrounds'[46] very often in contemporary Irish Catholic primary schools the structures are not in place to support and encourage this dialogue. Chapter Seven argues that there is a greater need for Catholic schools to become vibrant centres for inter-religious contact and dialogue. While many Catholic primary schools provide excellent support for intercultural and inter-religious initiatives there are also those who do not address the inter-religious needs of the school or wider community adequately.

4. A CATHOLIC VISION OF EDUCATION STRESSES AN ANTHROPOLOGY BASED ON THE DIGNITY AND MULTI-DIMENSIONALITY OF ALL HUMAN BEINGS.

Post-conciliar statements on education present a consistent, positive anthropology, a holistic understanding of what it is to be human which values the body, the emotions, the will, the mind and the spirit. Church teaching on education presents all humans as multi-dimensional beings whose physical, affective, volitional, cognitive and spiritual dimensions must be addressed and developed in any educational context. An educational process which ignores any one dimension of human life diminishes and devalues it.

It would be imprecise to suggest that the Catholic Church fails to recognise the rights of the individual to religious freedom. The Church consistently upholds the dignity of the whole human person who is 'to be guided by his own judgment' and who is never to be coerced in religious matters.[47] Vatican II presents the aims of true education as the harmonious formation of the whole human person through the development of their physical, moral, intellectual and social aspects.[48] Furthermore this anthropology presents all humans as being simultaneously private individuals with a public, social dimension. All Catholic education must address, appreciate and develop the individuality and uniqueness of the human being while simultaneously enabling them to live in society and to contribute to the cultural, social context in which they find themselves. A Catholic education is devoted to the full, complete development of the human being and a Catholic vision of education presents Catholic schools as intensely social institutions that work in the service of society. Vatican II sees that Christian education leads to 'the complete perfection of the human person, the good of earthly society and the building of a world that is more human.' [49] In 1977 an official Church document entitled *The Catholic School* presents the school as a privileged locus for the formation of the person.[50] It states that through a series of personal contacts and commitments, the school assists in the development of human intelligence, the formation of values, and the interpretation of human experience.[51]

'The school must stimulate the pupil to exercise his intelligence through the dynamics of understanding to attain clarity and inventiveness. It must help him spell out the meaning of his experiences and their truths. Any school which neglects this duty and which offers merely pre-cast conclusions hinders the personal development of its pupils.'[52]

Catholic schools are not mandated to transmit ideas and doctrines to unquestioning, passive pupils. The notion of a school providing pre-set answers to pre-rehearsed questions is totally out of synch with a Catholic vision of education. Any hot-housing of pupils or dissemination of materials which simply have to be regurgitated and replicated by pupils, falls short of the mission of the Catholic school. The mission of the Catholic school is the generation of autonomous, critical and independent thinkers who have a capacity to relate their own experience and understanding to the wisdom of the tradition that preceded them and to the culture and community that surrounds them. The school essentially offers a communal educational forum for the formation and development of the whole human being. Catholic schools should provide a creative environment where the teacher and pupils enter into dialogue with the received wisdom of the Catholic tradition. Catholic schools also facilitate dialogue with contemporary communities of scholarship so that students can become skilled practitioners in contemporary disciplines. As Pope John Paul II stated 'the promotion of the human person is the goal of the Catholic school'.[53] Catholic schools should liberate human beings, both teachers and pupils, from mass produced mentalities and depersonalised cultures and give them skills so they can freely and responsibly choose how to live their lives in accordance with their conscience.[54] In 1988 the Church again strongly affirmed that the aim of all Catholic education is the development and liberation of the human being to achieve their full potential.

'Future teachers should be helped to realise that any genuine educational philosophy has to be based on the nature of the human person, and therefore must take into account all of the physical and spiritual powers of each individual, along with the call of each one to be an active and creative agent in service to society. And this philosophy must be open to a religious dimension. Human beings are fundamentally free; they are not the property of the state or of any human organisation. The entire process of education, therefore, is a service to the individual students, helping each one to achieve the most complete formation possible.'[55]

The Catholic Church perceives that education is a central medium for the expression and development of an innate spiritual hunger for God. Of course many people fail to recognise and indeed actively deny their search for God. The Catholic Church argues that if the truth of the human search for God is denied then there is a 'breakdown', a diminishment, at the level of what it means to be human.[56] Any notion of Catholic education as bigoted, indoctrinatory, stultifying and narrow is not supported by official post-Conciliar teaching. Catholic education is presented as open-ended. It invites the human being into a voyage of self-discovery where each aspect of their personhood, that is, physical, affective, volitional, cognitive and spiritual, is given the opportunity to develop and grow to its full potential. Catholic education should liberate human beings from the slavery of ideological systems and externally imposed beliefs that the human being can neither assent to in freedom nor critique in detail.

Emerging Issues

The principle of Catholic anthropology raises the issue of how the child's physical, intellectual, emotional, moral and spiritual dimensions can best be nurtured and developed in Catholic schools. The 1999 Revised Curriculum presents the spiritual dimension in life as one of the key issues in primary education and perceives the function of religious education as the development of the child's spiritual and moral values.[57] However the term 'spiritual' is notoriously vague and conflicting and radically different interpretations of its meaning abound. While teachers in Catholic schools may well be committed to a holistic approach to educating the child and to developing each child's unique potential to the full, issues of resources, overcrowding and teacher-pupil ratio may make this very difficult to actualise.

5. CATHOLIC EDUCATION ENGAGES IN CRITICAL AND CREATIVE DIALOGUE WITH CONTEMPORARY CULTURE

The fifth principle underlying post-Conciliar teaching on Catholic education is that Catholics are called to engage in a creative and critical dialogue between faith and contemporary culture. Taking their lead from the Documents of Vatican II, especially the *Pastoral Constitution on the Church in the Modern World,* Catholic statements on education encourage Catholic educators to engage in significant and innovative dialogue with the modern world. A Catholic vision of education sees the Christian teacher working for the good of human society. The Church engages with the modern world and is legitimately concerned with the whole of human life. No dichotomous vision of faith and reason, sacred and profane, Church and world, religious community and society, is perpetuated in *Gravissimum Educationis* or indeed in subsequent Catholic teaching on catechesis and education.[58] Consequently the education of Christians, and indeed of all 'men (*sic.*)'[59] is of concern to the Church.

'The Church here states with utmost clarity that it has no desire to remain away *from* the world in a form of isolation but that Christian education is *in* the world and, in a sense, *for* the world, since man (*sic.*) must always work out his salvation in the concrete situation in which God has placed him and must achieve this not by protection but by contributing to the whole human community of which he is an integral and inseparable part.'[60]

The Church does not have a fortress mentality which erects a defensive barricade around the Catholic school and ignores the world surrounding it. Science, the media and technology are viewed as aspects of the world which can be used in the service of the gospel. In *Evangelii Nuntiandi* (1975) Pope Paul VI (1963-1978) addressed all the faithful of the entire world and focused on the relationship between evangelisation (proclaiming Christ to those who do not know him),[61] the Gospel and culture. In this document Paul avoids the two extremes of isolating the Gospel from culture or of making them both indistinguishable. *Evangelii Nuntiandi* illustrates the critical and creative tension that should exist between the Gospel, evangelisation and culture.

'Though independent of cultures, the Gospel and evangelisation are not necessarily incompatible with them; rather they are capable of permeating them all without becoming subject to any one of them.'[62]

Paul VI exhorts Catholics to evangelise culture and cultures and to renew them through proclaiming the Gospel in the midst of modern culture so that culture becomes regenerated by the Good News. Paul also stresses that the Church does not turn its back on contemporary culture and so technology and the media are suitable means of 'social communication for evangelisation'.[63]

However official post-Conciliar Church documents do not present a resounding and uncritical endorsement of culture. For instance in the introductory section of the more recent 1997 *General Directory for Catechesis* there is a realisation that 'some elements (of the culture onto which the seed of the Gospel falls) can prejudice the germination of the seed and indeed the very harvest itself.'[64] The Church warns that the globalisation of culture means that indigenous cultures are being devalued and eroded by the interests of mass communications or global economic and ideological interests. Traditional values and ways of life are being demeaned. The *General Directory for Catechesis* also states that 'in many places there is an acute awareness that traditional cultures are being assailed by powerful external forces and by alien imitations of imported life-styles, with the result that the identity and values proper to peoples are thus being gradually eroded.'[65]

One the Church's greatest contemporary challenges is to reject the elements of contemporary culture which impede the transmission of the gospel while accepting those elements which are harmonious with and beneficial to the spreading of its message.[66] This means that people involved in Catholic education must be able to 'read the signs of the times'. Catechists and religious educators must engage in acts of discernment in order to evaluate 'what may be genuine signs of the presence or the purpose of God'[67] and concomitantly they must reject as 'unhelpful and indeed harmful to the spreading of the Gospel' those elements of culture which contradict and obscure its message. The Church cites religious indifference, atheism (reasoned rejection of God), secularism (living without any reference to God), ethical relativism (all systems of moral reasoning being seen as equally valid) as examples of elements which impede the development of people's potential.[68]

Indeed the Church warns against an extreme over-emphasis on technology which can lead to an unbalanced functionalist and individualistic approach to life. For example the internet has brought huge benefits to the contemporary world in the form of a democratised, relatively cheap and accessible global communication and information system. For those involved in teaching religious education, the internet provides a tremendous opportunity to research and explore religious topics in an interactive and audio-visually stimulating manner. Virtual tours of places of worship, audio-files of religious chants, stunning images of religious symbols and personalities along with all of the traditional benefits of access to on-line books, libraries and collections make the internet an astonishing resource for religious education.[69] E-mail allows teachers and 'children from different national, cultural and religious backgrounds to share concerns'[70] and to enter into dialogue. The flipside of the advantages associated with Information and Communications Technology (ICT)[71] is the overwhelming lack of quality control and excess of information of doubtful origin and content value available on the internet.[72] Jim Robinson puts this succinctly when he reminds teachers that 'when you are only two clicks away from some undesirable site or other, you need to be sure that the site you are recommending to your pupils is appropriate in every sense of the word.'[73] Negative aspects of the internet include the proliferation of pornographic and paedophilic material, the unrelenting commercialism of sites and products which persistently target users, and the spreading of destructive viruses. Catholic teachers are called to read the signs of the times and to critique their culture while using its positive aspects to spread the gospel message of Jesus Christ. This can be a very difficult and sometimes confusing task.

The Catholic school aims to integrate faith and life intelligently and ethically so that teachers and pupils are encouraged to embody their Christian faith and values in their personal lives and in their service to the community.[74] Catholic schools are communities which attempt to translate the gospel of Jesus Christ into a living service to the community and culture within which they are located because they have as their fundamental task 'a synthesis of culture and faith, and a synthesis of faith and life'.[75] The Catholic school is not afraid of contemporary culture yet neither is it afraid to critique contemporary culture so that it uses positive aspects of culture to promote the full development of the human person and to infuse the world with the Gospel vision and values.

Emerging Issues

Dialogue with contemporary culture raises a number of important issues. In the post-modern world one does not speak so much of 'culture' as of competing and diverse cultures which challenge and confront the child and the teacher in the primary school. Oliver Brennan's research shows that Irish youth culture, like contemporary Western youth culture in general, is characterised by 'disaffiliation from the institutional Church, by relativism, undifferentiated pluralism and a deep suspicion of institutions'.[76] However Brennan is emphatic that the appropriate pastoral and religious educational response to the decline in Church affiliation and practice is not to ignore this reality, neither is it to deplore contemporary culture or to attempt to restore traditional forms of religious practice. 'Church leaders need to hear the cry of the young generation, listen carefully to what is being said, and respond appropriately.'[77] Catechists who wish to transmit the faith have to be aware of the culture of the community they address as well as use language and concepts that are meaningful to their listeners. Yet the use of contemporary youth culture in the classroom raises further issues.

Very often teachers are unsure of what aspects of culture they can legitimately use or should avoid in the classroom. Opinions vary. This raises the question of power. Who is going to read the signs of the times in relation to contemporary cultures and who will evaluate the appropriateness or inappropriateness of introducing various aspects of contemporary culture in the Catholic classroom? Will it be the Catholic parent, the child, the teacher, the school manager or the hierarchy? Catholic religious education must analyse and critique the exercise of power so that it can identify legitimate and conversely abusive exercises of power in the service of dialogue between the gospel and contemporary culture.

6. A CATHOLIC VISION OF EDUCATION VIEWS EVANGELISATION AND EDUCATION AS BEING INEXTRICABLY INTERLINKED

A sixth principle of Catholic education is that all Catholics are called to evangelise. In post-conciliar documents, especially *Evangelii Nuntiandi* (1975) and *Catechesi Tradendae* (1979) evangelisation and education are inextricably interlinked so that the school is both a location and agent for the work of evangelisation. *Evangelii Nuntiandi* states:

> ... it has been possible to define evangelisation in terms of proclaiming Christ to those who do not know Him, of preaching, of catechesis, of conferring Baptism and the other sacraments.[78]

In effect evangelisation means the call to conversion. At baptism each Christian is called to conversion in Jesus Christ and in turn is empowered with the possibility of living their faith as real and direct witnesses to the truth of the gospel of Jesus Christ and so leading to the conversion of others. Teachers play a crucial role in evangelisation and the document *Evangeill Nuntiandi* stresses the need for the gospel of Christ to be embodied in their own lives. As Paul VI pointed out:

> Modern man (sic.) listens more willingly to witnesses than to teachers, and if he does listen to teachers, it is because they are witnesses.[79]

The teacher who evangelises successfully bears witness to their own personal faith in Jesus Christ. A teacher who not only teaches, but practises what they teach has a far greater chance of successfully nurturing faith than someone who neither believes nor practices the message which they ostensibly profess. The dictum 'What I do tells you who I am, not what I say' is a challenging reminder to teachers that the issue of integrity, that is the relationship between what they teach and what they as individuals believe and practice, is crucially important in the area of religious education. The Church asks the question ' In the long run, is there any other way of handing on the Gospel than by transmitting to another person one's personal experience of faith?'[80]

Evangelisation is deeply ecclesial and yet also deeply personal since no evangeliser acts as an isolated individual, but rather 'acts in common with the Church and her pastors'. All people are called to the special work of evangelisation in the midst of their work and culture. The family is identified as a particular center of evangelisation where the parents evangelise their children and are in turn evangelised by them.[81] The document affirms the capacity of the receiver to become the giver and places the child being catechised at the center of the process of evangelisation. This cyclical dynamic where 'the person who has been evangelised goes on to evangelise others'[82] means that children in Catholic schools are not seen as passive recipients, but as active agents. Very often the teacher's own faith is deepened and nurtured through witnessing the simple but profound spirituality of the children. Likewise parents are often profoundly moved by the religious curiosity of their children. Children's capacity to appreciate and question the infinitely comprehensible and wondrous nature of life should not be underestimated. Often their questions concerning meaning, mystery and transcendence propel adults to search for answers to previously unasked questions. The parent or teacher who journeys with the child through preparation for the sacraments often has their own sense of God's sacramental presence deepened.

In conformity to the Christocentric principle the Church presents Christ as the prototypical and ultimate evangeliser.[83]

The Church was born of Christ's evangelising activity and having 'been sent and evangelised, the Church herself sends out evangelisers'[84]. This call to every believer to evangelise is at the heart of a Catholic vision of education.[85] Every believer is called to evangelise to the best of their ability. Now popular and indeed misguided images of evangelisation often centre around a clerical, imperialistic and aggressive imposition of a set of beliefs and practices on unsuspecting individuals. Brendan Kennelly depicts the missionary as one who fails to appreciate a country's indigenous cultures and religious traditions while aggressively superimposing an uninvited colonial and alien religious tradition on its people. The Missionary states,

> It is clear that all your gods must go / Back into the darkness from which they came. / I tell you this because I know /…Heaven's brightness flows to you from me / And on behalf of God I say, that's right.[86]

It is important to acknowledge that evangelisation is not to be equated with cultural intolerance, religious manipulation and spiritual coercion. The word 'evangelisation' is not used in the sense of extraneously imposing a set of doctrines on unwilling or unsuspecting children and teachers. Evangelisation is an on-going process where all members of the school community are called to give witness, in freedom, through their words and actions, to the Gospel of Jesus Christ so that they contribute to the faith development of their peers. In Catholic schools teachers who go about teaching children and serving their educational needs to the best of their ability are actively involved in evangelisation.

Emerging Issues

Post-modern societies reject the notion of one universally valid system of truth or overarching worldview which provides answers for all peoples. Many people in post-modern societies exhibit discomfort with the notion of converting or evangelising others. Some teachers express a discomfort with the notion of being agents for conversion and see that faith formation is best addressed by the parents at home or the priest and community in the parish. A small percentage of primary teachers have expressed the view that the school 'should have no role in the religious formation of the child'.[87] One teacher stated 'We feel that we are doing a service for both families and the Church, a service that is barely acknowledged and that neither are willing to do for themselves'.[88] New initiatives for parish based sacramental preparation go some way towards redressing the imbalanced school-centred approach to sacramental preparation but they are, as yet, in their infancy.[89] One has to ask whether the Catholic Church's call for each of its members to 'seek out the lost sheep, proclaim and heal at the same time'[90] is at odds with some contemporary teachers' understanding of their role in the Catholic primary school. The challenging issue of reconciling the call to evangelise with the reality of teaching in a religiously diverse school and society is dealt with in greater depth in Chapter Seven.

7. A CATHOLIC VISION OF EDUCATION IS CENTRED ON CATECHESIS AS A VITAL MISSION OF THE CHURCH

The preceding principle dealt with evangelisation because, both experientially and logically, in the lived process of faith formation evangelisation precedes catechesis. The process of initiation into faith (evangelisation) comes before a dialogue among believers leading to maturity of faith (catechesis) is possible. Even the etymology of the word *catechesis*, which means 'echoing back' or 'sounding down' mirrors this process.[91] Catechesis echoes back the faith that has been handed on to the initiated individual. Catechesis involves the ongoing faith formation of children, adolescents, young people and adults.[92] It is a vital 'means of evangelisation' which incorporates the fact that 'the faith demands to be known, celebrated, lived and translated into prayer'.[93] Catechesis is a systematic instruction in the fundamental teachings and the living content of the Catholic faith, aimed at initiating the receiver into a deeper personal relationship with Christ, a fullness of Christian life and a mature faith.

> A means of evangelisation that must not be neglected is that of catechetical instruction. The intelligence, especially that of children and young people, needs to learn through systematic religious instruction the fundamental teachings, the living content of the truth which God has wished to convey to us and which the Church has sought to express in an ever richer fashion during the course of her long history.[94]

Doctrinal content is important in a Catholic vision of education and catechesis should be cognitively challenging and intellectually coherent as well as being consistent with the best theological and educational principles. Catechesis is not synonymous with the communication of data or information concerning the faith. Catechesis moves beyond the notional or intellectual into the 'patterns of Christian living',[95] from doctrine into life,[96] from information to formation. Catholic education is not so much concerned with the dissemination of information (although this is a vitally important aspect of Catholic education and faith formation) as with the formation of the whole human person. *The Catholic School on the Threshold of the Third Millennium* (1998) puts this point succinctly when it states that 'in the Catholic school's educational project there is no separation between time for learning and time for formation, between acquiring notions and growing in wisdom.'[97] The aim of catechesis is 'to encourage a living, explicit and fruitful profession of faith'.[98] The *Catechism of the Catholic Church* (1994) presents catechesis as:

> an education in the faith of children, young people and adults which includes especially the teaching of Christian doctrine imparted, generally speaking, in an organic and systematic way, with a view to initiating the hearers into the fullness of Christian life.[99]

Since Vatican II there has been a revival of interest and research in catechesis. The Church recognises that Catholic faith formation poses significant challenges.[100] In contemporary society many baptised people are non-practicing and effectively live lives without formal reference to Christianity.[101] The Church sees that other baptised people are so engrossed in dialogue with various cultures and religions, or feel so hesitant about their own faith that they fail to 'give explicit and courageous witness in their lives to the faith of Jesus Christ'.[102] The Church also recognises that, for a variety of reasons, many baptised people are dissatisfied with the Church, and their sense of belonging to a Church community has consequently been weakened.[103]

There are two main complimentary categories of catechesis. These are (a) initiatory or basic and (b) continuing or permanent catechesis. (a) Basic catechesis involves the conversion and basic initiation of people into the Christian life and is closely linked to the sacraments of Christian initiation (Baptism, Confirmation and Eucharist). Like all forms of catechesis it is barren if it is not nurtured by the constant support and living witness of the Church, the Christian faith community. (b) Continuing catechesis or education in the faith refers to the progressive and continuing faith formation of children, adolescents and adults through a variety of media including the study of scripture (for example, *lectio divina*), the Church's social teaching, preparation for the sacraments (liturgical catechesis), spiritual formation (retreats/workshops) and theological instruction.[104] Often teachers will be involved in providing simultaneous basic and continuing catechesis to one class of children where different children have diverse religious or non-religious backgrounds and individual religious needs. A teacher may initiate some children into faith while nurturing other children's existing faith. Now while both basic and continuing catechesis occur within the primary school they cannot be exclusively confined to a school context for catechesis concerns a life-long journey in faith.[105] Faith formation in schools complements faith formation in the parish and home so that catechists do not act in isolation from the wider context.[106] This is why catechetical programmes such as the *Alive-O* programme place such emphasis on home-school-parish links.

In 1988 the Church attempted to clarify the relationship between catechesis and what it termed Religious Instruction.

> There is a close connection, and at the same time a clear distinction, between religious instruction and catechesis, or the handing on of the Gospel message…. The distinction comes from the fact that, unlike religious instruction, catechesis

presupposes that the hearer is receiving the
Christian message as a salvific reality. Moreover,
catechesis takes place within a community living
out its faith at a level of space and time not
available to a school: a whole lifetime.[107]

There is a certain ambiguity about what the Church means
when it refers to religious instruction. One possible
interpretation is that religious instruction is an aspect of
catechesis which focuses most specifically and systematically on
promoting knowledge of the faith without assuming that its
recipient is a believer.[108] As religious instruction is a scholastic
discipline it should be taught with the same systematic
demands and rigour as any other discipline.[109] In the post-
modern context the diversity of children's, teachers' and
parents' religious and non-religious backgrounds cannot be
ignored. When children are not operating from an active faith
background religious instruction is the most appropriate form
of catechesis that the teacher can use.[110] Religious instruction
focuses on the cognitive aspect of catechesis and appreciates
that faith formation does not bypass knowledge and content.
There is a body of belief, a *Credo* or Creed, to which Catholics
are called to assent when they say 'I believe' and any reduction
of the faith which by-passes its scriptural and doctrinal basis
does a disservice to pupils, teachers, the subject area and the
faith community.[111] Religious instruction ensures that children
are literate in the Catholic faith. John Paul II stated, children
"have the right to learn with truth and certainty the religion to
which they belong. This right to know Christ, and the salvific
message proclaimed by Him cannot be neglected."[112]

The Church realistically acknowledges that children have
different faith perspectives and it presents religious instruction
as a methodology appropriate to those who are i) believers, ii)

searching for belief and iii) non-believers.[113] The Church recognises that it has a ministry to each group of students and it has an approach designed to nurture and meet the needs of each.[114] The element of religious instruction reminds all those involved in faith formation that catechesis is not a uniform activity. Religious instruction can become part of a process of raising the potential believer's interest and thoughtfulness about life and so awaken their sense of the religious dimension of life. Religious instruction attempts to provide a basic, cognitive education in the Catholic faith without assuming that all children or teachers proceed uniformly.

Emerging Issues

There is a need to examine the assumption that the most appropriate form of religious education in Irish Catholic schools is a catechetical or confessional approach. The fact that a small but significant percentage of teachers have opted out of teaching religion or are unwilling to teach religion in primary schools raises the question of whether the category of religious instruction needs to be given greater prominence in Irish Catholic primary schools. Derek Bastide highlights three approaches to religious education: (i) the confessional, (ii) the giving them the facts and (iii) the understanding religion approach.[115] In theory Irish Catholic schools operate from within an exclusively (i) confessional approach which assumes belief on behalf of the teacher, the child, the parent and the community to which the school is attached. In recent decades Church affiliation and practice have declined steadily and there is a need for a variety of approaches to religious education in order to respond to this changing religious landscape.[116] Bastide's third approach, the understanding or empathy in religion approach, merits serious consideration in a context where either the teacher or child is a non-believer. This approach goes beyond the teacher providing the child with mere information or Gradgrindian[117] religious 'facts', as in approach (ii), but instead emphasises looking at religious beliefs and practices sensitively by enabling the child to empathise with the believers of a particular religious tradition without necessarily believing in that religious tradition themselves. The aim of the 'understanding religion approach' is not just to provide information about the religion in question but to get the child to step into the shoes of the believer and imagine what it is like for a believer to go on pilgrimage to Lourdes or Knock, to appreciate what it is like to celebrate Easter or to fast during Lent. The teacher does not necessarily expect the child to accept the truth of the faith tradition which he or she is teaching, but rather to understand its main beliefs and to respect the meaning which the faith holds in the lives of believers.

CONCLUDING REMARKS

A Catholic vision of education is largely positive and reveals the Church's very high esteem for teachers[118] and indeed for all who are working in Catholic educational contexts. The role of parents is acknowledged as being of crucial importance in the Catholic school community. Catholic education aims to develop the full potential of the human being and has a strong social justice agenda. The child is not the passive recipient of information but is actively and freely involved in the process of faith formation. Furthermore the child, and every member of the Catholic school community, is recognised as having the capacity to evangelise others. In Catholic schools the Church is committed to high academic standards, to interdisciplinary dialogue,[119] and to the formation of human beings with a capacity to think independently and to judge according to their own conscience. The Church is not overly prescriptive about the methods used to catechise students and acknowledges the academic integrity of different disciplines as well as the formative nature of all Catholic education. Religious instruction is a category that enables teachers to respond to the diverse faith backgrounds of their pupils.

While this chapter has presented a profile, a preliminary sketch of a Catholic vision of education, there are other aspects of Catholicity left unexplored. Catholic primary schools may partly or perhaps more fully recognise themselves in this profile. The manner in which individual Catholic schools embody a Catholic vision of education is complex and specific to each school community as it is negotiated at a local level between teachers, children, parents, school management and Church. This chapter does not attempt to reduce Catholicity to seven principles or to establish a definitive checklist against which schools should be evaluated. Catholic schools may well be committed to 1. Religious Freedom: 2. Academic integrity; 3. Christocentricity; 4. Catholic anthropology; 5. Dialogue with contemporary culture; 6. Mission to evangelise and 7. Catechetical orientation. Nonetheless the nature and implications of this commitment varies from school to school. Some teachers may be comfortable with an explicit mission to evangelise, while others may prefer an implicit emphasis on evangelisation through their witness as dedicated classroom practitioners. Likewise some teachers may respond to the call for initial and ongoing catechesis while others may feel that an emphasis on religious instruction is more appropriate in their classroom context. Catholic schools embody a variety of interpretations of what it means to be Catholic.

While the official Catholic documentation concerning education is very positive in orientation this chapter has focused on some of the multiple emerging issues which are central to a contemporary debate on Catholic education. Emerging issues include questions concerning: a state syllabus for religious education; the Catholic Church's majority control of the primary school sector; provision for non-Christian members of the Catholic school community; funding and pupil-teacher ratio; legitimate exercise of power; teachers' willingness to evangelise and the desirability of an exclusively confessional approach. While the Catholic vision of education is based on at least seven solid religious and theological principles it is true that no amount of good documentation can immunise an educational system from the need for effective critique, action and reform. Having a corpus of good documentation to back up the Catholic educational endeavor is one thing. Implementing and monitoring the Catholic vision of education in a manner which is true to the tradition, which sets high and achievable academic standards, which creatively forms the whole human being and orients the person to a life committed to social justice and a thirst for God, is entirely another.

NOTES

1   Vatican I (1859-60). Vatican II was convened by Pope John XXIII and closed by Pope Paul VI. It involved an updating of Catholic theology (*aggiornamento*) and produced 4 constitutions, 9 decrees and 3 declarations that brought far reaching changes in the Church's understanding of itself, its theology, pastoral and liturgical system and its relationship to other churches and religious traditions.

2   'The ideas proposed by the Second Vatican Council...influence profoundly the shape of religious education in Catholic schools', Ryan, M. & Malone, P., *Exploring the Religion Classroom A Guidebook for Catholic Schools,* Australia: Social Science Press, 2000, p.17. For an account of the impact of Vatican II on the Catholic church see GDC Introduction par. 27.

3   Texts such as *Gravissimum Educationis* Vatican II, 1965, paragraphs 1 to 10 inclusive; henceforth GE.

Evangelii Nuntiandi, Catechesis as a work of evangelisation in the context of the mission of the church, 1975, pars 17-20; 24, 40-47; 60, 70-71, henceforth EN.

The Catholic School, 1977, pars. 17-43; pars. 50-52; pars. 70 & 78-9, henceforth C.S.

1978 *Catechesi Tradendae*, Catechesis in the context of evangelisation, 1979, pars. 18-25; pars. 51-55, henceforth CT.

Lay Catholics in Schools: Witness to Faith, 1982, pars. 5-24, henceforth LCS.

The religious dimension of Education in a Catholic School, 1988, henceforth RDECS.

Catechism of the Catholic Church, 1992, Prologue pars. 1-10, henceforth CCC.

The Catholic School on the threshold of the Third Millennium, 1997, henceforth CSTTM.

General Directory for Catechesis, 1997, Part 1, Chapter 3; Part 3 Chapter 2; Part 4 Chapter 2, henceforth GDC.

Consecrated Persons and their Mission in Schools, 2002, henceforth CPMS.

4   This text was promulgated on October 28, 1965.

5   CT par.18.

6   Cf. Gerald Grace, *Catholic Schools: Mission, Markets and Morality*, London: Routledge Falmer, 2002. See Part 11 Catholic schools post-Vatican 11: A review of research studies pp. 80-110. See also Albert Price 'Turbulent Times – A Challenge to Catholic Education in Britain Today' in James C. Conroy ed., *Catholic Education inside out outside in*, Dublin: Veritas, 1999, pp.112-134.

7   Grace, *Catholic Schools*, p.108.

8   The RCIA document in 1988 stressed that all faith formation should follow the model of the catechumenate, in other words it should focus on pre-baptismal and post-baptismal catechesis, mainly on the sacraments of Baptism, Confirmation and Eucharist.

9   GDC par. 91.

10 The RCIA provides a model for all catechesis through its gradual character, its definite stages (pre-catechumenate, catechumenate, purification and illumination, mystagogy), its link between information and formation, its biblical and liturgical basis and the link between the initiated and the whole Christian community. GDC par. 88f.

11   There is no suggestion that the order in which these principles are presented in this chapter represents their importance in church documentation.

12   GE par. 1.

13   GE par 2.

14   GE pars 3 & 6. For the importance of parents as the primary educators of their children see CSTTM par. 20; LCS par.12.

15   GE par. 3. cf. CSTTM par. 17.

16   GE par. 6.

17   This idea was clarified by Pope John Paul II in *Centesimus Annus.* See also CSTTM par. 17.

18   CS par. 70.

19   GE par. 5.

20   GE par. 8.

21   CSTTM par. 16.

22   CSTTM par. 15.

23   *Teaching Religion in the Primary School: Issues and Challenges,* INTO, 2004, p.180.

24   Fintan O'Toole 'Catholics should go public' in *The Irish Times,* 12 October 2004.

25   *Shadow Report by Educate Together on The First National Report to the United Nations Committee on the Convention on the Elimination of all Forms of Racial Discrimination* by Ireland, January, 2005.

26   CS par 39.

27   CS par. 39.

28   CS Par.70.

29   Cf. GE Conclusion.

30   GE par. 10.

31   CSTTM par. 19. For an account of the importance of teaching see LCS pars. 15, 16.

32   EN par. 44. See also CT par. 51, GDC par. 148.

33   GDC par. 148.

34   GDC par. 30.

35   GDC par. 150.

36   GDC par. 151.

37   *Teaching Religion,* INTO, p.1.f.

38   *Teaching Religion,* INTO, p.72.

39   CS par 29.

40   CS par.33. For an account of the centrality of Christ to catechesis

see the GDC Part One par. 40, 80, 85.

41   CS par 35-6.

42   CT explores the christocentrism of catechesis in pars. 5 & 6. 'The definitive aim of catechesis is to put people not only in touch but in communion, in intimacy, with Jesus Christ...' CT par. 5.

43   In contemporary Western culture there is a tendency to emphasise the humanity of Jesus Christ at the expense of his divinity. Some people find the doctrine of the Immaculate conception (Mary was conceived by Joachim and Anna without original sin), the virgin birth of Jesus (Mary was a virgin when she gave birth to Jesus), the miracles of Christ and his resurrection from the dead, as implausible aspects of the Christian faith. Andrew Furlong, the radical Anglican writer, tends to stress Jesus' humanity at the expense of his divinity when he states 'I think that Jesus of Nazareth, without whom there would have been no Christian religion, was a human being like the rest of us, though a very extraordinary and inspiring one.' Andrew Furlong, *Tried for Heresy*, O Books, 2003, p.11.

44   GCD par. 30. Enda Lyons says, Christians recognise in Jesus the 'superabundance', the 'More', the 'Beyond' or the 'Divine' which they call God'. Enda Lyons, *Jesus: Self-portrait by God*, Dublin: The Columba Press, 1996, p167f.

45   GCD par. 30.

46   CSTTM par. 11.

47   DH par. 11. CS par. 29 states "It must never be forgotten that the purpose of instruction at school is education, that is, the development of man from within, freeing him from that conditioning which would prevent him from becoming a fully integrated human being. The school must begin from the principle that its educational programme is intentionally directed to the growth of the whole person."

48   Cf. GE par. 1. As children advance in years they are also entitled to a 'positive and prudent' sex education. Cf. Walter M. Abbott Ed., *The Documents of Vatican II*, London: Geoffrey Chapman, 1967.

49   GE par. 3. A Christian education introduces the baptised to the knowledge of the mystery of salvation so that, through the faith they have received and through liturgical action, they can develop as human beings who model themselves on Jesus Christ and contribute to the good of the whole society.

50 CS par. 26.
51 CS par. 27. See also 'the concept of school as a place of integral formation by means of a systematic and critical assimilation of culture' par. 26.
52 CS par. 27.
53 John Paul II Address to the National Meeting of the Catholic School in Italy in *L'Osservatore Romano*, 24 November 1991, p.4. cf. CSTTM par.9.
54 CS par. 31-32. See also LCS par. 18.
55 RDCS par. 63 cf. CS par 29.
56 GDC par. 23.
57 *Primary School Curriculum Introduction*, Dublin: Government Publications, 1999, p.9, p.58.
58 E.g. CS par. 44. cf. LCS. par. 20, 21.
59 GE par. 1.
60 Carter *The documents of Vatican II*, p.635.
61 EN par. 17.
62 EN par.20.
63 EN par. 45.
64 GDC par 20.
65 GDC par. 21.
66 'appropriate all the positive values of culture and of cultures and reject those elements which impede development of the true potential of persons and peoples.' GDC par. 21.
67 GDC par. 32.
68 GDC par. 22.
69 Cf. *RE today*, Summer, 2004 ,Vol. 21, No.3.
Virtual tours pp.46-7 and Input 8, RE and ICT, *RE today*.
70 Robert Jackson, *Rethinking Religious Education and Plurality Issues in diversity and pedagogy*, USA: Routledge Falmer, 2004, p.12.
71 'ICT includes the range of hardware and software devices and programmes such as personal computers, assistive technology, scanners, digital cameras, multimedia programmes, image editing software, database and spreadsheet programmes. It also includes the communications equipment through which people seek and access information including the Internet, email and video conferencing.' Cf. www.ncca.ie/j/index2.php?name =publ accessed 25/5/05.

72   In 2004 the NCCA launched the *Information and Communications Technology (ICT) in the Primary School Curriculum: Guidelines for Teachers* to help teachers use ICT effectively in the curriculum

73   Jim Robinson, 'Using the Internet Wisely' , Input 8, RE and ICT, *REtoday*.

74   CS par. 44 & par. 56.

75   CS par. 37.

76   Oliver Brennan, *Cultures Apart? The Catholic Church and Contemporary Irish Youth*, Dublin: Veritas, 2001, p.9.

77   Brennan, *Cultures Apart?*, p.161.

78   EN par. 17.

79   EN. par. 41.

80   EN par. 46.

81   EN par. 71.

82   EN par. 24.

83   EN par 6-12.

84   EN par.15.

85   CSTTM par.11.

86   Brendan Kennelly, *The Boats Are Home*, Meath: Gallery Books, 1989, p.53.

87   *Teaching Religion in the Primary School: Issues and Challenges*, INTO, 2004, p.53. 7.8% of teachers expressed this view.

88   Teaching Religion, INTO, p.55.

89   cf. Maeve Mahon & Martin Delaney, *Do This In Memory*, Dublin: Veritas, 2004.

90   GDC par.86.

91   P. Devitt, *That You May Believe*, Dublin: Dominican Publications, 1992, p.10.

92   GDC par. 33.

93   GDC par. 84.

94   EN par. 44.

95   EN par. 44.

96   EN par. 47.

97   CSTTM par. 14.

98   GDC par. 66.

99   CCC par 5.

100   GDC par. 24, 29.

101   GDC par. 25.

102   GDC par. 26.

103 GDC par. 28.
104 GDC par. 71.
105 GDC par. 73.
106 GDC par. 78.
107 RDCS par. 68.
108 GDC par. 85.
109 GDC par. 73.
110 GDC par. 73.
111 GDC par. 83.
112 John Paul 1, April 15, 1991, *Allocution on the Symposium of the Council of the Episcopal Conference on the Teaching of the Catholic Religion in the public school* cf. GDC par. 74.
113 GDC par. 75.
114 LCS par. 42.
115 Derek Bastide, *Religious Education 5-12,* London: The Falmer Press, 1987, p.7.
116 Brennan, *Cultures Apart,* p.160.
117 Cf. Devitt, *That You May Believe,* p.9.
118 Cf. LCS
119 GDC par. 73.

CHAPTER FOUR

Christian Religious Education:
Purpose and Process

• •

Christian religious education involves developing in students a religious commitment to Jesus Christ so that they become disciples.[1] It includes Christian formation in which Christian beliefs, attitudes and practices are appropriated, and critical education in which one learns to reflect on Christianity. Christian religious education is a life-long process carried out in many different settings including the family, the local Church community and in Catholic schools. Catholicism has developed a rich tradition of reflection around the task of religious education. This theoretical tradition includes reflections upon:

- the purposes of Christian religious education;
- the contribution made by theology and the social sciences to religious education theory and practice;
- the nature and capacities of the person being educated;
- the kinds of educational activity that are valued;
- the methods appropriate to the different contexts in which Christian religious education is carried out;
- the means of planning and assessing or evaluating the curriculum.

This chapter introduces the reader to some key theorists who inform current approaches to school-based Christian religious education in the Catholic tradition. It also outlines some broadly accepted insights from the theological and educational domains that have a significant influence upon contemporary religious education programmes and practice in the Irish context. An examination of these theoretical foundations will enable teachers to understand the professional rationale supporting current approaches to religious education in Catholic primary schools.

The chapter begins with some reflections upon a theological rationale. Christian religious education is trinitarian, christocentric and ecclesial. This means that it is rooted in the mystery of the Trinity, places Christ at the centre of the whole enterprise and promotes and services the needs of the Church. These theological foundations have profound implications for how one understands the goals or purposes of Christian religious education in any context. Christian theology also informs the curriculum (content and process) of Christian religious education. Nevertheless, this content and process must be given an educational framework if it is to serve religious educators adequately. Therefore the second section of this chapter outlines some general educational principles and values to be considered when devising religion programmes for the primary school classroom.

The third section is devoted to the question of methodology, that is the discussion of how one goes about Christian religious education. First, a theologically grounded approach to catechesis is presented. This method is found at the heart of many contemporary catechetical programmes such as *Alive-O*. Then, forms of planning and assessment appropriate to school-based religious education are discussed. Here planning and assessment are placed within the broader goal of ministering to the spiritual, moral and religious life of the child. Finally, the importance of developing students' capacities for a religious way of knowing is examined. In this regard, it will be argued that playful engagement with narrative, ritual and symbol are central to the religious education of children. The chapter closes with a brief examination of two areas which are key to the development of religious knowing in the primary school context: storytelling and ritual.

THE PURPOSES OF CHRISTIAN RELIGIOUS EDUCATION

The purposes of Christian religious education are shaped primarily by Christian theology, and secondarily by educational theory. The renowned American curriculum theorist Dwayne Huebner explains that religious education is a process by which educators introduce the young to the traditions which protect and illuminate the transcendent or religious dimension of the lives of humans. Our philosophical and theological interpretations of that transcendent dimension, and our understanding of how human beings relate to transcendence therefore has a major impact upon how the task of religious education is understood.

The doctrine of the Trinity is the starting point for understanding the purposes of Christian religious education. The claim that we believe in a relational God of love – the loving relatedness of three persons, Father, Son and Spirit – is 'the deepest claim that Christianity offers about the Mystery that undergirds our existence.'[2] Theologian Catherine La Cugna describes this as the mystery of 'God for us' because the Trinity reveals that God's relationship to us is one of care and love. In other words, God intends our salvation, desiring that we live our lives to the full, both here and hereafter. Therefore we religiously educate because God is *for* humanity. Because

God is for us and for all creation we risk engaging in the quest for that which will enable us to confront the patterns of destruction in the world and foster fullness of life for all. In sum, we religiously educate because Christian religious education can be a part of the process of salvation that God desires for all persons and for all creation.

The most important affirmation Christians make about God is that God's purposes have been fully expressed in the life, death, and destiny of one particular person, Jesus of Nazareth. For Christians, Jesus is the central symbol and norm for understanding God. This means that Jesus' person, teachings and actions can all be considered a parable of God, teaching us who God is and the kind of salvation God desires for us. This has a number of implications for our understanding of God, of Church and hence of the purposes of Christian religious education.

First, as the notion of the reign (or kingdom) of God lay at the heart of Jesus' message, the idea of God he mediates cannot be divorced from what he meant by the reign of God.[3] Jesus used the symbol of the 'reign of God' to suggest that God's deepest desire is to bring all of reality to fulfilment out of love. Second, Jesus' teaching and healing actions revealed that God acts against that which diminishes or negates human wholeness. Third, Jesus' actions showed that God's concern for salvation, while universal (Lk 1:29-37), reveals itself in a partiality towards those who are weak, dependent and oppressed, particularly the economically poor. Finally, Jesus clearly wanted to form a 'people of God' who are themselves concerned for humankind and all creation. Today this community of disciples is called the Church.[4]

The Church, as the community of disciples of Jesus, is both the seed and the sacrament of God's salvation in the world today.[5] This means that the Church community seeks to be an effective sign of the presence and transforming power of God for all humanity. Through word, sacrament and action, the Church affirms God's saving presence in human history. Religious education is one way in which the Church participates in God's work of salvation in the world. It does so by helping people to enter into a personal relationship with Jesus Christ, so that they become his disciples and participate in the fulfilment of the reign of God.

The Irish-born theologian and religious educator, Thomas H. Groome, suggests that the over-arching purpose of Christian religious education is the reign of God which he describes as the symbol of God's ultimate purpose for humankind and creation.[6] People learn what it means to serve God's reign when they participate in the Church community as it strives to promote love, compassion, peace, justice, mercy, forgiveness, integrity, inclusion and freedom from oppression for all people. In this way, God's reign is to be realised on every level of human existence – personal, interpersonal, and socio-political – so that God's presence permeates and transforms every aspect of life.[7]

When serving the reign of God becomes the ultimate purpose in religious education, this has repercussions not only for *what* is taught but also for *how* it is taught, as well as for the *context* in which it is taught. Everything that is done in religious education should help realise the values of the reign of God for all people and throughout all of God's creation. Nothing that is done should hinder students from exploring the presence and call of God in their own lives and in the lives of others, particularly the poor and the oppressed. Groome emphasises that the reign of God suggests the need for a holistic kind of faith that includes cognitive, affective and behavioural aspects.[8] Such faith is nurtured by an approach to religious education that invites people not only to know *about* God, but to 'know'

God in a personal relationship so that God transforms their perspectives and ways of acting in the world.

Professor John M. Hull agrees that the purpose of Christian religious education is to promote the following of Jesus in serving humanity. This aim is truer to the nature of Christian faith, says Hull, than any emphasis on making people religious and Christian. Hull distinguishes between religious education that seeks to propagate Christianity and religious education that seeks to serve the reign of God. Two contrasting approaches towards a theology of evangelism help to illustrate this distinction. On the one hand, there is an approach to evangelism that involves convincing people of other faiths to become Christian. This approach, according to Hull, builds up certain religious identities while obliterating others. On the other hand, an examination of what Jesus did suggests another approach to evangelism. Jesus did not seek to force people to accept his religious views: he sought to bring about peace, justice and well-being for all, particularly the poor and marginalised. He announced a new humanity, in which Greek and Jew, circumcised and uncircumcised, male and female, slaves and free, would all be one (Gal 3:28; Col 3:11). Consequently, the community of Jesus' disciples – the Church – continues to invite people to live God's good news of salvation in Jesus Christ as an essential part of its mission of following Jesus in serving the world.[9] The emphasis in this new approach to evangelisation is not upon making non-Christians into Christians but upon Christians living their faith as credible witnesses in the world. This work of evangelisation is carried out in conversation with other Christian churches and with religious faith communities that acknowledge the human responsibility toward the oppressed and the poor of the world.

A COMMUNITY AFFAIR

Learning a religious language which enables one to relate to God is a central part of the process of becoming fully human. Initially children learn to speak one such language by becoming part of a religious community. This community nurtures them as they acquire a sense of the way that religious language works. Becoming religious in a Catholic Christian way involves immersion in the narratives, symbols, beliefs and practices of the Catholic religion to the extent that children feel a real sense of belonging to a strong community of memory and hope.

Being part of a community where people care for and love one another is a precondition for true belief in the God of Jesus Christ. For Christians, love of God and love of neighbour are inextricably entwined. The Church strives to be a loving community which supports the faith of its members through a rich tradition of Scripture, liturgy, prayer, story, parables, and symbol as they learn to live the way of Jesus. It offers believers reliable and trustworthy access to the person of Jesus Christ, to the story of his life and to the 'good news' of his saving acts for us. Catholics believe that the Church has the authority to protect the revelation of Christ as it is symbolised and expressed in Scripture, doctrine, liturgy and moral teaching. These symbolic expressions of Christian revelation are authoritative sources for people in the present as they try to discern who God is and how they are to live as people of God.

Catholic religious educators sometimes differ in their understanding of and vision for the Church, as well as in their understanding of how religious education serves that vision. On the one hand those who favour the model of the Church as 'the people of God' will see the primary purpose of religious education as nurturing the personal faith of people in their encounter with the person of Jesus. They therefore tend to emphasise the importance of educational activities that foster discipleship of Jesus. On the other hand, those who favour an institutional model of Church tend to emphasise the goal of helping people become faithful members of the Church, by providing them with solid education in the 'truths' of the faith. These people place a high value on knowledge of religious doctrines, as well as on the induction of learners into current Church practices and ethical codes. Clearly, both models of Church will inform the development of an appropriate curriculum of religious education for Catholic primary schools. Discipleship always needs the support of established guidelines, structures and practices. Similarly, the institution always needs to remain open to new forms of discipleship in order to avoid the pitfalls of authoritarianism and legalism.

CURRICULUM

The educator's purposes in religious education shape and influence decisions about the intended curriculum. Curriculum (from the Latin *'curriculare'*, 'to move along together') deals with *what* needs to be taught. This 'what' need not be understood exclusively in terms of religious *content*. It can also include an understanding of curriculum as *process*. This means that one allows for kinds of learning such as an ability to meditate, to participate in ritual, to express oneself through art, and to use religious language and symbol to make meaning and explore mystery. In summary, the curriculum of Christian religious education describes all valued educational activities in the realm of the Christian religion. Decisions about the kinds of educational activity to be valued in schools depend upon the value frameworks (technical, scientific, political, aesthetic, ethical and theological) which teachers use to assess this activity and understand its meaning.[10]

As noted above, Christian theology articulates the nature of the Christian religion. It therefore defines many of the authentic and valuable Christian attributes, knowledge and ways of knowing that a Christian religious education curriculum should promote.[11] The primary subject matter to be taught is God. God cannot be known directly however but only through sacred narrative, symbol and ritual. 'Knowing' God in this mediated way is not like learning to solve a problem; it is more like responding to a call. And by our response we are brought into an intimate relationship with God whose creative and life-giving Spirit continues to call us forward to fullness of life. Consequently, the curriculum of Christian religious education is not only the stories or materials the teacher presents to the students, but the *processes* through which students learn the art of using religious language to effectively meet and foster their relationship with the God of Jesus Christ.

RELIGION PROGRAMMES

Educators bring various criteria to bear when deciding upon the content and processes of religion programmes for primary schools. Ideally, the curriculum will reflect both the formative and critical educational dimensions of religious education that were outlined in chapter one. Four key areas make up the curriculum of Christian religious education in its directly formative (catechetical) dimension: scripture, beliefs, morality, and liturgy/prayer. Classroom-based religious education enables children to develop in all four areas, for example, understanding and reflecting on Christian beliefs, Church teachings and doctrines; interpreting scriptural stories; playing with religious symbols and metaphors; participating in prayer, rituals, liturgy and other expressions of Christian spirituality; and developing the knowledge, attitudes, values and thinking skills necessary to become a moral person.

This kind of formative religious education in the Christian religion is an important basis for the critical dimension of religious education in the primary school. As Jeff Astley argues, 'Education in general – and Christian religious education in particular – should recognise that, logically and psychologically, the formation of a person's identity and worldview must happen before [critical analysis and evaluation of knowledge claims] develops.'[12]

In other words, a rich grounding in one's own religious tradition is a necessary prerequisite for many of the skills of critical religious education. These include the ability to comprehend and appreciate the place of religious belief and practices in human life; to understand the need for dialogue among Christians; and to explore the beliefs and practices of different world religions. Inter-religious education should enable children to develop powers of empathy for and sensitivity towards people whose religion differs from their own. Furthermore, content and activities that enable pupils to learn *about* and *from* other spiritual traditions, such as Judaism, Buddhism and Islam, enhance their own skills of religious literacy. For example a Christian child might learn a Buddhist method of meditation which enhances their capacity for spiritual awareness. The child learns something extremely valuable *from* Buddhism while remaining grounded in their own religious tradition. In this way the encounter with Buddhism enhances the child's participation in the reign of God.

The first step in drawing up a religious education programme for the primary school is to devise a core syllabus which takes account of the prior knowledge, needs and interests of the students. It will also take account of the particular contribution of Christianity to religious education. Then a syllabus is drawn up that provides a general outline of the key religious narratives, concepts, beliefs, symbols, prayers, rituals, practices, procedures and experiences that will enable students to enter into and develop a personal relationship with Jesus. The syllabus should also indicate how progression within the curriculum is to be achieved. This progression refers to increasing conceptual complexity as well as to the breath and extent of the content and processes to be taught.[13] The syllabus would then be used as a guide for formulating learning objectives and choosing educational activities for the primary school.

METHODOLOGY

Methodology is 'the means by which we seek wisdom about method.'[14] It answers the questions: *how* do we go about teaching religion and *why* do we choose to go about it in that particular way? In other words, methodology involves the development of a reflective theory about the educational task. Important methodological questions include: How will I engage students in curriculum content and processes, and in what order and sequence? How will I help students to explore the Mystery at the heart of religion? How will I cultivate religious knowing? How will I go about teaching the skills of religious literacy I wish to teach? How do I help pupils interact creatively with Scripture and tradition? How do I engage the lived experiences and culture of the learners? How will the Christian tradition be interpreted?

The methodology of primary religious education is informed by pedagogical principles which draw upon psychological theories of learning and of human development. Ideally these principles provide a rationale for the development of both the formative and the critical dimensions of religious education in the primary school. Furthermore, religious educators work from certain assumptions concerning knowers, knowledge and the activity of knowing. These assumptions influence teachers' choices of educational methods, tools and strategies, as well as their approach to writing objectives, the planning of questions and assessment. Methodology will also be informed by theology. For example, one's theology of culture would have an important impact on one's approach to the culture of students.[15]

Once teachers have decided upon learning objectives they employ a variety of methods or strategies to assist them in carrying them out. Among these may be included the use of critical reflection, dialogue, drama, art, music, story, ritual, guided imagery and action. Often religious education programmes suggest particular methods and provide materials and strategies to enable teachers to realise them in their own classroom context. For example the current *Alive-O* programmes (*Alive-O – Alive-O 4*) suggest the methodological framework: focus, reflect, respond.

Catechetical Methodology

The *Alive-O* framework is one expression of the method that is widely used in catechetical programmes throughout the world.[16] This dynamic method or process has the goal of fostering a relationship between the pupil and Jesus Christ. It involves linking the lived experience of pupils with scripture and the Church's tradition. The method starts with the learners' experience and leads them to reflect upon it in the light of the Gospel. By bringing the light of scripture and tradition to bear upon the lives of pupils they learn new ways of *being* Christian in the world.[17]

This catechetical method is called alternatively *correlation* or *praxis*. The goal is to set up a profound relationship between life and faith.[18] Every aspect of the Christian tradition is an expression of the experience of people of faith in the past. Correlation involves making the faith experience of these people my own so that I can freely choose to respond to the call of God in my own time and place. Through coming in contact with various mediations of the faith experiences of other Christians (scriptures, doctrines, art, liturgies, icons, lives of saints), I find a language to express and extend my own experience in the present. In appropriating these mediations for myself, I become aware of how they affect me and of what they enable me to understand. I allow this encounter to affect my own knowing and my desire for loving action in the future.

One's approach to the Christian faith tradition depends largely upon one's understanding of the theological concept of revelation. Christians understand religion as a lived response to a Divine initiative or revelation. In other words, we believe that God seeks us out and calls us into relationship with him. God reveals Godself to us and we are invited to respond. The Catholic theologian, Karl Rahner (1904-1984), described revelation as the ongoing communication of the mystery of God to the world. This revelation comes to us through concrete actions and symbols in history and in our daily lives. The central sign of Christian revelation is the life, death and resurrection of Jesus (the Paschal Mystery). Jesus is our ultimate guide for understanding who God is and how, as human beings, we are invited to relate to God. When Jesus died he sent this Spirit to be with us as we discern God's presence and call in our lives. God can be found therefore in the experience that comes from God's Spirit bringing about healing, liberation or salvation in peoples' lives today.

Within various catechetical methodologies the place of pupils' lived experience depends largely on the religious educator's understanding of revelation. Some theologians see revelation as a series of propositions containing information. Religious educators influenced by this perspective will tend to emphasise the content of doctrines rather than pupils' lived experience and accompanying existential questions. In contrast, theologians following Rahner, point out that God continually reveals Godself to people in the midst of their everyday lives and history. This is because the risen Christ is still with the people of God as they seek to encounter and recognise God's presence and will for their lives in the world today. Doctrines and statements of faith, they assert, must continually be interpreted in dialogue with the reality of God's presence in students' lives.

Christian faith has two aspects: revelation and response. Revelation refers to what believers accept as divinely revealed. Response refers to the believers' commitment to and trust in this revelation. Christian faith begins therefore with the fact that God has revealed and continues to reveal Godself to humanity. For this reason, we must understand, reflect upon and study the *content* of the Christian faith. While we cannot objectify this content (i.e. God), it is mediated by symbols or signs given by God in salvation history. These include scripture, sacraments, Church creeds, doctrines, dogmas and the lives of the saints.

Each of these signs of revelation discloses its meaning when interpreted and appropriated with the help of God's Spirit. As Christian symbols and signs, they have the power to transform our perspectives and ways of living in the world. Furthermore, Christian narratives, beliefs and symbols raise questions about aspects of our experience that may have gone unnoticed. For instance, the Christian's faith in a providential God raises the persistent question of why there is so much pain and evil in the world. Similarly, Jesus' teaching about the privileged place of the poor in the reign of God directs our attention to the poor and oppressed of the world today. The mysteries of the Trinity, the Incarnation, the Cross and Resurrection, and the Eucharist draw us into an exploration of the mystery at the heart of our existence and enable us to reflect upon our human experiences of ambiguity, suffering and hope. Moreover, the scriptures and traditions of the Church offer us images of love, of hope and of promise as we try to follow the way of Jesus in our own lives.

The second aspect of Christian faith is the human side of the faith relationship. If God continues to speak, to communicate Godself to the world, it makes sense that God speaks in the lived experience of people today. As God is present and active in peoples' experiences and actions, pupils must be enabled to explore their experiences and to interpret them in the light of the Gospel. Christian religious educators, believing that there is no evident contradiction between religious experience and ordinary experience, place considerable stress on encouraging children to deepen their awareness of the religious dimension of everyday experience. They are convinced that exploration of human experience can assist or provide an opening out to religious understanding. This is not to say that Christian faith can be *deduced* from human experience alone. There is something, however, in human experience that points to the mystery which Christians believe is revealed in the life, death and resurrection of Jesus, the Christ. A key task of religious education is to help students recover the deep questions of existence to which Christian faith responds.

Christian religious education is about setting students' imaginations free to explore how God meets their desire for truth, meaning and reality in the particularity of their own lives. Immersion in the richness of the Christian religious tradition enables them to discover the presence of God at the heart of their existence. Consequently, the primary goal of Christian religious education cannot be accomplished by the teacher. The best that teachers can do is to create the conditions and offer support so that people can hear God's call and develop the personal resources needed to respond.

PLANNING AND ASSESSMENT

It is important to consider the value of contemporary approaches to planning and assessment for religious education. Each approach contains underpinning assumptions about the nature of the person to be educated, the goals of education and the nature of the learning process. The prevailing mode of studying teaching today is the scientific. This means that teachers generally speaking use the scientific knowledge of generalisation, prediction and control in thinking about teaching. The prevailing idea is that if a teacher can master the principles of learning and child development; if objectives are clearly outlined and lessons planned accordingly; then teaching will be effective. A brief outline of this scientific approach to planning and assessment, as it applies to religious education, is provided here.

Objectives

'Objectives' refer to the reasons for including certain educational activities in the curriculum. We can distinguish between teaching objectives, behavioural objectives and learning objectives. Teacher objectives describe the things the teacher wishes to do to facilitate pupil learning. For example she may wish to *read* a scripture story, *explain* a worksheet, or *teach* the words of a hymn. Behavioural objectives describe the exact pupil behaviour teachers want students to perform. For example the objective 'that the students will complete a worksheet' is a behavioural objective. Behavioural objectives of this nature are easily observed and verifiable though they can lead teachers to focus on very narrow goals.

Learning objectives are broader than behavioural objectives. They illustrate how pupils are to *use* content (what teachers teach, educational material and activities) to demonstrate *learning*.[19] The focus here is on what teachers wish students to learn. Learning objectives are statements that describe the things pupils are expected to be able to do during or after instruction or teaching (broadly defined). The key is to describe the specific process or behaviour the pupil will perform so that their learning activity can be observed and assessed. However, while the learning objective is stated in behavioural terms the intention behind the objective may be broader than the explicit behaviour itself. For example, the objective 'that the student will *demonstrate empathy* with Jesus in the garden of Gethsemene by *stating* how he might have felt at that time', reveals that the intention of the teacher is to help students to develop the capacity or disposition of empathy. She will ensure that this learning objective is achieved by exploring the story of Jesus' in the garden of Gethsemene; by asking pupils how Jesus might have felt; and by suggesting words to describe Jesus' emotions where required. In this way, the teacher plans appropriate educational activities in order to fulfil his/her goal.

Learning objectives generally describe the concepts, skills, attitudes, and behaviours that need to be learned in particular religion lessons. They enable teachers to set immediate educational goals, to select appropriate instructional methods and resources, to communicate the purpose of lessons to students, and to plan some forms of assessment appropriate to the study of religion. In addition, the articulation of objectives enables teachers to conceptualise how teaching and learning in religion complement or contrast with learning in other areas of the primary school curriculum. This scientific mode of planning requires teachers to pay attention to the quality of teaching and learning in the classroom and helps them avoid a form of religious education that is at best vague and haphazard and at worst lacking in substance. It is important to remember however that we cannot always plan for pupil's learning in accordance with pre-determined levels of attainment. The idea of curriculum as *process* suggests the need to be open to learning that we may not have foreseen when drawing up objectives for a lesson.

Assessment

When one decides on the curriculum content and processes suitable for a religious education programme, one may then consider some formal and informal means of assessing whether that curriculum serves the educational needs of one's particular class. Various forms of assessment reflect different goals for learning. The assessment of learning objectives, for instance, is one way of measuring and evaluating student's immediate performance in the classroom. Teachers are generally able to assess whether learning objectives have been achieved if empirical evidence of knowing and doing can be observed. For instance, the objective given above ('that the children will demonstrate empathy with Jesus in the garden of Gethsemane by *stating* how he might have felt at that time') describes a pupil behaviour that can be observed and assessed. If the children imagine and describe Jesus' emotions the teacher will know whether her intention to promote Christian attitudes in the student is being achieved or not.

The primary kind of assessment appropriate to religious education is that which supports and enhances learning. Assessment *for* learning can be distinguished from assessment used to assign grades to students or to satisfy the demands of external authorities.[20] The word assessment derives from the Latin *assidere*, which means 'to sit by'. Therefore, religious educators will seek forms of assessment that enable them to accompany students as they learn what it means to be religious. The use of assessment *for* learning enables teachers to examine the learning processes engaged in by students as well as the learning outcomes achieved. It also enables them to assess whether children are developing the important dispositions and attitudes which are a central part of becoming Christian and developing a Christian character and world-view. Teachers using assessment to support learning can make useful observations from classroom discussions and presentations, quizzes, worksheets, games, verbal and written accounts, created prayers and rituals, role plays, dramatic expressions, computer-generated presentations, artwork, reflective journals, projects, musical performances, students' self-evaluations, as well as from the day-to day interactions of students working with others in a variety of situations. Other helpful forms of assessment include moral dilemma discussions, debates, and open-ended questions in general. In sum, a holistic approach to assessment in religious education is based on the assumption that human beings learn through multiple avenues – through the senses, feelings, intuitions, rational thought – and that learning can be expressed in many ways – through image and symbol, poetry, drama, dance and story, as well as through writing and conversation.

Objectives and Assessment: a Caution

Scientific methods of observing, planning and assessment in education are important tools for religious educators as they provide ways of valuing many of the educational activities carried out in religious education. It is important to remember, however, that a scientific form of valuing is only one mode of reflection on teaching and learning. It does not provide a comprehensive framework for specification of the entire curriculum of religious education. One can also reflect on teaching and learning using an aesthetic model or guide.[21] While a scientific mode of understanding concerns itself primarily with the predictability of teachers' actions to influence objectively observable learning, the artistic mode concerns itself with skilful and competent use of language, of material, of colour and design, of movement and the flow of events in the classroom. For example teachers will engage in ongoing reflection on the atmosphere created in their classrooms when children are invited to engage in ritual. The teacher's own spirituality will probably be the most significant factor influencing children's experience of ritual in any context. The teacher's ongoing awareness of his/her own spiritual journey will constitute an important part of his/her reflection on and understanding of religion teaching in this regard.

It is important to be aware that some valued educational activities in religious education cannot be easily accommodated to current models of educational objectives. This is because these activities do not lend themselves easily to forms of analysis based on empirical evidence of 'learning'. Indeed, precise scientific planning for some of the most important outcomes of religious education (for example, the ability to use the religious metaphor 'the Lord is my Shepherd' to grow in one's trust and love of God, or the ability to play with religious language as a way of resolving ultimate existential questions) is impossible and the attempt to do so may even be counter-productive. Finally, learning objectives generally relate to learning outcomes which can be assessed in the immediate term. Many of the valued goals associated with religious education however, such as the development of virtues, are longer-term goals and are not so easily verifiable.

Religious educators by and large, have a broader view of the role of education in personal development than that which can be empirically measured. The primary aim is to develop the moral, spiritual and religious capacities of the person being educated, rather than providing for the performance of skills. In other words, religious educators are less concerned with overt performance than with how religious knowledge, attitudes, language and skills are integrated with the personal development of the individual. Therefore, they will always be wary of viewing education solely in terms of transmission and accountability. They will also refuse any approach to educational objectives that causes them to narrow their goals to fit a truncated understanding of human knowing and learning.

The kind of knowing which religious education seeks to foster does not sit easily within the scientific model of education. Religious knowing has an inherently imaginative aspect to it and is taught using poetical, metaphorical, and narrative strategies which stimulate depth of understanding, creativity, wonder and awe. Therefore, many activities in religious education (for example, artistic play with religious imagery) are to be valued precisely because they enable children to immerse themselves imaginatively *in* religious language without having to produce anything that can be seen or measured by an objective observer. Learning how to be *in* religious narratives, symbols and ritual practices in this way is not the same as learning information that can then be assessed, as if one were checking if a message has been received. It is more akin to responding to the experience of God at the heart of one's life and learning how to place God at the centre of all of one's knowing and loving in the world. Consequently, knowledge, skills and behaviours that can be objectively planned and assessed in religious education are always placed in the context of the broader goal of ministering to the religious, moral and spiritual capacities of the child.

In summary, while the aims of Christian religious education cannot be guaranteed, either by the prescription of curriculum content, or by the way this content is outlined, it is nevertheless important that teachers approach the teaching of religion in an intentional fashion. This requires the articulation of clear learning objectives and the use of ongoing assessment which forms part of the teaching – learning process. Religious educators will be aware however of the need for balance between clear intended outcomes of the teaching and learning process and those outcomes that cannot easily be predicted or measured. Furthermore, attention must be paid at all times that the forms of planning and assessment used, genuinely reflect the different kinds of knowing that are valued in the religious domain. In this regard, the curriculum should be supported by a flexible pedagogy in which genuine connections between knowledge, understanding, attitudes and skills are nurtured and sustained.

Fostering Christian religious knowing[22]

Christian religious faith is a whole-bodied act of trust in the activity and presence of God within human life. It is primarily an affective response to the invitation of God to see reality as God sees it and to love all people as God loves them. Therefore, the kind of knowing which religious education seeks to foster is primarily an affective, behavioural mode of knowing, an engaged relational way of knowing. In this chapter this kind of religious knowing will be distinguished from religious knowledge. Christian religious education fosters the art of religious knowing by means of a system of *Christian* religious language. This religious language comes mainly from scripture, the liturgy of the Church and the symbolic aspects of both.

Christian religious imagery, myth, symbol, parable and story enable us to engage with the deep existential questions that need to be brought to awareness and explored if we are to be true to our humanity. When we reflect on our human existence we realise that we are finite creatures of earth and clay and yet we yearn to be in relation to something that transcends our finite existence; we are born and yet we die; we seek freedom and yet we flee from it; we need to be autonomous yet we crave to be in relationship. These paradoxes define who we are as human beings. Religious knowing enables us to live in these paradoxical tensions, freeing us to continue living creatively in the world. The symbolic language of religious stories, poetry and rituals enables us to be grasped by a meaning which is bigger and newer than that which we create by ourselves alone. Christianity draws our attention to dimensions of reality that we might easily overlook and enables us to decipher and to contemplate the mysteries of life and death.

When we teach through liturgy, sacred image, sacred story and parable we are teaching more than we can say in scientific language or in logical conceptual discourse. We invite students to open themselves to the possibility of being met by a God who requires them to see reality in a new way. Christian religious symbols, narratives, rituals and practices draw our attention to the holy dimension of all reality and encourage alternative ways of seeing ourselves, others and the world. They enable us to see reality in its depth as permeated with the presence of God; to see everything and everyone as held in being by love. When we learn to see reality through the eyes of the Christian religious tradition, we become aware of the presence of God in the most mundane human experiences and begin to participate in God's work of salvation in the world. Further, the use of creative activities enables students to develop varied expressions of loving response to God.

Religious knowing is to be distinguished from knowledge *about* religion which may be understood as conceptual knowledge of religious facts, stories, beliefs, doctrine and theology. Religious knowledge is the 'content' of religious knowing. Religious doctrines and creeds are important because they articulate truths that draw our attention to key aspects of God's revelation. Children need to be introduced to these doctrines and creeds in a way that is appropriate to their developing capacities for understanding. Their ability to *explain* Church doctrines and their ability to engage in theological reflection will differ from that of adults because their ability to think abstractly develops with time. This does not mean that we do not introduce children to religious doctrines and creeds. It means, however, that we must be aware of how children's understanding of religious concepts changes over time. For instance, while the small child should not be asked to explain the doctrine of the Trinity, she can come to 'know' and relate to the Trinity through practising the sign of the cross and reciting 'In the name of the Father, and of the Son and of the Holy Spirit.' While religious knowledge involves talk *about* religious language, religious knowing is being *in* the language, in such a way that one's imagination is freed for new insight and understanding.

In conclusion, Christian religious education is somewhat similar to teaching a language with which one is endeavouring to express and explore experience of oneself, of others and of God. Many of the methods used in primary religious education seek to develop the language of religious knowing. The key is to find ways to teach children the creative potential of religious symbols and religious language so that they encounter religious meaning and develop a personal language for religious expression. The ability to use religious language in this way is deeply rooted in the imagination and therefore one could say that it is an art that children 'catch' rather than 'learn'. And similar to learning any artistic process, there is no one methodology that ensures the kinds of imaginative insight and discovery that are possible when children are invited to explore religious symbols and narrative through their imagination.

TEACHING THROUGH SYMBOLIC PLAY AND NARRATIVE

A central task of religious education for children is to invite them to encounter religious symbol and imagery on the level of their senses. This enables them to think symbolically in a concrete rather than in an abstract way. Children's ability to use symbols and to engage in symbolic activity is nurtured though symbolic play and ritual activity. Symbolic play is a way of engaging with reality as a way of understanding it.[23] It is a key way that children discover more about themselves and about life itself. It is also the primary way humans learn the ways of being, feeling, and thinking that are congruent with the Christian community's understanding of what it means to be human.[24] Symbolic play helps children to interiorise the faith tradition but also allows them to extend the tradition in creative ways.[25]

Play utilises a mode of knowing that is closer to artistic creativity than the kinds of intellectual problem-solving and theological reflection *about* God which require logical or abstract thought. It engages imagination and wonder to enable us to find meaning in life and death and to imagine new ways to live. Symbolic play begins at the place where we encounter the deep questions of life and where we meet the mystery that surrounds all of our existence. It enables us to develop a new way of being in the world and a way of creatively coping with our human limits within the context of a system of religious language. The ability to do this does not come as a *product* of play but rather it comes to us in the *process* of play itself. In other words, the art of using religious language is learned while playing with it. In this sense religious play should not be seen as a teaching tool from which we demand some measurable or visible product or outcome. Religious education is about teaching the art of playing so that children can discover the presence of the Creator playing with them as well as expressing their deep identity as creatures who create.[26]

Examples of activities that engage children in creative religious play include: dramatic improvisation, modelling with clay, painting, weaving, dancing, juggling, listening to music and developing rhymes, chants and songs. Poetry also offers innumerable opportunities to play with and enjoy religious language; a process which nurtures children's creative and spiritual imagination. Children also learn how to play with religious symbol through their participation in religious rituals, both inside and outside the classroom. Ritual involves learning by doing. Through participation in classroom rituals, children learn the Christian language of ritual – praise, thanks, confession, and mourning.[27] These languages enable children to worship God and to express the deepest desires and movements of the human heart. In addition, individual ritual actions (such as lighting a candle before a statue) and communal ritual actions (for example, the sign of the cross) offer children a whole-bodied way of articulating the mystery of God.

Children also learn the language of religious ritual as they participate in the liturgies celebrated in the local Church, the most important of which is the Sunday Eucharist. The readings, prayers, gestures and symbols of the Eucharist work together over long periods of time to shape children's attitudes, understandings and faith commitments. Ideally education in religious narratives, symbols and rituals in the primary school classroom should allow children to practice the patterns of language and behaviour they are acquiring through their experience in the local Christian faith community.

Narrative

Telling the stories of faith is another important part of the work of primary religious educators. Christian religious education is rooted in the central stories of scripture and, in particular, the story of Jesus Christ. Stories of Abraham and

Sarah, of Moses and Miriam, of Rachel and Jacob, of Jesus and Mary, reveal a God who cares deeply for us and who comes to meet us in our everyday lives. These religious stories awaken children's spiritual imagination and prompt them to look within and beyond their own experience to discover something of the 'truth' of reality and of the presence of God in it. When children listen to a story they enter into the imaginative energy of the story, and so allow the story to organise their experience in a new way. Kevin Nicols notes that,

> A good story is one of the major embodiments of the creative imagination. It is a prime example of that subtle relatedness of character and event, of symbol and pattern which has the power to draw our feelings into new places. It is also an outstanding example of the way in which religious formulations (or philosophical or moral ones) can be embedded in a web of character, happening and image. Entering into this web we identify with characters and happenings and see how the principles so embodied echo in our own experience.[28]

Christian stories nurture a distinctly religious imagination enabling us to see things differently from the ways to which we have become accustomed. Jesus understood the power of images to change peoples' way of seeing reality and so he often chose to teach people in parables, ritual, images and metaphor. Through the vehicle of the parable he gave his listeners a glimpse of his experience of God, an experience which radically upturns one's ideas and values. Furthermore, Jesus understood that to see reality differently means that you alter the way you live. As Douglas Sloan explains,

'Whenever we want to understand, integrate, and interpret the world, whenever we seek to infuse our actions in the world with vitality and purpose, we draw upon our images. Whenever we look to the future, we are guided by images.'[29]

Religious narratives and parables serve to nourish and protect the image-absorbing and image-making capacity that enables students to discover new and vital images for action.

CONCLUSION

In this chapter some of the theoretical foundations for Christian Religious Education in the Catholic primary school were outlined. We began by situating all Christian Religious Education within the overarching theological vision of the Trinity and the reign of God. We saw that all decisions concerning curriculum, religion programmes and methodology should serve the larger goal of inviting students to become disciples of Jesus in serving humanity. We then proceeded to examine some ways of valuing the kinds of educational activity carried out in Christian religious education. First, a Catholic theology of revelation suggested the particular value of educational activities that enable students to relate their life experiences to scripture and the Church's tradition. Second, we noted the ways in which religious education depends on the educational languages of psychology and other social sciences in the articulation of objectives, the drawing up of syllabi and in the structuring of assessment. Third, aesthetic ways of valuing educational activity were deemed to be of particular importance as the form of knowing one wishes to foster in primary religious education is closely akin to that of artistic creativity. In summary, this chapter offered a professional rationale for Christian religious education in the primary school by drawing insights from theology, educational theory, psychology, philosophy, art and ethics. Reflections such as these should enable teachers to develop their own particular professional rationale for the challenging task of religious education in the primary school.

NOTES

1   While Christian religious education has a clear formative aim – learning to be and become more Christian—it is not exclusively confessional in character. In other words, Christian religious education can be carried out in such a way as to include non-Christian students who wish to learn from the Christian religion. Furthermore, Christian religious education includes elements of critical education including ecumenical education, inter-religious learning and the ideological critique of religion.

2   Michael J. Himes, 'Living Conversation: Higher Education in a Catholic Context', *Conversations on Jesuit Higher Education*, 8 (1995), p. 22.

3   Roger Haight, *Jesus Symbol of God*, Maryknoll, New York: Orbis Books, 1999, chap., 4.

4   See chapter 6 for a detailed explanation of God's preferential love for the poor.

5   LG nos 5, 1.

6   Thomas H. Groome, 'The Purposes of Christian Catechesis' in Thomas H. Groome, and Michael J. Corso (eds), *Empowering Catechetical Leaders*, Washington, DC.: National Catholic Educational Association, 1999, pp. 3-27. Groome outlines his Shared Christian Praxis approach in Thomas H. Groome, *Sharing Faith*, San Francisco: Harper & Row, 1990 and in Thomas H. Groome, *Christian Religious Education*, San Francisco: Harper & Row, 1980.

7   For Groome's inspiring description of the reign of God see his *Sharing Faith*, pp. 14-18.

8   Ibid., pp. 18-21.

9   John M. Hull, 'Religion and Education in a Pluralist Society,' p. 4. Essay from his website: www.johnmhull.biz/ accessed 16/02/04.

10 Curriculum theorist Dwayne Huebner suggests that the central notion of curricular thought is that of 'valued activity'. Huebner moves from this central notion to the clarification of the value frameworks or systems which may be used to value educational activity. He suggests five such value frameworks: technical, political, scientific, aesthetic and ethical. Much current curricular ideology reflects a technical value system which draws on a economic model of rationality. Educational activity should be valued more for its aesthetic and ethical values where the concern is 'not on the significance of the educational act for other ends, or the realization of other values, but the value of the educational act per se'. Dwayne Huebner, ' Curricular Language and Classroom Meanings' in Vikki Hillis (ed), *The Lure of the Transcendent: Collected Essays by Dwayne E. Huebner*, Mahwah, New Jersey: Lawrence Erlbaum Associates, 1999, pp, 106, 110.

11 Jeff Astley, *The Philosophy of Christian Religious Education*, Birmingham, Ala.: Religious Education Press, 1994, p. 122.

12 Ibid., p. 274.

13 P. Adey, 'Dimensions of Progression in a Curriculum', *The Curriculum Journal* 8:3 (1997), pp. 367-392. Some models for the measurement of increasing conceptual complexity (Piaget, Fowler and Kohlberg) are introduced in chapter five.

14 Mary Elizabeth Mullino Moore, *Teaching from the heart: Theology and Educational Method*, Minneapolis: Fortress Press, 1991, p.20.

15 See chapter six for a Catholic theological approach to the dialogue with children's culture.

16 The teaching strategy suggested for the junior programmes consists of three steps. First an initial focusing activity explores some aspect of the child's life. This is followed by reflection in which the child is invited to learn something from the Christian tradition, relating this to his/ her own experience. Finally the child is offered an opportunity to respond to what was learned.

17 For a fuller description of the Catholic tradition see chapter six.

18 Praxis describes a dialogue between theory and practice, between faith and reason, between human experience and Christian faith, with the intended outcome of lived Christian faith.

19   Peter. W. Airasian, *Assessment in the Classroom*, 3rd edition. New York: McGraw Hill, 1997, p.78-79.

20   Lorrie A. Shepard, 'The Role of Assessment in a Learning Culture', *Educational Researcher*, 29:7 (2000), p. 4.

21   For this idea and for reflections on the need for different curricular languages see Dwayne Huebner, 'The Art of Teaching' and 'Curricular Language and Classroom Meanings' in Hillis (ed), *Transcendent*, pp. 23-35; 101-117.

22   I am indebted to Dr Andy McGrady (Mater Dei Institute of Education, Ireland) for my understanding of the distinction between religious knowing and religious knowledge. See glossary. For an extended discussion of children's religious thinking see Chapter Five.

23   Symbolic play is the form of play that emerges during the (Piagetian) stage of preoperational thought (2-7 years) when a child is capable of symbolically representing an object that is absent from his/ her view.

24   Ronald H. Cram, 'Knowing God: Children, Play, and Paradox', *Religious Education*, 91:1 (1996), p. 58.

25   Diane J. Hymans, 'Let's Play: The Contribution of the Pretend Play of Children to Religious Education in a Pluralistic Context.' *Religious Education*, 91:3 (1996), p. 372.

26   I am indebted to Jerome W. Berryman for this description of religious play and for the suggestion that the primary organising image for religious play is that of the creature and Creator God at play together, creating. Jerome W. Berryman, *Godly Play*, Minneapolis: Augsburg Fortress, 1991, pp. 12-13.

27   Maria Harris and Gabriel Moran, *Reshaping Religious Education: Conversations on Contemporary Practice*, Louisville, Kentucky: Westminster/ John Knox Press, 1998, p.34.

28   Kevin Nichols, 'Imagination and Tradition in Religion and Education', in Jeff Astley and Leslie J. Francis (eds), *Christian Theology and Religious Education: Connections and Contributions*, London: SPCK, 1996, p.194.

29   Douglas Sloan, 'Imagination, Education, and Our Postmodern Possibilities', *Revision*, 7:2 (1992), p. 46.

CHAPTER FIVE

Understanding the Child: Potential and Promise

• •

Christian religious education is first and foremost the religious education of persons. Its central aim is to bring human beings to the fullness of their humanity by fostering their encounter with and free response to the God of Jesus Christ. It is therefore of critical importance that religious educators are aware of the gifts, capacities, experiences, developmental stages and educational needs of the children they teach. This means that teachers will ponder questions like: Do children have an innate capacity for intuitive, affective religious experience? Are children spiritually aware? If so, how do children express their spirituality today? How can religious education contribute to the holistic development of students? What vision of moral, spiritual and religious development is offered by the Christian religious tradition? These questions frame the area of enquiry for this chapter, which considers the children who are to be religiously educated in the Catholic primary school.

A basic principle of child-centered education is that education must be grounded in knowledge and understanding of the child. To honour this principle for *religious* education teachers need to study the cognitive, affective, aesthetic, moral, social, and spiritual dimensions of the child's life. They will consider for example, how children relate to symbol; how their faith growth is connected with their personal growth; how they become moral; and how they understand religious concepts. Religious educators will also consider how the wider social environment – children's familial, cultural, ethnic and socio-economic background – affects children's capacity to be religiously educated. Finally, teachers need to be aware of the extent to which formative religious influences affect children's capacity to learn. Of critical consideration, therefore, will be children's lived experience of Christian community today.

This chapter begins by identifying some foundational theological assumptions that are made about children as subjects of Christian religious education in the primary school. This is followed by an outline of some of the research on the cognitive, moral and spiritual capacities of children that enriches our understanding of their educational needs. Four contemporary approaches to nurturing the spirituality of children which seek to take account of this research will then be examined. These include 'The Gift to the Child Approach', the Montessori tradition of religious education, the work of American psychiatrist Robert Coles, and a way of exploring children's spirituality developed in the British context by David Hay and Rebecca Nye. The chapter ends with a consideration of the variety of familial, cultural, economic, social and educational backgrounds from which students in Irish primary schools currently derive. An appreciation both of individual differences and of the unique socio-cultural contexts in which religious education is carried out today is imperative for the development of approaches which are tailored to the needs and capacities of students in primary schools.

CALLED BY GOD...

Christian religious educators seek to nurture the transcendent or religious dimension of children's lives. Their first theological assumption is that the child has an innate capacity for transcendent experience. This means that the child is naturally open to being drawn into communion with something more than herself, and ultimately with God. But who is this God? The doctrine of the Trinity enables Christians to appreciate that God is in a loving, life-giving relationship with us. God is the relationship of the three persons (Father, Son and Spirit) among themselves, but also continually moving toward us in loving relationship. God has revealed Godself as a God 'for us'.[1] In other words, God is not removed from us; God is present with us, inviting all to be in loving relationship with the Divine. This presence of God in our midst is described as grace. Furthermore, this invitation to be in relationship with God is totally free and prior to any action on our part. God has created us simply because God wants to be in relationship with people who can respond.

The notion that children have an innate capacity for transcendent experience or spiritual awareness is supported by faith in the creation of each individual in the image of God (Gen 1:26-30). This means that there is something intrinsic to our very being that connects us to God's own way of being: we are made for loving relationship and communion with God, with others and with the world around us. In other words, we are invited to discover our true selves as we strive to be in ever-greater communion with others and with God.

Karl Rahner helps us to understand this natural capacity for relationship with God. He explains that if we examine our human capacity to love, to question, and to hope, this investigation points to our potential for the Divine. For instance, our capacity to ask the deeper questions – of the meaning of life and of our own significance in the universe – points to our natural openness to hearing the ultimate meaning offered by God. Similarly, our fundamental desire for value and love is ultimately fulfilled when we transcend ourselves in loving relationships with God and with other people. In other words, God's love builds upon our natural human gifts and upon our basic desire to transcend ourselves through love of God and neighbour. To be human is to have a radical desire for self-transcendence – a radical desire that is, fundamentally, a desire for God.[2]

Christians believe that human beings are 'flawed' creatures with a capacity for sin. Consequently human beings are in need of the salvation brought about by Jesus. Through his life, teaching, death and Resurrection Jesus revealed that God's deepest desire is to pour his healing love and peace into our hearts. God holds out an offer of relationship and enables human beings to respond through freedom and love. Each one is called to play a unique part in God's loving plans for the world and everyone has a free and personal response to give to the unique call of God. One of the key tasks of religious educators accordingly is to use the resources of the Catholic tradition to invite pupils to notice, understand and freely respond to the presence and call of God in themselves, in their relationships with others, and in the world. Religious education also involves creating a space within which pupils can be freed from everything that diminishes them as human beings, and which prevents them from freely responding to the call of God.

...TO FULLNESS OF LIFE

The second theological assumption made by Christian religious educators is that the child has unending capacities to grow and develop and so become more fully human. While every person conceived is a human being, one can also act in ways that damage one's basic humanity, thus becoming dehumanised. In this sense human personhood is something to be developed right throughout lives. Humans are created in the image of a relational God. To be and to become human is therefore to be and become a person-in-relation. This means that every child is continually learning how to enter into ever-deeper relationships with others, with the world around them, and with God. Religious education aims to enable the child to reach her full potential and to live a full life as the unique person she is. Hence, each child is encouraged to become fully alive at each and every age and stage of development.

The Christian commitment to the integral development of the child has its theological foundation in the doctrine of the incarnation. Through the doctrine of the incarnation, Christians make the radical claim that the absolute Mystery of God became a human person and lived a fully human life. Christians believe that Jesus not only shows the way to full humanity but transforms the very meaning of being human. Indeed, it was precisely in living his humanity to the full that Jesus in fact revealed his divinity. In other words, disciples of Jesus strive to become fully human in the way of Jesus, becoming thereby more like the God in whose image they are created.

MORAL, SPIRITUAL AND RELIGIOUS DEVELOPMENT

Religious educators, in their attempt to understand the child, are challenged to make use of the best psychological, educational, philosophical and sociological resources available. This section will outline some of the contemporary research which informs religious educators' understanding of the child's moral, spiritual and religious capacities. For instance, the idea that children *develop* in their moral and religious thinking and in the way they 'hold' their faith is proposed. While this description of contemporary theory is not exhaustive, it is intended to introduce teachers to some research perspectives that will enable them to understand, appreciate and interact with the children they teach.

Erikson and virtue

For the past forty years, the Freudian ego-psychologist Erik Erikson (1902–1994) has provided a rich resource for religious educators interested in the tensions that give shape to human life and identity, as well as the implications of those tensions for moral, spiritual and religious development. Erikson was interested in the operations of the psyche, the largely unconscious shaping of meanings that underlie emotional and personality growth. At the same time, he focused upon the fact that human development always occurs in the context of particular communities and societies and continues through the whole of one's life. Because Erikson attended both to the individual psyche and to the social dimensions of a person's development his theory is described as a psychosocial developmental theory.

According to Erikson, every person takes in the norms, values and worldview projected by the society around them, yet each has an individualised set of potentials unlike those of any other. Out of these different ingredients the person creates a unique identity as they journey through life. Erikson outlines eight stages or phases of psychosocial development which he claims are experienced by all people from birth to death. At each stage a crisis must be faced in which the person must work out a favourable balance between the counterplayers of the stage (See Table 1). If people succeed they develop key human qualities such as the ability to care, to hope and to love. This developmental process is unvarying and if each stage is not successfully traversed one must return and complete the developmental task involved at that particular stage. Erikson's eight stages are outlined here.[3]

Table 1.

Stage	Crisis	Virtue
One	Trust vs Mistrust	Hope
Two	Autonomy vs Shame and Doubt	Will
Three	Initiative vs Guilt	Purpose
Four	Industry vs Inferiority	Competence
Five	Identity vs Identity confusion	Fidelity
Six	Intimacy vs Isolation	Love
Seven	Generativity vs Stagnation	Care
Eight	Integrity vs Despair	Wisdom

The first task in the human life cycle is to develop a fundamental sense that oneself and the world outside oneself are basically trustworthy. Before and after the child is born, a child's caregivers (often the mother and father) must be able to communicate to the child a deep conviction that there is a meaning in what they are doing as they care for the child's needs. When the child consistently receives this kind of care, she learns to trust in someone outside of herself and develops the virtue of hope. Eventually the child will imaginatively transfer her trust in the caregiver to the transcendent God. In this way the foundations for the capacity to 'have faith' are laid down in the basic rituals of care between the child and her caregiver. This, says Erikson, is the paradigmatic religious stage, as it provides the basis from which humans develop the ability to hope in the promises of God.[4]

Erikson alerts educators to the fact that the origins of faith lie in the process whereby a child develops a sense of self in relation to significant others in her life. One of the crucial tasks of the small child is to develop a sense of self as someone who is capable of dynamic interaction with others throughout the lifespan. Human beings are constituted by the whole network of relationships into which they are born. The quality of these relationships is highly significant for the development of children's spiritual and religious capacities. Caregivers who do not relate to the child as a unique being severely compromise her ability to transcend herself in loving relationship with another, including the capacity to be in relationship with God. If she doesn't have a sense of self, her capacity to freely relate to God may be adversely affected. Young children who experience healthy and relatively secure relations with caregivers will be open to the religious dimension of experience and to life-giving images of God. Erikson believed however that while the origin of religious experience lies in these early experiences with primary others, development depends upon how the person negotiates the remaining seven critical pairs of issues found at each of the eight stages of life.[5]

In 1964 Erikson proposed a 'schedule of virtues' to correspond to the eight stages of development. He asserted that if each stage is successfully negotiated people develop a particular virtue or strength. In infancy and childhood one develops the virtues of hope, will, purpose and competence; in adolescence, fidelity; and in adulthood, love, care, and wisdom. Those virtues are most decisive at such times but they are not limited to these stages in the lifecycle. In using the word 'virtue' for these qualities, Erikson recovers the old English meaning of virtue as *inherent strength* or *active quality*. Virtues are closely connected to the presence of the Holy Spirit in people's lives. Donald Capps notes that as Erikson's schedule of virtues culminates in wisdom, his moral perspective has profound affinities with the wisdom tradition of ancient Israel, especially as reflected in the Book of Proverbs as well as in Jesus' proverbial sayings.[6]

Moral formation

Catholic moral theology provides an additional dimension to our understanding of how people develop Christian moral virtues. In his book, *Making Disciples*, moral theologian Timothy O'Connell explains that a virtue describes the *inclination* and *ability* to act consistently in such a way that one brings about the goal of that particular virtue. So, for example, the courageous person has the inclination and ability to make judgments enabling him or her to act courageously in most situations; a loving person chooses consistently to act lovingly and is able to do so when required; an honest person regularly tells the truth and so on. So becoming a virtuous person is about developing personal styles of being *and* characteristic ways of behaving. Moreover, a person's character shapes the particular form virtues take. A Christian might for instance decide to overlook an insult because of Jesus' exhortation to 'turn the other cheek'. The reason for this is that Christian faith gives people distinctive perspectives, attitudes, dispositions, intentions, purposes and norms which are brought to bear on particular moral decisions to act virtuously. It also provides motivation as articulated so pointedly by Saint Paul when he says, 'The love of Christ urges us' (2 Cor 5:14), inspiring us to act in a virtuous manner.[7]

O'Connell explains that people can be helped to develop Christian character and Christian moral virtues both when their commitment to behave in certain ways is reinforced and when their ability to choose and act in a way that truly incarnates the goal of Christian virtues is developed. This involves educating people's emotions as well as their intellects. One way in which people's inclination to behave in moral ways is nurtured is that of story. This is because it engages their imaginations and enables them to experience situations from another point of view, what some commentators term perspective-taking. Story encourages movement away from a self-centered worldview to a worldview open to others. Furthermore, through story people develop a vision of what is truly real and truly worth striving for in the world. Moral development requires a decision and a conversion to a vision. Often religion offers this vision, for example, the vision of the reign of God. This vision was presented by Jesus at the beginning of his ministry when borrowing from the prophet Isaiah he spoke of a world in which the blind would see, the prisoners would be released, and there would be an end to the suffering of the poor and oppressed (Lk 4: 16-21).

Creating opportunities for students to interact in groups with people who live Christian values and offering them exciting role models to follow is another way of nurturing Christian moral action. This, notes O'Connell, arises because 'it is by our experiences of and with other persons that our moral sensibilities are most decisively shaped'. We develop morally out of the emotional, interactive experience of moral-social conflict with others and by imitating people whose way of living we admire.[8]

O'Connell also makes the interesting claim that moral formation is less about teaching the intrinsic importance of different moral values as it is about teaching their *relative* importance. People are formed in Christian values as they learn to re-order their value priorities. Consequently, one of the goals of Christian religious education is to convince people of the *relative* importance of the Christian perspective and way when compared with the other perspectives and lifestyle options offered by their culture.[9] This means that teachers need to recognise the values that appeal to children and the reality of the value conflicts they encounter. For example, the pursuit of happiness is an important value in contemporary Irish culture. The pursuit of happiness at all costs, however, conflicts with the gospel value of justice and compassion for the poor. To deny the value of happiness while extolling the virtue of justice would be to deny the real appeal of happiness as a value. Instead, the task is to teach children how to decide for example, when, on balance, money spent on personal pleasure or on material goods is morally justified.

O'Connell argues that it is important that people not only develop a Christian identity: this identity must be *central* to the numerous identities they have. Identities become central to persons to the extent that their important relationships depend on them. Consequently, to educate for Christian moral identity means to educate for ever more life-giving relationships: relationships with self, with others and also with God's own self.[10] One clear implication for Christian religious educators is that the home, school and community must work together to educate for Christian identity. Moreover, the school, as one locus for the creation of identity, must be in tune with the way in which children seek and find identity in other social contexts.

Moral thinking

The development of children's capacity for moral thinking and moral judgement coincides with their acquisition of moral virtues. Moral development occurs when we reflect upon our actions. This ability to reflect upon what we do is something that can be learned and developed. Studies of children's moral thinking derive mainly from the field of developmental psychology and depend upon the Swiss psychologist Jean Piaget's (1896-1980) studies of intellectual development. Piaget is described as a cognitive-developmental theorist because he suggested that children's mental development proceeds by moving through predictable sequential stages. His stage-theory describes how this movement from immature to more complex structures or forms of thought occurs. Piaget's theory enables educators to help children move beyond their present stage of thinking to reach higher, and hence, more mature forms of thinking.

Piaget also studied the way children play and soon began to discern predictable changes in the way they thought about right and wrong as they negotiated the rules of their games. This research enabled him to describe a two-stage progression in children's moral judgment. His first stage of moral development is known as 'heteronomous morality' in which children depend upon adults for rules and focus on the consequences of actions with no awareness of the importance of intentions. Here children regard actions as right if adults approve of them. Actions are considered wrong if the child makes a mess, regardless of whether this is intended or accidental.

In Piaget's second stage, 'autonomous morality', children develop the capacity to develop their own rules and co-operate with their peers. The focus at this stage is upon the intention behind actions. Here children begin to apply rules based upon a goal of mutual respect and co-operation. The change from the heteronomous to the autonomous stage comes about, Piaget claimed, through a process of cognitive restructuring of the ways in which the children are thinking morally. Piaget's theory suggests an approach to moral education that provides students with opportunities for personal discovery through problem-solving rather than indoctrinating them with moral principles and norms.[11]

Moral development

Theories of the development of moral thinking tend to be based upon Piaget's cognitive-developmental approach. These theories emphasise children's reasoning or thinking about moral issues rather than their moral behaviour. For instance,

Harvard educator, Lawrence Kohlberg built upon Piaget's cognitive developmental base to develop a theory of 'levels and stages of moral development'. He examined the ways in which people think through moral decisions in order to make judgments about actions. Moral reasoning, says Kohlberg, develops through three levels and six distinct stages. These stages are universal and human persons proceed through these stages in an irreversible and predictable fashion. Because individuals offer different reasons for their actions they are assigned a different stage. They move from one stage to another when their current understanding no longer fits with their experience and moral intuitions. Kohlberg's stages of moral development culminate in the virtue of justice. This means that the goal of moral thinking, in his view, is an ability to think about moral issues using universal ethical principles that promote the dignity of all.[12]

Kohlberg's stage theory is useful for understanding the moral reasoning of children. In Kohlberg's first stage children follow rules so as to avoid being punished and in order to obey people in authority. These children have an egocentric point of view and so don't consider the outlook or perspectives of others. Avoiding physical damage to persons and property is of more importance than their psychological interests. Children in Kohlberg's second stage follow rules when they meet their own needs or those of others. Here individuals are moral in order to get something or to earn rewards. These children are aware that everyone has his own interest to pursue and that these may conflict, so that what is right is relative. Hence the need to do deals with others to get what one wants, and the desire for fairness whereby each person gets the same amount. For children at Kohlberg's stage three, right is playing a good (nice) role, being loyal and trustworthy, and keeping rules. Here individuals are moral to get approval from others and to avoid social rejection. This stage also understands and uses the Golden Rule: one does what one would like the other to do for oneself. These children are 'aware of shared feeling, agreements, and expectations which take primacy over individual interests.' Therefore they are orientated towards shared norms of behaviour, as well as shared moral and religious laws.[13]

Kohlberg's theory has been criticised by commentators who note that young children may have a far richer sense of morality than Kohlberg allows. For example, Jeff Astley claims that children do not act solely out of fear of punishment, but also from considerations of fairness and for other reasons.[14] Another Harvard educator Carol Gilligan also challenged Kohlberg's research findings. She wondered why more men tended to be found in the higher stages in Kohlberg's schema. She suggested that perhaps this is because women perceive and value in different ways. While men emphasise the values of individual rights and justice, women place a higher value on responsibility, service, interdependence and care in relationships. Gilligan criticises any theory of moral development that assumes that the male way of thinking is normative for all humanity. She argues for an 'expanded ethic' that would encompass compassion, tolerance and respect.[15] These qualities echo Erikson's moral perspective which, we noted above, has close affinities with the biblical *wisdom* tradition. In contrast, the ultimate virtue in Kohlberg's schema is justice, a virtue of primary importance to the *prophetic* tradition of ancient Israel.

It seems therefore that an inclusive approach to moral formation will include insights from both the wisdom and prophetic traditions of the bible. Both traditions share the insight that the key to moral growth and change lies in our interactions with and care for other people. Moral education therefore involves not only teaching ways of reasoning through moral dilemmas and making moral judgments. People must also be taught to direct their attention to the concerns of others by developing the skills of imagination, empathy, compassion, respect, tolerance, discipline, fidelity and care.

Religious thinking

The study of children's religious thinking has undergone much development over the past forty years. In the 1960s, British researcher Ronald Goldman created a highly influential theory of cognitive religious development. His landmark study *Religious Thinking from Childhood to Adolescence* was published in 1964. Goldman focused upon the religious thinking of six- to sixteen-year-old British children and youths. He asserted that religious thinking is no different from non-religious thinking: it is thinking towards a religious object (for example, the concept of God). Using Jean Piaget's cognitive developmental theory and research approach, Goldman found that children's cognitive development placed certain developmental limits on learning religious concepts. For example, he proposed that religious analogies and metaphors are beyond the capabilities of the child who thinks in a literal or concrete manner, and who hasn't yet developed the ability for abstract thought.[16] In his subsequent book, *Readiness for Religion* (1965), Goldman advised against introducing children to religious concepts too early. The emphasis in primary school, he claimed, should be on affective development rather than on conceptual development.

Irish researcher Andrew McGrady of the Mater Dei Institute of Education disagreed with Goldman. He argued that difficulties arise if one equates religious thinking solely with Piaget's operational thinking. A broader definition of the nature of religious knowing must take account of children's ability to interact with metaphor as part of such knowing.

McGrady outlined some elements of thinking that are unique to religious knowing including the ability to recognise, comprehend, produce, extend, interrelate and evaluate religious metaphors. Irrespective of the child's stage of general cognitive development according to Piaget's schema, she thinks religiously by constructing or inheriting metaphors.[17] In research carried out with Irish secondary school pupils, McGrady found that pupils are able to think metaphorically before the onset of Piaget's formal operational thought. Consequently, he urged that teachers be encouraged to facilitate the development of religious thinking at all levels by taking account of the distinctive metaphorical nature of religious language.[18]

Following researchers such as McGrady, religious educators are now paying more attention to the distinctive elements in children's religious thinking, which distinguish it from other forms of thought. The goal is to offer a more inclusive consideration of childhood religious thinking which does not silence or disempower the voices of children. Researchers emphasise, for example, that the small child develops a capacity for symbolic representation in the first months and years of life. As Goldman did not measure this aspect of children's religious thinking, he underestimated children's capacity to engage with religious metaphor. In addition, psychologist Shellie Levine argues that children's cognition includes skills of thinking such as 'metaphoric logic', which are essential to the spirituality of experienced spiritual practitioners in Christianity, Judaism and Buddhism. She finds that children demonstrate many of the cognitive skills exercised by people who are highly developed spiritually. Therefore the challenge, says Levine, is to nurture the spiritual capacities of children by building upon the cognitive skills children tend to have acquired naturally.[19]

FAITH DEVELOPMENT

Faith development theory helps us to understand the psychological processes by which people develop faith. One well-known faith development theory was devised by American Methodist theologian and psychologist of religion James W. Fowler III. Fowler wrote the classic book on the subject of faith development, *Stages of Faith* – in 1981. According to Fowler's theory faith 'develops' as one becomes capable of more sophisticated kinds of thinking and valuing. Fowler's theory is a useful tool for educators who wish to discern the blocks to authentic faith and to understand the different ways in which people relate to religious traditions throughout their lives.

Relying strongly upon the work of Erikson, Kohlberg and Piaget, Fowler describes faith as the universal capacity for making meaning. It also describes the activity of knowing, valuing and relating to that which we find meaningful. More precisely, faith is a way of knowing and interpreting one's experiences in relation to some 'unifying centre of meaning and value'.[20] Prior to being religious or irreligious every person places his or her trust in a transcendent centre (or centres) of value, an image (or images) of power, and a narrative or story which orients her/him to what is of ultimate importance in the world. Faith is a response of commitment to that transcendent value or power because the person perceives it to be most true and real.

On this account faith is broader than *religious* faith or belief. All persons have an image of what they take to be of ultimate concern and of ultimate value. For example a humanist may be committed to human life and this commitment may be described as a 'faith' even though, consciously, it has no religious dimension. Many people's basic orientation or worldview is *religiously* informed. For example, the reign of God is the vision of reality to which Christians commit their lives. Jesus, the revelation of God, is the centre of value and power which unifies this vision. In this view, God's desire for peace and harmony, for justice and equality is the ideal which Christians work towards and the ultimate source of meaning in their lives.

Fowler distinguishes the content of one's faith – *what* one believes in – from the way in which one has faith, or the 'how' of faith. For example, the way a Muslim and a Christian think about and relate to Allah or God may be very similar although they believe very different things about the deity. Similarly, a Hindu and a Jew may relate to religious symbols in the same way, though the symbols themselves will differ, being unique to their respective religions. In each case the *structure* or *form* of faith may be the same though its *content* differs. Fowler is interested in those patterns or structures of thought, of valuing, and of knowing which underlie the specific content of people's faith and of how these patterns change over time.

Stages of faith

Fowler proposes six 'stages of faith' in addition to a pre-stage which together describe the kinds of thinking and valuing people may experience as their faith grows and changes throughout their lives. A faith stage describes 'the set of abilities which support a person's believing, valuing, committing and acting'.[21] Each stage is an average of seven sets of structures covering skills such as thinking and reasoning; understanding and responding to symbols; constructing a world-view; reasoning and judging morally; locating and relating to authorities in respect of one's faith; adopting another person's perspective; and setting the limits to one's own 'community of faith'. At each stage, a person's faith will reflect a particular form of reasoning, of perspective-taking, of moral decision-making, and so on. The earlier stages (1-3) in Fowler's theory are based upon Piaget's developmental stages of thinking, and enable us to identify predictable developmental turning points in the ways people construct meaning in relation to what is of ultimate value and power for them.

Some of Fowler's findings concerning children of primary-school age will be outlined here. Fowler's stage one (intuitive–projective faith) begins at about age three and a half to four and generally lasts until age six or seven. This is parallel to Piaget's pre-operational stage. At this stage children do not yet think in a logical fashion and have a limited ability to differentiate and co-ordinate their perspective from others. Children's emotional, cognitive and faith development depend upon their relationships in early childhood and there needs to be a sense of order in their world that they can trust. These children begin to interpret the events of daily life in terms of the religious and other meanings that adults attach to these events. Therefore, they need to develop a sense of belonging and it is through this experience of belonging to a particular nurturing community that they gradually learn to take the perspective of others.

Children's faith at stage one is made up of magical thinking, fantasy, ritual actions, as well as ideas and images formed through their relationships with key authority figures, especially parents. They put their ultimate worldview together in bits and pieces of stories drawn from religion, fairy-tales, film and television. Children's power of imagination is key to faith development at this stage and they are very open to religious stories and symbols. They particularly enjoy mythic stories with clear distinctions between good and evil. At the same time, since these children are particularly influenced by visible signs of power, their imagination can easily be hijacked by terrifying images of power, for example the devil. Educators need to be alert to the ways in which religious doctrines, moral taboos and frightening imagery can be used in a way which is detrimental to the children's well-being at this stage. This abuse can have a long-lasting effect upon the emotional and cognitive foundation of faith in children's lives.

When children reach Piaget's concrete operations (usually between five and seven years) they are ready to move into the second or narratising stage of faith development (mythic–literal faith). At this stage the child begins to identify with the stories, belief and practices of a religious community. Although this development may occur naturally, the transition can be supported and deepened by a teacher sensitive to faith development theory. Children at this stage are described as 'concrete thinkers' meaning they measure perceptions by appeal to concrete, or lived, experience. They also begin to think logically, to unify experience and to trace patterns of cause and effect. As a result, these children tend to view God as a parent who will reward the good, and punish the bad.

The major strength of stage two is the growing capacity of children to use narrative as a means of organising meaning. This means that children can begin to create stories and to retell the stories they have heard. They continue to be affected deeply and powerfully by story, symbol and drama at this time. Furthermore, Fowler claims that their capacity for symbols is still quite literalistic and that they understand stories and myths in a mythic and literal way.[22] Nevertheless, these children are beginning to distinguish between fantasy and reality (the tooth fairy and the Easter Bunny don't exist!). Teachers can aid this process, for example, by helping them to understand that Jesus is a real person who lived through childhood like themselves, thus enabling them to distinguish between Jesus and various magical and mythological figures they have encountered. These children identify readily with the heroes and heroines of books, film, music, sport and comics, great characters of the bible, along with mature adults in the community who elicit their admiration and love.

Children at stage two also begin to use classes and categories to order the world, sorting out people and groups that are like them and different from them. They need to hear the story of their community and religious group – the great stories from the Hebrew scriptures and the Christian scriptures – as well as the rules, teachings and beliefs of the Christian tradition. Religious educators can support children as they develop an affiliation with their own particular religious group while simultaneously learning to distinguish, respect and learn from the religious traditions of others.

Children in Fowler's stage two are beginning to understand that people's intentions are important and that they are responsible for the decisions they make. Teachers can help them to examine their motives and to appreciate the underlying values behind the community's rules. Furthermore, children are now better able to take the perspective of another and so benefit greatly from hearing the stories of other children, the poor, the elderly, those who have different abilities and lifestyles to themselves. Finally, children at this stage have an acute sense of fairness and justice; something which can be supported through human rights education and when children are invited to get involved in social justice activities in their own neighbourhood.

Religious educators should avoid seeing Fowler's stages as an achievement scale or a model with the aim of pushing people to the next stage. Rather, the theory enables them to better understand the children they teach and challenges them to provide a strong nurturing environment which will enable children to remain open to questions of meaning in their lives. Furthermore, Fowler's theory alerts educators to the power of religious language, rituals, stories, and ethical teachings to awaken the child to the domain of faith. The religious educator uses the resources of the religious tradition to provide learning experiences that will help the child to complete any developmental transition she is going through. Finally, it is important to remember that religious faith is richer and more complex than any faith development theory can describe. The ongoing challenge is to discover rich flexible multi-dimensional imagery for discussing moral, religious or spiritual change. A number of attempts to develop a rich language for children's spirituality will be examined in the sections that follow.

NURTURING SPIRITUALITY: FOUR APPROACHES

The idea that children have deep spiritual awareness before they are taught a religious faith is now widely accepted. Indeed, many studies suggest that more children have spiritual experiences than anyone had previously expected.[23] Four different approaches to understanding and nurturing the spiritual and religious capacities of children will be examined here. They illustrate the contemporary approach that seeks to learn from children's actual spiritual lives: by examining the ways in which they use religious and non-religious language and symbol to make sense of their world and of their place in it. Paying attention to children's lived spirituality is crucial for those who wish to introduce them to the resources of religious traditions today.

1. Theological conversation and 'The Gift to the Child Approach'

In the mid-1980s a number of researchers at the University of Birmingham School of Education introduced a new approach to the religious education of children. They developed this approach because they felt that children's religious capacities were being underestimated at that time. In particular they criticised approaches to religious education that drew upon

Goldman's research which, they claimed, was based upon 'a misunderstanding of the nature of religion, which was more concrete than was often realised.'[24] The Birmingham researchers argued that children who think in a concrete manner are capable of engaging with abstract religious concepts such as God, heaven, and angels, if they are engaged in theological conversation at a concrete level. Therefore, they wished to shift the concern from seeing religious education of children as a matter of teaching them religious concepts to engaging in theological conversation with children in such a way that they become flexible religious thinkers.

In order to understand this approach one needs to appreciate the distinction between having an abstract idea and thinking in an abstract way. As John Hull explains, a child may think in a concrete pattern but still understand an abstract word. For instance, the idea of God is abstract because it relates to something which cannot be touched or seen. It is also a generalisation by which people refer to the One who is the source of everything and the essence of love. Concrete thinkers such as young children, however, think about abstract words such as 'God' only in relation to the objects, people and situations they have experienced. For example a child can enjoy and understand a story about God speaking to the child Samuel just as he or she can appreciate a story about Harry Potter or what granny did when she was at school. In other words, the word 'God' will have meaning according to the situations in which it is encountered. God is appreciated as the friend of Moses, as a loving shepherd, as the father of Jesus, and so on. Therefore, the child thinks about God mainly through the images of God she is offered through story and in theological conversation with others. As the child builds up a repertoire of stories, songs, poetry and conversations about God, an ability to generalise and a sense of the intangible aspects of God will build up over time.[25]

John Hull and his co-researchers at the University of Birmingham devised a method of inviting children into theological language in this way called 'The Gift to the Child Approach'. This approach emphasises the role of images in children's religious thinking and the importance of nurturing the child as a theological image-maker. For example, children are provided with a rich variety of images of God so that they learn how a wide variety of symbols can point to the Divine. The technique accepts the literal nature of religious imagery in the thinking of the young child, proliferating images so as to enrich the child's creativity.[26] An example of a useful game used in this approach is where children are invited to look at objects (a rose, a ring, a picture of a woman) and asked whether God is a bit like that object or not. They are then invited to suggest ways in which God is not at all like the object chosen. This teaches children that almost anything can become a symbol of the divine, but that symbols never entirely exhaust the Mystery of God.

Religious educators can learn from the Birmingham project that children think religiously in ways that are appropriate to their needs. This ability will be nurtured or hampered by the kinds of theological conversations they are invited to engage in. Some of the deepest questions asked by children are religious questions: questions about death and dying, about personal identity, about the reasons for being moral, about the idea of God. It is important therefore to enable children to acquire an appropriate vocabulary which will enable them to carry out conversations about God and about the important issues of human life.

2. The Montessori tradition and Godly Play

Another perspective on the spirituality of children comes from the Montessori tradition of education and is best exemplified today by 'Godly Play'. Godly Play is an approach to religious education developed by Texas-based theologian Jerome W. Berryman. Like Hull, Berryman challenges those writers who suggest that children cannot think theologically because they are incapable of thinking abstractly until they reach adolescence. Furthermore, he notes that faith development theories approach the phenomenon of faith and its language from the standpoint of the scientific method. He submits, however, that scientific methods cannot explain the realm of the spirit which lies beyond ordinary sense experience and thought.[27]

Berryman opposes existential knowing and scientific knowing, saying that scientific meaning is very different from religious meaning. For example, when someone dies science wants to know why in terms of what caused the death. Religion, however, explores the deeper existential issue of death and tries to make religious meaning with the help of the language of liturgy. The signs, symbols, music and ritual gestures of the funeral liturgy make present, in a uniquely powerful way, the mysteries of faith. When believers participate in the liturgy, their personal grief is gathered into the faith of the Christian community. They experience the healing touch of God, and so it becomes possible, in the midst of despair, to hope.

Berryman has developed his own method of catechesis with children aged between two and twelve years which he outlines in his book, *Godly Play* (1991). He emphasises that if we communicate to children our belief in the presence of a benevolent God, they develop the capacity to face existential issues in their lives. Some of the existential issues faced by children include death, freedom, aloneness and meaninglessness. Religious educators can enable children to sense the presence of God when they respect children's religious lives and the existential issues they grapple with. Without this respect for the children's unique spirituality, they are less likely to reveal their experiences to others or even to themselves. Christian religious education can enable children to use religious language and symbol to make sense of these experiences, by engaging them in the language of parables, sacred stories and liturgical acts by which they can know God and experience God's presence.

Maria Montessori

Berryman draws upon a strong tradition in the religious education of children that has its origins in the work of Maria Montessori (1870–1952). Montessori saw all of her teaching as *religious* education and was committed to nurturing the inner spiritual power of the child. Her view of the child is that of a human person creatively unfolding from within. 'We know', she says, 'how to find pearls in the shells of oysters, gold in the mountains and coal in the bowels of the earth, but we are unaware of the spiritual gems, the creative nebulae, that the child hides in himself when he enters this world to renew mankind.'[28]

The key to Montessori's education is the immense influence the environment has upon the growing child. She saw the classroom as a place of 'spiritual rest'. Furthermore, Montessori was convinced that creative imagination is developed through the senses and that only such a base can lead on to creative and life-giving intelligence. Therefore she designed sensorial materials that children could use to learn by trial and error, choosing their own activities and discovering for themselves what could be done with the materials. In her school in Barcelona the children learned about worship and the sacraments in a chapel with child-scaled furnishings and using hosts for the Eucharist made by the children themselves.

Montessori made much of the symbol of 'Jesus as The Good Shepherd' with younger children. This was developed by one of her pupils – Sofia Cavalletti – into an actual approach to religious education which later became known as 'The Catechesis of the Good Shepherd'. Cavalletti began developing this approach in Rome in 1954, and it is still used in many parts of the world today.

Sofia Cavalletti and the Catechesis of the Good Shepherd
The goal of religious education, according to Cavalletti, is to minister to the religious life of the child. Consequently, the primary focus of 'The Catechesis of the Good Shepherd' is the child's personal relationship with God. In her book, *The Religious Potential of the Child* (1983), Cavalletti writes beautifully of the natural spiritual capacity of the child. She believes that children have a profound sense of the majesty of God which is reflected in the language they use when speaking of God. The young child is drawn to God because of his wealth of love that seeks to be matched by the love of God. Notably, Cavalletti also finds that children can appreciate religious metaphors and analogies, even if they cannot express their meaning in abstract terms.

The Catechesis of the Good Shepherd focuses on the *exigencies* or vital needs of children, as opposed to their *experiences*. The name of the catechesis which is taken from the image of the Good Shepherd (Jn 10:1-30) illustrates this point. This symbol seems to meet the existential needs of the three-to six-year-old child for love, for protection, for care, and for the presence of God. Furthermore, the joy of the child before God serves as the catechist's guide in choosing materials, because it is an indication that some deep religious need of the child is being met.

The teaching of parables is central to the Catechesis of the Good Shepherd. When using the parable method the teacher does not attempt to explain the parable. Instead, through the use of carefully chosen meditative questions, s/he begins to explore the meaning of the parable with the children, pointing to the limitless richness the parable contains. Children are then given concrete materials (biblical figurines, backgrounds, art materials) with which to make theological meaning from the details of the parable. For example, a child who hears the story of the Good Shepherd (Lk 15: 3-7) might wish to play with the image of herself as the lost sheep either by drawing the story or by manipulating figurines as she retells the story in her own way.

The Montessori tradition of religious education, as developed by Cavalletti and later by Berryman is a fine example of how children can be introduced to the Christian faith tradition in ways which attend to the inherent richness of the children's own spiritual lives. Both Cavalletti and Berryman emphasise children's capacity to meet with the living God through imaginative activity such as play, story, ritual and art and this emphasis is their particular strength.

3. Robert Coles and The Spiritual Life of Children

In recent years, there has been renewed interest among researchers in children's capacity for intuitive affective religious experience or spiritual awareness. Earlier studies of children's religious cognition tended to be carried out in formal research settings such as university campuses or schools. Today, new methods of qualitative research enable researchers to adopt a participant-observer role in conversations with children in different settings. One attempt to understand in naturalistic terms what children mean when they talk of their experience of God comes from the American Robert Coles.[29]

Coles is a professor of psychiatry and medical humanities at the Harvard Medical School in Boston and is noted for his many books in which he outlines his conversations with children all over the world on spiritual, moral and political issues. As a psychiatrist Coles is interested in the close connections between the psychology and spirituality of the child. He claims that there is an overlap between the psychological, moral, spiritual, and religious dimensions of the child's life. Therefore, to understand children's spiritual lives requires that one understand how children use the spiritual and religious dimension of experience to help them make meaning in the world.

Coles' work is contextual: it aims to learn from children as they go about their lives; in the home, the playground, and the classroom. In *The Spiritual life of Children (1992)* he recalls his conversations with children in the United States, Central and South America, Europe, the Middle East, and Africa, following the three major world religions: Judaism, Christianity and Islam. He was interested in the ways particular children incorporated the religious traditions (or secular ideals) of their family into their ordinary conversations. From his experiences he concluded that spiritual awareness is a 'universal human attribute'. 'Children', he declares, are 'seekers… young pilgrims well aware that life is a finite journey and as anxious to make sense of it as those of us who are farther along in the time allotted to us.'[30]

Children talked to Coles about 'their desires, their ambitions, their hopes, and also their worries, their fears, their moments of deep and terrible despair'.[31] These were connected with biblical stories, religiously sanctioned moral rules, rituals, and religious images in children's imaginations. In other words children called upon the resources of their religious communities as they tried to understand their lives. Coles places particular emphasis on the way children embrace religious stories, linking them to their own personal stories. He observes,

The stories are not mere symbolism, giving expression to what people go through emotionally. Rather, I hear children embracing religious stories because they are quite literally inspiring – exciting their minds to further thought and fantasy and helping them become more grown, more contemplative and sure of themselves.[32]

Christian children, Coles noted, have a common desire to picture God. For many, drawing God's face enabled them to experience the presence of God. These children reported 'seeing the face of God', usually at times of heightened emotional response whether of joy or fear. Furthermore, children often summon God and evoke God's actions, expressing the belief that God listens to all the prayers He hears. Coles also found that many young children experience 'intense visionary moments', a form of psychological transcendence in which the child experiences the interconnectedness of all of reality, of humans dead and alive, of the world of nature, and of the entire universe. In the section which follows a further examination will be made of children's innate sensitivity to this mysterious dimension of reality.

4. Spiritual Awareness and the Core of Children's Spirituality

A strong tradition of looking at spirituality or spiritual awareness as a natural human predisposition, that is as a biological reality, is to be found in the British context and in work carried out at the Alister Hardy research centre at Oxford. In 1965, the zoologist Alister Hardy proposed the idea that there is a form of awareness which has evolved through the process of natural selection which has a positive function in enabling people to survive in their natural environment. This basic awareness can be characterised as being in the sphere of holiness, awe, and wonder. It can be described as a sense of presence that enables one to transcend and yet enter more deeply into the ordinary or mundane aspects of one's life. Once experienced, this awareness stays with the person: once known it cannot be unknown. Finally, this awareness is universal but finds expression in a multitude of languages, beliefs and religious, non-religious and even anti-religious ideas.

In 1969 Hardy set up *The Religious Experience Research Centre* at Manchester College, Oxford, (now called The Alister Hardy centre) so that research could be carried out into people's experiences of heightened spiritual awareness. Edward Robinson, the second director of the centre, paid particular attention to accounts of childhood spiritual experiences submitted to the centre. Robinson calls these experiences – 'the vision of childhood' and he reflects on them in *The Original Vision* (1977). The title of his book derives from Edwin Muir who wrote in his autobiography:

> A child has a picture of human existence peculiar to himself, which he probably never remembers after he has lost it: the original vision of the world... Certain dreams convince me that a child has this vision, in which there is a completer (sic) harmony of all things with each other than he will ever know again.[33]

According to Robinson, the original vision is made up of feelings of wonder and awe, of intuitive knowledge, of oneness with all things, of meaning, and of personal significance. Religious education has an important role in 'providing suitable experiences and spaces to allow children to reactivate and reintegrate' these experiences.[34] For example, contemplative prayer can nourish the child's awareness of the unity of all things. Similarly, the mystery experienced in ritual can help strengthen the sense of awe and reverence a child has already experienced in nature or in other experiences.

Robinson also points to the importance of religious images and words that are stored in children's subconscious and which can enrich their religious awareness at a later period when they are ready for it. This means that not all that children are exposed to in religion need be immediately understood. As Robinson explains, 'not only can the memory be enriched with things recalled later with gratitude but words themselves can have an incantatory power that operates at a level deeper than any logic'. Religious traditions keep the original vision of the child alive as they enrich and focus the child's natural capacity to be open to the spiritual dimension of experience. Religion can offer 'a language, a means of interpretation, for an awareness of something already sensed, however dimly, to be real'.[35]

The Children's Spirituality Project at the university of Nottingham is an example of more recent research in this tradition and was shaped by the director of the project, David Hay. Together with Rebecca Nye, Hay published results of a three-year investigation of children's spiritual consciousness in *The Spirit of the Child* (1998). They report that results of this research support Hardy's view of spiritual awareness as a natural human predisposition. Every child, they found, has a spiritual potentiality, no matter what the child's cultural context may be. This natural human capacity can either be obscured or enhanced by the culture the child lives in. Indeed, while Hay and Nye found that spirituality is 'massively present in the lives of children' they claim that it is hidden because of what they term 'a culturally constructed forgetfulness' which causes children to suppress their natural spirituality. In other words, as religion has been largely removed from the public to the private domain in modern western societies, children learn very quickly that the language of spirituality is thought to be of little value, and so tend to hide it.[36]

Hay and Nye outline a continuum in children's expressions of spirituality. First, they note that as many children today are not brought up in an explicitly religious context, their spirituality may be expressed in secular terms. For example, some children perceive spiritual matters in terms of questions or principles. Others display an insightful emotional sensitivity to their experience or a deep awareness of mystery. Some children may find ways of making conscious or unconscious associations between their questions and experiences and the traditional spiritual language of religion. Still others 'experience their spirituality directly and personally in the form of religious insights'. Finally, in some cases children use religious language 'as a means of detaching themselves from the reality of their own experience'. In this regard Hay and Nye's research points to a worrying disconnection between children's experience in modern secular societies and the way in which the language and wisdom of the Christian community is conveyed to them.[37]

Rebecca Nye had numerous conversations with children in an attempt to understand the shape and form of their spirituality. Even though each child's spirituality was found to be unique, Nye gradually began to discover that there was something uniform about 'the resounding sense of children's spirituality'. This required that she develop a core category namely, *relational consciousness,* to provide an interpretative key to children's spirituality. Relational consciousness describes a particular kind of mental activity, which entails 'some degree of *awareness* on the part of the child of the remarkable nature of her own mental activity' when she is *relating* to things, other people and God. So spirituality has something to do with being drawn into relation with something or someone outside of oneself and with the capacity to be objectively aware of oneself as the subject of these experiences. This apparently objective insight into one's subjective response fosters a new dimension of meaning in the child's life.

Hay and Nye suggest that this 'relational consciousness' is a biologically in-built constituent of what it is to be human. To this extent it cannot be taught. What the teacher can do is to help children 'become aware of their awareness' and to reflect on this experience in the light of the language and culture within which it emerges.[38] Hay also suggests ways of directing children's attention to 'those aspects of human experience through which spiritual awareness most easily comes to light', for example, worship, prayer, silence, contemplation, meditation, mantras, and koans.

CONTEXTUAL AND OTHER EXPERIENCES

Having explored several different understandings of the religious potential of the child and several corresponding approaches to religious education this chapter concludes with a consideration of how children's familial, cultural, ethnic and socio-economic background affects their capacity to be religiously educated. It is now widely agreed that the society into which someone is born, the styles and values of the family in which one lives, the kind of education one receives and the culture created by communications media, exert an enormous influence upon the kind of person that each one becomes. Students in Irish primary schools come from a wide variety of cultural, economic, and familial backgrounds. Knowledge of these backgrounds will necessarily impact upon the religious images, language and methods religious educators use, as well as upon the expectations they have of students' religious knowledge, understanding and experience.

Increasing Diversity[39]

The student population in Catholic primary schools is now increasingly diverse. One source of such diversity is the differing intellectual and physical abilities of students. Another is ethnic diversity as evidenced for example in the Travelling community. Irish society is also increasingly multicultural with immigrants from Asia, the Middle East and Africa, as well as from Europe. Some of these are refugees and asylum seekers. Others have freely chosen Ireland as an alternative place to live their lives. These different races bring with them a variety of languages, customs, practices, ethical principles, cultural beliefs and religious affiliations, all of which impact the work of religious education in the school.

Irish society is also becoming more economically diverse given that the expansion of the economy has failed to meet the needs of some social groups excluded from the wealth of the majority. As the gap between rich and poor widens, many children find themselves caught in a poverty trap, which hinders their capacity to reach their full potential either in a social or in an educational context. Unfortunately, children from culturally and socially different families may encounter a school culture and language that clashes with and even devalues the culture and language of their homes.

Religious education has a pivotal role to play in promoting knowledge, respect and responsibility towards people whose cultural, socio-economic and religious backgrounds are different to one's own. Growing up in a diverse society, children become religious side by side with children who are being formed in different religious faiths. This means that teaching children to become Christian needs to be carried out using the principles of intercultural education and of inter-faith dialogue.[40] For Christians a stance of openness to 'the other', and in particular to the marginalised and oppressed other, is inspired by the teaching and actions of Jesus who lived a life of radical inclusive love. Religious educators need to become particularly attuned to the ways in which the Christian tradition can be used to promote and advance the radical vision of inclusivity and equality which was Jesus' vision for the world.

Mass Media and Popular Culture

Mass media culture and popular culture have a significant impact upon children's values and ways of understanding life. In the most recent survey carried out in Ireland, for example, two thirds of the children surveyed spent more than two hours watching television and videos on school days.[41] When this is combined with time spent playing computer games, watching films, listening to pop music and reading magazines, the influence of popular culture upon children's worldviews cannot be underestimated. The challenge to religious educators is to understand the ways in which children make meaning using the resources of the popular culture, becoming attuned to the religious, non-religious and even anti-religious nature of the messages children receive. In this way children can be taught to be discerning agents and creators of culture in their own right.[42]

Family

It is within the family that the foundations for faith are nurtured and brought to life. Here the child experiences the love, care, hope, understanding, belonging and wonder that form the basis for religious education in the primary school. Unfortunately, the family can also be a place that is detrimental to children's moral, spiritual and religious growth. This happens for example where the punishment of children is given a religious legitimation or where children are introduced to religious ideas that are inherently tormenting. But even more fundamentally, the degree of trust, security and loyalty an infant experiences in the first months and years of life has a profound effect upon the foundations of faith.

The nature of family life is changing. While most students live in a traditional family, an increasing number of children are growing up in stepfamilies, blended families, single-parent families, gay and lesbian families or families based upon *de facto* relationships. Furthermore, families may struggle with personal and social problems that put considerable strain on children and limit the stability of the home. Parents or caregivers may feel inadequate to nurture their children spiritually. Their biblical and theological knowledge may be limited and they may struggle with negative experiences of Church. Nevertheless, many young adults reject a materialist approach to life and desire a different sense of meaning for their children and themselves than that of materialist secularism. They long for a community of loving, trustworthy people with whom they can find meaning and make a difference with their lives. The religious education carried out in a Catholic primary school can support this search for meaning and for values, precisely when it acknowledges the gifts offered and the challenges faced by those it serves.

CONCLUSION

Every child is unique and every child is formed at a crossroad of influences. Each individual student is passing through a series of identifiable developmental stages while at the same time every one is unique, possessing different personalities, abilities, experiences and capacities for learning. Most importantly, each is invited to give a personal response to the loving call of God. Educators who pay attention to the ways in which children express their spirituality and moral awareness today will be able to offer the resources of religion in ways which promote and enhance children's spiritual and moral lives. Such attention is crucial if educators are to find ways of giving children access to the Christian faith tradition of ritual, communal narrative, doctrine and social teaching, such that children will find there rich resources for the expression, extension and transformation of their own authentic spirituality. The Christian tradition provides not only a structure of ideas and forms of expression which enable children's growth, but also religious images and stories which suggest worthwhile ways of being human. The individuality of the child and the complexity of the social reality in which education is carried out today calls educators to adopt a humble yet hope-filled stance in respect of religious education which serves to enhance the moral, spiritual and religious development of the child.

NOTES

1   Catherine Mowry La Cugna, *God For Us: The Trinity and Christian Life*, New York: HarperSanFrancisco, 1991.

2   Walter E. Conn, *The Desiring Self*, New York/Mahwah: Paulist Press, 1998, p. 72.

3   For a detailed description of these stages see Erik H. Erikson, *Identity and the Life-Cycle: A Reissue*, New York: W.W. Norton, 1980; *Identity Youth and Crisis*, New York: W.W. Norton & Co, 1968; *Childhood and Society*, New York: W.W. Norton, 1963; *Insight and Responsibility*, New York: W.W. Norton & Company, 1964.

4   'Faith' refers here to the human side of the relationship with God as studied by psychology. Of course, for Christians, the act of religious faith is brought about by the grace of God and in this (theological) sense faith is understood as a gift. Here we are interested in the psychological processes whereby persons put

their trust in someone/ thing beyond themselves. For this understanding of faith see James W. Fowler, *Stages of Faith: The Psychology of Human Development and the Quest for Meaning,* San Francisco: Harper & Row, 1981, pp. 4-35.

5   Jerome Berryman, 'Children's spirituality and Religious Language', *British Journal of Religious Education,* 7:3 (1985), p. 121.

6   Donald Capps, 'Erikson's Life-Cycle Theory: Religious Dimensions', *Religious Studies Review,* 10 April (1984), p. 121.

7   The description of virtues here is that of Timothy J. O' Connell, *Making Disciples,* New York: Crossroad, 1998, pp. 39-42.

8   O'Connell, *Making Disciples,* p. 76.

9   Ibid, pp. 57-64.

10   Ibid, p.99.

11   Jean Piaget, *The Moral Judgment of the Child,* London: Kegan Paul, 1932.

12   Lawrence Kohlberg, *Essays on Moral Development,* San Francisco: Harper & Row, 1981; *The Psychology of Moral Development,* San Francisco, CA: Harper Row, 1984; *The Philosophy of Moral Development: Moral Stages and the Idea of Justice,* San Francisco: Harper & Row, 1981; 'Stages of Moral Development as a Basis for Moral Education' in C. M. Beck et al., (eds), *Moral Education: Interdisciplinary Approaches,* New York: Newman Press, 1971.

13   Lawrence Kohlberg, *Philosophy,* pp. 409-10.

14   Jeff Astley, 'Moral Development', in Jeff Astley and Leslie J. Francis (eds), *Children, Churches and Christian Learning.* London: SPCK, 2002, p. 72.

15   Carol Gilligan, *In a Different Voice: Psychological Theory and Women's Development,* Cambridge, MA: Harvard University Press, 1982.

16   Piaget's central concern was with the processes by which the act of knowing was determined by internally organized structures within the developing human organism. The individual constructs cognitive schema through interaction with the environment. Particular logical operations characterise successive schema. The stages of cognitive development outlined by Piaget are: 1.Sensori-motor stage (0-2) years; 2. Pre-operational (2-7 years); and 3. Operational thinking. Normally, between the ages of 7 and 11 the child engages in *concrete operations,* i.e., s/he tends to think within the limits of the

objects, people and situations which have been encountered. As the child becomes capable of formal operations (often around 11-12 years of age) s/he is able to think in abstract terms.

17   Andrew G. McGrady, 'A Metaphor and Model Paradigm of Religious Thinking', *British Journal of Religious Education*, 9:2 (1987), pp. 85, 92.

18   Andrew G. McGrady, 'Glimpsing the Divine: Metaphor and Religious Thinking' in Dermot A. Lane ed., *Religion and Culture in Dialogue*, Dublin: the Columba Press, 1993, pp. 151-182.

19   Shellie Levine, 'Children's Cognition as the Foundation of Spirituality', *International Journal of Children's Spirituality*, 4:2 (1999), pp. 121-140.

20   James Fowler, 'Introduction' in J. Fowler, and R. W. Lovin (eds) *Trajectories in Faith*, Nashville: Abingdon Press, 1980, pp. 19-20.

21   Gary L. Chamberlain, *Fostering Faith*, New York/ Mahwah: Paulist Press, 1988, p. 18.

22   As regards the limit Fowler puts on children's capacity for symbolic thinking McGrady's research provides a necessary caution. McGrady reminds us that what Fowler may have measured is the effect of general elements of thinking that influence religious thinking. It might be better, he suggests, to restrict discussion of 'stage development' to general cognitive processes and not to apply the notion directly to the distinctive processes within the area of religious thinking, for example metaphor usage. McGrady, 'A metaphor and model paradigm', p. 92.

23   G. Klingberg, ' A Study of Religious Experience in Children from 9 to 13 years of age', *Religious Education* 54 (1959), pp. 211-216. D Elkind and S. Elkind 'Varieties of Religious Experience in Young Adolescents', *Journal for the Scientific Study of Religion*, 2 (1962), pp. 102-112. E. Robinson. *The Original Vision: A Study of the Religious Experience of Childhood*, Alister Hardy Research Unit, Manchester College, Oxford, 1977. K. Tamminen, 'Religious Experiences of Children and Young People', *Research Reports on Religious Education*, Helsinki, 1983.

24   John M. Hull, 'Religion in the Service of the Child Project: The Gift Approach to Religious Education' in Michael Grimmitt (ed), *Pedagogies of Religious Education*, Great Wakering, Essex: McCrimmons, 2000, p 112.

25   John M. Hull, *God Talk with Young Children*, Birmingham: University of Birmingham and the Christian Education Movement, 1991, pp.7- 9.

26   John M. Hull, 'Theological Conversation with Young Children', *British Journal of Religious Education*, 20:1, Autumn 1997, p. 8.

27   Jerome W. Berryman, 'Faith Development and the Language of Faith' in Donald E. Ratcliff (ed), *Handbook of Children's Religious Education*, Birmingham, Alabama: Religious Education Press, 1992, p. 25-28.

28   Maria Montessori, *The Absorbent Mind*, Oxford, England: Clio Press, 1997, p. ix.

29   Coles' concern is with the psychology of the child and the way in which children 'use' religion as a way of maintaining a stable sense of identity. For more on this psychoanalytical perspective see Ana Maria Rizzuto, *The Birth of the Living God*. Chicago, IL: University of Chicago Press, 1979. Coles' works include:
       Robert Coles, *The Moral Life of Children*, Boston: Houghton Mifflin, 1987. *The Call of Stories: Teaching and the Moral Imagination*, Boston: Houghton Mifflin, 1989. *The Moral Intelligence of Children: How to Raise a Moral Child*, London: Bloomsbury, 1997. *The Spiritual Life of Children*, Boston; Houghton Mifflin Co, 1990. *The Political Life of Children*, New York: Atlantic Monthly Press, 1986. *In God's House*, Grand Rapids: Eerdmans, 1996.

30   Robert Coles, *Spiritual life*, p. xvi.

31   Ibid, p.108.

32   Ibid, p.121.

33   Edwin Muir, *Autobiography*, London: Faber, 1938, p. 33.

34   Edward Robinson, *The Original Vision*, Oxford: The Religious Experience Research Unit, Manchester College, 1977. Two other collections were published under the titles: *This Time-Bound Ladder*, Oxford:Religious Experience Research Unit, 1977, and *Living the Questions*, Oxford: Religious Experience Research Unit, 1978.

35   Robinson, *Original Vision*, p. 82, 96.

36   David Hay and Rebecca Nye, *The Spirit of the Child*, London: Harper Collins, 1998, pp. vi, 20.

37   Ibid, pp. 110, 143.

38   For an example of this approach see John Hammond, David Hay et al, *New Methods in Religious Education Teaching: an Experiential Approach*, London: Longmans/ Oliver & Boyd, 1990 and Hay and Nye, *Spirit*, pp. 159-175.

39   The topic of religious, ethnic and cultural diversity in Ireland is examined more extensively in Chapter Seven.

40   Dr Roland Tormey, *Intercultural Education in the Primary School: Guidelines for Schools*, Dublin: NCCA, 2005.

41   Judith Cosgrove, Thomas Kellaghan, Patrick Forde, Mark Morgan, *The 1998 National Assessment of English Reading*, Educational Resource Centre, Dublin: E Print Ltd, 2000, pp. 62-63.

42   See Chapter Six for further exploration of the topic of culture and of an approach to inculturation.

CHAPTER SIX

Educating for Catholic Identity: Contemporary Challenges

• •

All human beings possess a natural desire to develop a personal identity. We all have some sense of what it is that makes us unique in addition to having a sense of belonging to specific communities or groups. Every person belongs to particular families and local communities. We also participate in Irish society, in the wider European community, and in the global community conveyed to us through communications media such as television and the internet. In a world of so much diversity and choice, the formation of a clear sense of identity is at best partial and never quite complete. Nevertheless, identity formation is a central part of human development and is a task with which all persons are concerned right throughout their lives.

Catholicism offers a particular vision of human identity and of the goals of human development. It proposes that the process of identity formation has an essential religious dimension. In other words Catholicism asserts that we are ultimately dependent on God for our deepest sense of self and that our emerging self-identity is intrinsically related to religious questions.[1] Furthermore it suggests that full human identity is formed to the extent that one transcends oneself in relationship to other people, to the created world and to God. This view of human identity sees Jesus Christ as the model of the human person. Catholics develop full human identity when they have a sense of themselves as closely related to Jesus Christ. The promotion of integral human identity in this sense is the goal of the Catholic school.

This chapter offers a broad vision of the kind of personal identity proposed by Catholicism and of how one educates for 'Catholic identity' in schools. The chapter begins with an exploration of how people form identity in contemporary society. Next, it proposes the value of having a Catholic identity today. It is argued that the development of a contemporary Catholic identity does not mean that Catholics cut themselves off from people of other religions and philosophies, but rather they relate with them and are open to the questions that they pose. A number of key characteristics that distinguish the Catholic religious tradition are then described. It is suggested that these characteristics will inform the way one educates for Catholic identity in schools. Finally, some of the contemporary issues that need to be addressed by religious educators are discussed. These challenges are presented here as opportunities to develop new educational strategies appropriate to the task of educating for Catholic identity today.[2]

IDENTITY FORMATION

People form identities today in ways that are quite different from the past. While our grandparents grew up in fairly close-knit communities, where most people had more or less the same world-view or scale of values, this is no longer true for many people today. We grow up in a global village, in which we meet very different kinds of people. As a result personal identity in modern societies can be quite fragmented and diffuse as people participate in multiple communities at the same time. In other words, the encounter with 'otherness' is central to the process of identity formation today. 'The other' is a term used to describe people who are different from oneself because of social, racial, ethnic, religious, gender, sexual or other significant difference. Perhaps more than at any other time in history contemporary persons form their identity in dialogue with people who are different from themselves.

The pace of change in contemporary societies makes it very difficult to sustain commitments to particular traditions, practices or communities. Nevertheless human identity can only be developed through commitment to some vision of what is true and good, and through affiliation to particular communities. For the young person there are many stages where these commitments are being worked out and there is much trial and error. Different kinds of identity are tried on like costumes. A young person tries out as a Manchester United fan, then as a rapper, then as a computer geek, then as a young professional. What does this mean for the teacher? They need to be indulgent with the try-outs or try-ons, to give feedback as to how the youngster looks and behaves, but not to squelch the fun of experimentation. The development of self-identity is important work and the task of identity formation is one that people today will undertake repeatedly over the course of their lives.

In this situation of constant change and multiple belongings it is important to explore the value of having a specific *religious* identity, that is, of allowing one's human identity to be informed by religion. Two perspectives help us to situate the particular kind of religious identity proposed by Catholicism. One of these is relativism, the other fundamentalism. Relativism describes the perspective that there are no objective standards by which to evaluate any culture or religion. All religions and worldviews are equally valid it claims. Hence relativists refuse to commit themselves to any particular religious community or group.

These people may live with a very ambiguous and uncertain sense of identity. They may become isolated as they lack connections to an historical community which nurtures their capacity to respond to the Transcendent (God).

Besides relativists there are other people who respond to a changing world by seeking a clearly defined moral universe and visible sources of authority for their lives. They may be tempted to join various fundamentalist groups who appear to offer clear solutions to the complex questions of modern living. Fundamentalism is a cultural–theological worldview that stands in defence of fixed beliefs and strict moral codes. Fundamentalists tend to read Scripture through a conservative traditionalist, ideological lens. They also tend to create sharp boundaries that distinguish them from other groups.

CATHOLIC IDENTITY

In contrast to both relativists and fundamentalists, Catholicism invites people to enter a way of being religious that avoids the extremes of both positions as ways of approaching the question of human identity. Catholicism acknowledges pluralism and diversity, but it also recognises the need for discernment of cultural practices and various worldviews. All worldviews are not the same. They can be evaluated according to their capacity to promote genuine human development. Catholicism upholds an understanding of the human person in relationship to God. This perspective on humanity is quite distinct and must be distinguished from a generalised humane understanding. Many educators have a clear notion of 'genuine human development', but it would omit the Christian understanding of humanity-in-relation-to-God.

Contemporary thought is particularly tolerant and sensitive to 'the other' and to difference. This is because secular states require peace and tranquility to prosper economically.

Furthermore, as the 'global village' has enabled people to recognise how similar all people are, there is a desire to accord others the same rights and freedoms as the majority in society. Hence the culture – global and local – favours relativism and discourages fanaticism or dedication or even conviction about ideals, unless these ideals are in harmony with secular humanism. In contrast Catholics are committed to the vision that it is God rather than ourselves who gives human life meaning and purpose. The Catholic perspective on the human condition is inspired by the revelation of scripture and by Church tradition. The Catholic community offers people distinct values, practices, ethical principles, symbols, spiritualities, religious language, as well as some recognised norms and authority, which support them in the development of a sense of self and a sense of purpose in the world.

Catholicism invites people to be part of a Church community and to draw from the wisdom of its religious tradition both past and present. The Church claims it offers access to the revelation of God as mediated through Christian scriptures and traditions. In other words, the Catholic religious tradition is seen as a source of trustworthy guidance for anyone who desires to respond to the love of God and to Jesus' call to discipleship in the contemporary world. Catholicism differs from fundamentalism, however, in that it is open to dialogue with contemporary culture and appreciates the signs of hope therein. Furthermore, it is possible to develop a distinct Catholic identity and a pluralistic and ecumenical openness to other religious faiths at the same time. Catholicism is a particularly rich tradition for the kind of engagement with 'the other' that is a central aspect of the struggle for identity in the world today.

The core of Catholic identity is a living relationship with God, who has been revealed in Jesus Christ and whose Spirit continues to be present in the Church. We reach our fullest potential as persons in relationship with Jesus as he is the one from whom we learn how to live a fully human life. Education for Catholic identity then involves the promotion of *catholicity* – God's free and open invitation to all human persons to fullness of life, through participation in, and celebration of the universal redemptive activity and power of Christ in the Holy Spirit.[3] The etymology of the term *'catholicity'* is from the Greek *'kata holos'*, meaning 'including everything and everyone'[4] and so catholicity is openness to the saving action of God wherever it may be found. Catholic education seeks to promote catholicity by inviting students to know and respond to God who transforms the world from a place of suffering, oppression and inequality to a place of healing, liberation and radical equality for all.[5] It also enables students to recognise and celebrate their divine origin and eternal destiny in God.

Characteristics of Catholicism

We can outline some notable characteristics, strengths or principles of Catholic Christianity which give to the Catholic tradition its particular character and purpose. These provide teachers with some resources as they educate for Catholic identity today. One characteristic to be noted is that the Catholic tradition has a commitment to the place of reason in the process of coming to faith. Reason provides the basis for that further leap of commitment which is faith. It also uncovers continually the meaning of Christian beliefs, teachings and practices. These are continually interpreted by contemporary people of faith, using the best of critical biblical and theological scholarship. Likewise, Catholics seek to harmonise the understandings of history, science and philosophy with the tenets of Christian faith. In this, Catholicism provides an alternative to fundamentalism which often requires that its adherents avoid the difficult questions raised by these disciplines. One difficult question, for example, is how to understand the differences between the biblical account of creation and modern scientific evolutionary theory. The biblical fundamentalist will set up an irreconcilable conflict between these two accounts, whereas a more moderate Catholic view aims to reconcile scientific discoveries with a faith perspective since all knowledge ultimately comes from God.

Another characteristic of note in Catholicism is its abiding commitment to 'handing on' a body of religious language, interpretations of Scripture, religious ritual and religious truths. This cumulative wisdom of the past is generally referred to as 'tradition'. The core of this tradition is the offer of an encounter with the person of Jesus Christ and his 'good news of salvation'.[6] This encounter is mediated now through scripture and practices that have been handed down through the ages as the Church has continued to live and reflect on the Christian faith. The tradition includes beliefs, doctrines, ethical principles, rituals, symbols, spiritualities, theologies, stories of the saints, music, art, architecture and so on. These mediations offer people a language which enables them to understand their experience of self and the mystery of self, others and God. The Catholic tradition is constantly renewed and developed as new generations of Catholics respond to the living presence of God in their lives and bring their own experience of the encounter with the Divine to bear upon it.

A number of key philosophical and theological principles are found at the heart of the Catholic tradition. These include the sacramental principle, the principle of communion and the theological option for the poor. The sacramental principle means that human communication with God is not direct, but is mediated by the created world. People experience God as a creative, healing, transforming power in the ordinary experiences and things of life – in their minds and bodies, in their relationships and friendships, in their work and leisure activities, in nature and the whole created order. The seven sacraments are ritual high points that draw our attention to and strengthen such everyday experience of God's life and love.

When we become attuned to the divine presence in the world, we acquire an ability to see the Transcendent in the immanent, the 'beyond in the midst'. Such an ability to discern that God is present and active in the world is referred to by commentators as a 'sacramental imagination'. This is an imaginative capacity to glimpse God's presence and providence in particular moments, places, memories of persons and events. These experiences remind us that everything and everyone is held in being and loved by God. The sacramental principle also helps us to understand that we *respond* to God through the ordinary experiences of our lives. The most important way in which we respond is through our love of neighbour. In this way we participate in God's saving activity in the midst of our lives and communities.

The Catholic principle of communion affirms that to be human is to be made for relationship with others and with God. Indeed, Catholicism is characterised by a sense of peoplehood and community that reaches backward in time and outwards towards all of humanity. Catholics understand themselves to be rooted in a unified community because they recognise that both sin and salvation are communal realities. The Catholic doctrine of the Communion of Saints is one expression of this understanding of salvation. Catholics see themselves as being connected with all people of faith redeemed by Christ down through the ages. The Catholic commitment to community is also reflected in its broadly inclusive approach to Church membership which allows for infant baptism and in its efforts to retain people who are not strongly committed in the Church.[7]

The Catholic view of community is expansive and inclusive. This is because it recognises that all human beings share a common vocation to eternal life and so all are oriented to Christ and the Church.[8] Therefore, to be Catholic means to embrace all people in a hospitable and inclusive community of faith, hope and love. Catholics affirm the inclusivity and diversity of God's family by remaining open to the diversity and richness of both Christian and non-Christian traditions. Tom Groome summarises this understanding of catholicity as inclusivity in the following manner:

> Becoming a Catholic Christian means growing to love and care for all humankind – cherishing their diversity, relishing life and maturing into its fullness – for oneself and others, embracing the world as gift and responsibility – convinced that you can make a difference for life for all. ... It requires letting go of parochialism to embrace everyone as brother and sister, replacing narrow-mindedness with openness to learn from those who are very different. ... A true Catholic is convinced that God loves every person equally and God's family embraces all humankind.[9]

Another expression of this community emphasis is Catholicism's strong commitment to overcoming divisions among rich and poor. Catholics view themselves as disciples of Jesus in serving humanity, in particular the poor and oppressed of the world. This commitment has been crystallised for our time in the theological option for the poor. This principle states that God's love for all implies God's special attention to the weak and poor, precisely because they are most threatened by suffering and death. This option is one of the central themes of contemporary Catholic spirituality and has profound implications for religious educators as will be explored below.

Developing Catholic identity

While it is possible to outline abiding commitments or principles of Catholicism, Catholic identity is not so easily recognised and described. In a way it is incorrect to speak of *a* Catholic identity: it is more correct to think of multiple Catholic identities that share some key elements in common. Different understandings and interpretations of what constitutes 'Catholic identity' abound. It is precisely as people argue about the nature of that identity, however, that new forms of Catholic identity begin to emerge.

A person's self-understanding includes a sense of how his particular religious identity differs from other identities in his social-cultural milieu. It is natural to try to understand the boundaries that differentiate oneself from other people and groups. The basis of Catholic identity is the fact that God has revealed and continues to reveal Godself to humanity and that this revelation invites a particular kind of response. Likewise, the incarnation suggests a distinct way of being fully human and of developing human identity. Therefore, there are some clear boundaries that distinguish a Catholic worldview from that of other religious and non-religious worldviews. Catholics need to understand the unique particularity of Catholic faith if they are to have a viable and vibrant sense of religious identity in the modern world.

At the same time, it would be dangerous to define one's religious identity only in terms of what distinguishes it from others. To do so would be to ignore the presence of the Holy Spirit calling us to discover new possibilities for Catholic identity in our time. Catholics seek to find the ways in which the gospel is mirrored in the beliefs and lives of non-Christians thus challenging them to live their own Christian spirituality more deeply. Furthermore, Catholics are never content simply to co-exist with others in society who have completely different identities. The intensity of multi-culturalism today creates an ever-greater need for real communication and understanding between people. Together all seek to find common goals in the struggle against poverty and all forms of oppression in the world.

EDUCATION FOR CATHOLIC IDENTITY

Education for Catholic identity uses the resources of the Catholic tradition to promote the individual's relationship with Jesus Christ. The process of educating for Catholic identity will ultimately result in new expressions of that identity for our time.[10] Catholic religious practices will not only be adapted and amplified through the educational process but sometimes it will be completely new practices that will give adequate expression to the abiding values of the tradition. For example the promotion of the Catholic *principle of communion*, the belief in the unity of the human race and human solidarity, has been given new impetus and shape with the new cosmic consciousness of our time. Catholics are now committed to the promotion of cosmic well-being, recognising that the fate of the human community is intimately connected with that of the entire cosmos.[11] In the same way Catholic identity is continually shaped in interaction with different cultures and ways of life. One's approach to religious education therefore should enable people to become critically conscious of their power to create and shape their own identity. It should also furnish them with critical and inventive resources so that they will be able to extend the Catholic tradition, disclosing new aspects of the values, goals and purposes the tradition has been pursuing for centuries.[12]

Sometimes the Church fails to educate for and live out of the best of its own traditions. For example, people may be taught in ways that don't allow for thoughtful and committed examination of Church teachings or practices. They may also be taught to disparage the religious beliefs and traditions of others. Catholic women face the particular challenge of participating in a religious community that excludes them from priesthood. They continue to point out the ways in which some interpretations of the tradition can cause suffering for women and for the poor across the world. To point out the limitations in the living tradition in this manner is part of being faithful to the tradition itself. It is through this process that the Catholic tradition is faithfully renewed for the next generation.

A Challenge and a solution

The point has been made by some that Catholics have often failed to educate their own in the riches and depth of the Catholic tradition. The challenge therefore is to discover how education for Catholic identity can be carried out in a way that avoids the pitfalls of parochialism and sectarianism, indoctrination, sexism and uncritical socialisation. A number of key questions frame the challenge for Catholic educators here: Can the Catholic tradition provide a language that enables people to engage the complexity of human experience in our contemporary world? Can students be educated to interpret the faith tradition in life-giving ways? Can we educate in a way that people's rootedness in the Catholic tradition is a positive resource for their encounter with the traditions of others in a pluralist, multicultural society?

The solution lies, it has been suggested, in developing educational strategies that both nurture and reflect the dynamic character of Catholic identity today. The key aspects of Catholicism outlined already in this chapter will inspire these strategies. Such strategies ought also to be context-sensitive, recognizing the unique cultural context in which religious education is carried out in Irish primary schools. Finally, the fact that there are different interpretations of the tradition both within and outside of Catholicism will have to be taken into account in the very process of constructing a viable vision of Catholic identity for religious education today. [13]

We turn now to some important challenges facing religious educators in Catholic primary schools. The topics to be examined include globalisation, cultural change, media and communication technologies, educational disadvantage and special education. First the issues that emerge in relation to each topic and the particular challenge posed by these issues for religious educators will be explained. Then an examination will be made of some educational strategies that respond to the issues in question, drawing on the resources of the Catholic tradition in doing so. These challenges are central to the task of educating for Catholic identity in primary schools.

CONTEMPORARY CHALLENGES

Globalisation

We live in a changed world. Globalisation is a word used to describe the way in which cultures, nations, political and economic systems all over the world are becoming increasingly interconnected and interdependent. Advances in communication technologies along with improved transportation technologies have led to new connections between the political, economic, and social life of all the peoples on this planet. This compression of the world has coincided with increased consciousness of and reflection on global interconnections and on different cultures within the global whole. Globalisation has created new opportunities for genuine encounters between peoples, cultures and religions. It has also created new instances of injustice, prejudice, marginalisation and interreligious strife. In short, globalisation has created a completely new environment for the development of human and religious identity at this time.

Robert J. Shreiter defines globalisation as 'the extension of the effects of modernity to the entire world and the compressing of time and space, all occurring at the same time.'[14] The compression of time in globalisation describes the way in which we experience very little time lapse between events happening in the world and our perceptions of them. Millions of television viewers, for example, observed the second plane hitting the World Trade Centre in New York. In this way the reporting of the event coincided with the event itself. Similarly, reality television shows allow us to live simultaneously with the people whose ordinary lives we watch. When we give the present a heightened significance in this manner, the past is seen as less important and the future is perceived as arbitrary and full of risk. This poses a particular challenge to religious traditions which place great value on the knowledge and wisdom handed on by past generations as well as on moments of promise which await fulfilment in the future.

The compression of space in globalisation describes the way huge distances between places can now be easily bridged through transport or communications technology. One consequence of this is that boundaries of territory are not as significant for the formation of identity as in the past. The stable forms of community experienced by our parents and grandparents, in which people who lived in the same geographic area shared the same basic values and worldview, do not exist any more. Every person growing up in this globalised world faces an ongoing challenge to construct a personal identity from the myriad of values, ideals, cultural mores, religious practices and lifestyle choices available in their society. In this context, people need to understand what distinguishes them from others, but also what brings them together with others as they live together in a smaller world.

Religious education and globalisation
People develop religious identity where their experience of local faith communities and global communities meet. Religious education must place itself at this juncture providing people with the skills and resources to develop religious identity in creative and life-giving ways. Educating for Catholic identity in the context of globalisation involves two vital tasks. The first task involves giving people access to the narrative, sacramental and symbolic resources of the Church community. The Catholic tradition should be handed on and reinterpreted in such a way that students experience and learn the values inherent to Catholic practices and traditions. The second task entails the dialogue with the globalised world in which the first task is accomplished. This involves working out Catholicism's stance *vis-à-vis* other interpretations of reality offered to people in contemporary society. It also involves teaching people how to engage in an authentic encounter with cultural and faith traditions different from Catholicism.

The first task of religious education is to introduce students to the stories, rituals, practices, doctrines and forms of religious knowing of the Catholic faith tradition. Having a religious faith is essentially about belonging to a 'community of memory', engaging in its practices, using its language, inhabiting the tradition from the inside.[15] Inheriting a religious tradition in this way is not only about the stories, values, behavioural rules, rituals and customs that are handed down, but also about the *process* of handing down these religious meanings so that they can be taken up anew, retold, and actualised.[16]

Central to Catholicism is the assertion that God ordinarily comes to us through religious structures that we have been given, especially the incarnation, scripture, sacraments and apostolic ministry.[17] The first attitude of the believer towards this tradition ought to be one of trusting receptivity. Faith implies trust and a willingness to assent. Through their creative engagement with symbol and ritual, story and sacrament, poetry, play and dance students learn to appreciate and engage the wisdom of the Catholic tradition. Students who are immersed in this tradition should, over time, develop a sacramental consciousness – an ability to see God's presence and providence in their lives, and an ability to respond to it in positive ways. They should also begin to develop a critical and creative social consciousness, becoming people who can see and respond to the growing inequalities in their society and world.

The Catholic understanding of catholicity provides ample warrant for the second task for religious education in a globalised world. This task is to teach people in such a way that they understand how the Catholic worldview differs from others while nevertheless remaining open to learning from other cultures and religious traditions. It is neither realistic nor adequate to pretend that people develop Catholic identity in isolation from other faiths, traditions and cultures. Indeed, it may be that religious identity is developed precisely on the frontier where one's religious experience and beliefs create a boundary between one's own worldview and that of others.[18] Religious educator Fayette Veverka has argued that religious education should seek to respect pluralism and diversity by helping students to explore the 'boundaries' that differentiate them from other people. This calls for a commitment to conversation in religious education. Students should be helped to acknowledge the strengths and limits of their own particularity while, at the same time, intentionally exploring perspectives different to their own. Such conversation enables them to affirm and transform their own particular religious identity in ways which promote religious harmony in the world.[19]

Culture

The quality of our cultural environment has a direct influence on our ability to develop religious identity. Culture refers to 'that set of symbols, stories, myths, and norms for conduct that orient people cognitively, affectively, and behaviourally to the world in which they live.'[20] It is a socially constructed system of messages and images which socialises individuals and shapes their imagination and understanding of themselves, other people and the world. All persons are formed in social communities and their ways of seeing the world are profoundly shaped by the shared images and constructions of particular cultures. Educators who wish to educate for religious identity need to pay attention to the broader cultural environment of those they teach.

The stories, myths, and symbols of various religious and non-religious cultures have a powerful influence on children's imaginations, their interactions as social beings, and their developing sense of identity. Pope John Paul II stated that 'different cultures are basically different ways of facing the question of the meaning of personal existence.'[21] In other words, cultures present a worldview within which individuals locate their identity and explore the deep questions of meaning surrounding their lives. Religion is one culture among the many possible cultures one participates in throughout one's lifetime and has a crucial role to play in the processes whereby people receive and generate meaning for their lives.

Students and teachers in Irish primary schools are immersed in many different cultures – the culture of their homes and local communities, Irish national culture, as well as diverse religious, social and ethnic cultures. Most children are also exposed to mass media culture and popular culture, which send them persistent messages about the meaning and purpose of human life. Furthermore, the increasing dominance of North American culture, together with various attempts of resistance to it, is a pervasive aspect of children's lives today. Each of these cultures influences children's perspectives on reality, and has profound implications for their capacity to create and maintain stable identities and commitments throughout their lives.[22]

The issue of culture has become increasingly urgent for the Church and for religious educators for a number of reasons. On the one hand, there is a concern that the Church is failing to communicate Christian meaning and truth to people in such a way that they see Christian discipleship as a credible lifestyle option among the many offered by contemporary society. Some of the cultural aspects of Christian faith (institutional structures acquired over the centuries; certain customs and ritual forms; as well as the abstract language of various doctrinal formulas) may be hindering people from understanding and embracing the essential meaning of Christian discipleship. On the other hand, contemporary popular culture can suppress the human desire for religious meaning. As Michael Paul Gallagher explains,

> the pressures of the dominant culture leave many people blocked in a cultural desolation on the level of disposition or readiness for faith. This is because it kidnaps their imagination in trivial ways and therefore leaves them unfree for Revelation – or more precisely, for the hearing from which faith comes (c.f. Rom 10:17).

As a result, many people are no longer able to use religious language as a way of understanding what it means to be human.[23]

Religious education and culture

In relation to culture, Catholic religious educators need to answer a simple question: how can *these* students in *this* culture be effectively invited to enter into a personal relationship with Jesus Christ so that God's vision and promises for the world become their own? Religious education must reach people at the very heart of their culture because this is where Jesus Christ is encountered. If students are helped explore their own culture and lives they will encounter the Mystery at the heart of reality. The Catholic tradition enables students to name that Mystery as the God of Jesus Christ and invites them to explore the Christian faith story so that it illuminates their culture in a new way. Ultimately, students will go on to express their experiences of God through the forms of their own culture. In this way their culture will be transformed and redeemed by the gospel of Jesus Christ.

One way to nurture the dialogue between people and the gospel is through the methods of adaptation. *Adaptation* involves adopting language, imagery, materials, methods and styles that will appeal to the cultural or age-group we are working with. For example, as students are constantly exposed to attractive images by media culture, our methodology must expose them to quality Christian imagery; if music is valued by a particular age or ethnic group, we need to provide religious songs that will appeal to their music tastes and so on. When we adapt our materials to the culture of students we follow the teaching methods of Jesus himself. Jesus' parables, for example, were often based on the everyday activities and lives of the people listening to him. The aim for each generation of

Christians is to find a fresh new language that resonates with students so that they encounter Jesus at the heart of their lives and culture.

Most religious education programmes adapt religious materials using the best media and communication technologies available today. While this is a basic pre-requisite for modern programmes, however, the adoption of language, imagery and methods that appeal to students will not of itself ensure that the reign of God becomes an integral part of their worldview. For this to occur, the gospel must be announced and re-told in a manner that resonates with the way students of today discover and create meaning. Such a process is known as 'inculturation'.

Inculturation

Inculturation describes the creative and dynamic encounter between Christian faith and culture. It is the process whereby the gospel penetrates a culture in such a way that members of the culture begin to live and express their Christian faith through the forms of their own culture.[24] The challenge of authentic inculturation is to find out how students discover and create meaning through their own absorbing and reshaping of whatever cultural materials and expressions they are exposed to. In the light of this discovery educators can then invite students to draw in similar fashion from the symbolic, narrative and sacramental resources of the Catholic Christian faith community as they form and reform their identities, relationships and lifestyle commitments. For example, messages are often carried in children's popular culture through likeable characters such as Barney, the Tweenies, Yu-gi-oh, and Pokémon. This cultural pathway can be used to great effect in religious education programmes for children. It is critical that through the inculturation process the essential meaning contained in God's revelation to humankind in Jesus be preserved, presented and proclaimed. When the gospel is faithfully proclaimed, students can begin to forge their own unique and indigenous expression of Christian faith.

The imagination of the world and of the human person's place in it which is offered by any culture, can be life-enhancing or life-destroying, grace-filled or sinful. Catholics affirm that Christ is present in every culture and is responsible for everything true and good in them. This suggests the need to discern those values, ideas, concerns and practices already present in a culture which are compatible with the gospel and the reign of God. For example, we can examine popular children's literature, music and film in a search for echoes of the gospel in the themes, images, heroes, heroines, symbols, and narratives therein. Using this approach, we can begin to identify the values and ideas the students already possess that are in harmony with the gospel and that promote children's well-being. These concepts and values can serve as an entry point for our dialogue with them.

At the same time, the gospel cannot be equated with any culture. Every culture stands in need of redemption by Christ. During his life, Jesus illustrated that God does not side with death or with evil in any cultural tradition, including the religious traditions of his time. Consequently Christian inculturation challenges believers to adopt a critical stance to any aspect of culture that is contrary to the gospel and which hinders the advancement of God's reign in the world. Today, television and communications media control most of the stories to which children are exposed. They offer a different understanding of the true nature of reality and of the purpose of human life within it to that offered by Christianity. For instance, consumerist culture offers the ideal of material success as the goal of human life. It suggests to people that a good and happy human life is synonymous with beauty, wealth and the fulfilment of one's every need. This ideal is countered by the Christian vision of human development, which suggests that full personhood necessitates self-transcending love of other people and is fully compatible with the experience of sickness, failure and even death.

The religious educator needs to equip students with the tools which will enable them to criticise the storytellers and image-makers of the culture of their time and so resist any meanings which endanger genuine gospel values and perspectives. For instance, students can be helped to examine the heroes proposed to them by the electronic media as well as the criteria upon which the status of such celebrities is based. Furthermore, students' attention can be drawn to those who are excluded from participation in affluent society and whose stories are often overlooked by a culture obsessed with celebrities and winners. The sufferings of the poor and oppressed shatter any complacency one might have about the existence of evil in our world. Their stories leave no doubt that God's reign will only come in the struggle against all forms of injustice, suffering and oppression.

Inculturation describes a two-way conversation between students' lives and the Catholic tradition. This dialogue between faith and culture should lead to an enrichment and transformation of the tradition. For example, students can be very accepting of difference whether of gender, colour, class or creed. They thereby challenge interpretations of the Catholic tradition which breed intolerance, sectarianism, sexism and the idolisation of any laws and practices. In this way students can challenge Catholicism towards greater transformation for the sake of the reign of God.[25]

What will be the outcome of this dialogue between Christian faith and culture? Ultimately inculturation invites

Christians to action for transformation toward the reign of God. Inculturation has failed if the culture of our students remains unchanged by the gospel *and* if the tradition stagnates and remains the same. We cannot predict how our students will embody Christian faith in their lives. All we do know is that it will involve some expression of the central Christian values of faith, hope, and love. Just as they allow themselves to be formed and transformed by the gospel, so too the gospel will be reflected upon and interpreted by them in new and unique ways.

Media and communication technologies

The vast expansion of media and communication technologies – radio, television, video, DVDs, fax, CDs, satellite – has important implications for religious education. Catholics believe that God is a God who communicates with them and who invites response. Jesus is the ultimate communication of God – the Word made flesh (Jn 1:14) and God continues to communicate through the Spirit of Christ, present in the world. The *Catechism of the Catholic Church* emphasises this point: 'The Christian faith is not a "religion of the book". Christianity is the religion of the "Word" of God, 'not a written and mute word, but incarnate and living' (no. 108).[26] The advent of new technologies engenders new possibilities for communicating the Word of God and for responding to it in the world today.

The pastoral instruction *Aetatis Novae* (Dawning of a New Era) issued by the Pontifical Council for Social Communications, states that 'as the Church always must communicate its message in a manner suited to each age and to the cultures of particular nations and peoples, so today it must communicate in and to the emerging media culture' (no. 9). This is because individuals today learn, communicate, form values, and shape their identities using the resources of electronic media. The mass media of communication not only condition individuals' ways of knowing and communicating but also provide the interpretative paradigm which individuals use to negotiate meaning.[27] At the same time, electronic media are human productions and individuals can learn to interact with and use them in humanising or dehumanising ways. Hence the importance of reflection on the ways in which technology impacts education for Catholic identity today.

Religious education and media

John Shea has suggested that Catholic identity is both expressed and created by the particular cultural forms people use. In other words, there is a distinction between Catholic identity as constituted by a living relationship to God and the various historical forms which mediate that relationship.[28] What this means is that creations in the areas of liturgy, doctrine, ethics and communal structure have been the key 'carriers' of Catholic identity up to now. Important carriers of Catholic identity into the future will also be found in the sphere of media and communication technologies. For example internet-based cyber-communities of faith may be one way the Catholic vision of inclusivity and care will be 'carried' into the future.

Shea proposes that one set of 'carriers' of Catholic identity in the future will focus on the person's reception of divine love. These carriers will help students to attend to God's loving presence and providence in the world. Electronic media serve this goal when they are used to communicate the gospel in symbols, models, images and words which are accessible to and understood by those immersed in media culture. One of the greatest strengths of contemporary media culture is its capacity to communicate a good story. Well-produced television programmes, cartoons and films re-imagine and retell the stories of faith, in ways that connect with people today. For example, a film such as *The Prince of Egypt* provides for the current generation an attractive re-telling of the classic Exodus story of faith and salvation.

Good documentaries and films introduce students to the stories of strong people of faith who practice gospel values all over the world. These films carry the prophetic voice of Christianity; help students develop a global consciousness; and elicit compassion for the plight of the world's citizens and the created environment. Contemporary films can also provide an excellent focus for moral formation. When students are encouraged to reflect on the intentions and actions of characters on screen their capacities for moral reasoning and judgement are enhanced.

Electronic media may also enhance students' reception of the gospel when they are used to increase their active participation in the educational process. Specially designed websites require students to interact with data in ways which allow for critical and creative appropriation of religious material. Similarly, interactive video and computer games introduce students to traditional Christian symbols and practices. For example, a CD-Rom on the Holy Land takes students right into the sacred sites they are studying through an interplay of maps, video, other visual images and text.

The media can also be a place within which students dream and learn to engage in ritual behaviour.[29] As Gregor Goethals notes, 'through our games and our arts, we momentarily transcend social structures to play with ideas, fantasies, words … and social relationships'.[30] Students who have learned to play computer and video games can become very skilled in reading visual symbols and understanding religious codes. The challenge for religious educators is to build on this 'secular' ritual behaviour as they introduce students to the embodied rituals of religion.[31]

A second set of carriers of Catholic identity into the future, according to Shea, will focus on the ways in which Christians struggle for transformation, for the reign of God. Media and communication technologies can become a medium through which people respond to the loving invitation of God to transform the world from a place of suffering and oppression to a place of healing and liberation for all. For example, during the Asian Tsunami disaster in 2004–5, the power of television to transmit the scale of the tragedy contributed enormously to making possible a truly generous global response. Similarly, the internet can be used to develop students' critical consciousness of various forms of inequality all over the world. Cybercommunities of faith could provide students with resources and a focal point for prayer, fellowship, and various forms of social engagement on both local and global levels.

Communication technologies will become a stimulus to and an expression of lived Christian faith if students exercise their critical faculties as media-users and media-creators. This means that students and teachers need to understand how they receive and interpret the information and images produced by media technologies. They should also be able to locate reliable information on religious issues; to recognise when religious imagery is appropriated, manipulated or distorted by the media, by entertainers, or by religious organisations; to examine the different ways religious experience, religious questions and religious practices are portrayed on television, film or the internet; and to choose wisely from the abundance of information available to them in electronic form.

Over time students and teachers can be helped to discern whether media technologies are serving the goal of authentic human communication and interrelatedness. As Irish educator Andy McGrady argues, 'human social communication depends primarily upon the relational and spiritual quality of human culture and only secondarily upon technological systems.' Hence, the importance of alerting people to the need for a balance 'between immediate and mediated experience and between the real and the virtual'.[32] The difference, for example, between a real and a virtual community of faith may lie in the quality of embodied presence each affords. The forms of mutuality and self-giving that are possible in a real community may be supported but not replaced by the interactions in a virtual community one 'inhabits' in cyberspace.

Knowing the strengths and weaknesses of the various electronic media enhances our ability to use them efficiently. For instance, teachers need to consider the effects that the media technologies they use have on the development of children's imaginations. The power of a religious story or parable as told by a teacher in a way that attends to the particular context and language style of the students she teaches cannot easily be replaced by a machine, no matter how sophisticated. Teachers need to discover how students make meaning from the non-religious stories offered to them by the media and which can usurp the role of religious stories in students' lives. This should enable teachers to recraft the Christian stories so that they gain a deeper echo in the hearts and minds of students immersed in media culture.

Educational disadvantage and poverty

The gap between the rich and the poor in Irish society is growing all the time. Relative poverty has increased over the course of the last decade and Ireland has one of the highest levels of income inequality in OECD countries.[33] This inequality is also reflected in the educational system and in the phenomenon of educational disadvantage. In this section an attempt is made to outline why educational disadvantage is an important issue for religious educators. The Catholic tradition will then be examined to see what it has to say about the disadvantaged in society and the way Catholics ought to respond. Finally, some implications of this teaching for religious education in primary schools are noted.

Students who are educationally disadvantaged derive less benefit from the educational system than their peers.[34] Under the umbrella term 'educationally disadvantaged' one may include immigrants, refugees, Travelling people, children growing up in areas of social and economic disadvantage and individuals from disadvantaged backgrounds not living in designated areas of disadvantage. The educational needs of disadvantaged children are not being fully met in primary religious education at present. Two areas in which this inadequacy is most clear are those of language and culture.

Language contributes to educational disadvantage when the language of the classroom does not reflect the home experiences of children. Children who speak a non-standard dialect at home are consequently at an educational disadvantage when the religion curriculum assumes familiarity with standard (middle-class) vocabulary. Culture contributes to educational disadvantage when the culture of the school clashes with the culture of children's homes. Children derive a sense of meaning and identity from the various cultures in which they are immersed. Every child is socialised into certain cultural understandings, rules, mores, attitudes and behaviours in the home. When some children enter school they are exposed to a new culture – an unfamiliar system of values, beliefs and standards, which conflicts with the culture of the home. The Irish National Teachers' Organisation explains:

> the culture of the school, predicated on middle class language style and behavioural norms, makes it appear an inhospitable place. In this case, the

onus is very firmly on the school to develop an ethos, a curriculum and practice which recognises and values the cultural milieu of the child.[35]

The option for the poor

Catholics' concern for the weaker and oppressed members of society is crystallised in the theological principle of the 'option for the poor'. This principle states that God's unconditional love for all people implies divine special attention to the weak and poor precisely because they are the ones most threatened by suffering and death. Catholics are committed to a mission of preferential love for anyone who is poor and oppressed, excluded, or voiceless. God's preferential love for the poor does not imply that God does not love the rich: the poor are the privileged addressees of revelation *because* of their situation of suffering and misery. When we consider that God loves the poor simply because they are poor we encounter 'the mystery of God's revelation and the gift of his kingdom of love and justice.'[36] This is because God reveals Godself in history precisely through the divine predilection for the weak. As liberation theologian Jon Sobrino notes, 'it is not that God reveals himself first as he is and then shows himself partial to the oppressed. It is rather in and through his partiality toward the oppressed that God reveals his own identity.'[37]

The option for the poor is an option for the God of the reign of life as proclaimed to us by Jesus.[38] Anointed and empowered by the Spirit of God, Jesus devoted his ministry to healing and reconciling, to building up human beings, especially the poor and the downtrodden. Perhaps the most scandalous aspect of Jesus' life was that he revealed a distinct partiality for those who were weak, dependent and oppressed; particularly the *economic* and *sociological* poor. He believed that the reign of God is open to all but not in the same way to all. It is addressed directly only to the poor (Lk 4:18; 7:22; Mt 11:5; Lk 6:20). Jesus' deepest desire was to create a social-political situation in which people could be free and so fulfil God's wish that they might have life and have it to the full (Jn 10:10). His deepest concern was for the victims of sinful structures, prejudices and practices. Consequently, he called for the transformation of persons and institutions in the present, precisely because unjust structures or practices delay the fulfilment of the reign of God.[39]

Because God wishes all to have life, disciples of Jesus concern themselves especially with those whose lives are threatened. Indeed, a commitment to the poor is seen as 'a witness on which the authenticity of the preaching of the gospel message depends.'[40] The 'option' refers to the free decision of disciples to commit themselves to side with the powerless in their fight for justice and to oppose all persons and structures that hinder their liberation. Theologian Gustavo Gutiérrez notes that 'this option for the poor is not optional in the sense that a Christian need not necessarily make it, any more than the love we owe every human being, without exception, is optional.'[41] To be Christian *is* to make an option for the poor.

The 'option for the poor' is necessitated by the fact of social conflict in our world. Catholics cannot avoid facing up to the reality of inequality in society, nor can they disregard the causes that produce it. In the educational sphere this conflict manifests itself in the unequal opportunities for attainment within the school system, a conflict which is either combated or exacerbated by the kinds of curricula teachers try to implement. Teachers working in areas of educational disadvantage know better than most how education can exclude the poorer sections of society, especially when children's language and culture are not reflected in national curricula and programmes.

When faced with this reality we experience an ethical reaction: we realise that this is a situation in which the Christian message allows only one course of action. Here the Church is under the obligation of decisively taking sides.[42] We must let God be who God is – one who is partial toward the disadvantaged of this world. How might religious educators respond to this as God's Word and put it into action? How can religious educational practices reflect the Catholic commitment to the educationally disadvantaged poor?

Religious education and the option for the poor

An education worthy of Christian discipleship must be one that educates students to social responsibility, encouraging particular concern for the marginalised and suffering of society. Catholic education at its best raises a critical consciousness in learners about structural injustices in society and the imperative of working to eradicate them. Even small children can be helped to decide what constitutes injustice in their context and then to act in such a way that this injustice is undone and that structures of justice are created. For example, children can be helped to examine the way they pick teams at break time to see if those strategies serve to exclude rather than include children who are different. Children can also be taught to be conscious of and attentive to the concerns of the poor, the marginalised, and those discriminated against in their own communities, in the wider society and throughout the world.

Teachers working in areas of educational disadvantage need religion programmes that allow them to plan a flexible response to children's individual needs and differences. They will examine religious education programmes to see if they address the educational needs of the children they teach. They will ask questions such as: What kind of child and what kind of lifestyle is assumed by this programme?; Does this programme help disadvantaged children to realise their capacities for full human development?; Does the language offered resonate with the way children speak in areas of educational disadvantage?; What opportunities are offered to teachers to adapt materials to particular socio-cultural contexts?; Does this programme seek to connect the gospel to the reality of children's lives and to the tensions inherent to living in an unequal society?; And finally, does the programme enable children to use religious resources to counter the negative impact on them of societal racism, prejudice and classism? All children deserve to have a positive and constructive experience of religious education in Catholic schools. Teachers ask the Church to take sides by producing programmes which, in fostering the full flourishing of the disadvantaged, promote the equality and well-being of all.

Religion programmes should be constructed in such a way that teachers can accommodate differences in culture, class, and levels of educational ability. They should reflect equally the daily lives of *all* children – including children from dominant Irish, Traveller, asylum-seeker and refugee backgrounds, as well as children with physical and intellectual learning disabilities. Furthermore, religious education programmes should enable children to build on the fundamental strengths of their own home culture.[43] For example, teachers can be invited to incorporate children's own vernacular language into religious education curricula, while paying attention to the ways in which they can be helped to change to a more standardised form of English. Finally, teachers in areas of educational disadvantage require extra resources which will enable them to respond to different learning needs.

The option for the poor also helps determine the curriculum of Catholic religious education. For instance, the fact that the poor are the first ones to whom Jesus' mission is directed (Lk. 4:18-21), should be strongly reflected in the way students are introduced to the reign of God. Similarly, an awareness of the concrete reality of God's salvation of the poor should influence the approach one takes to teaching about the Church and the sacraments. The Church will be presented primarily as a people of the poor, as a people committed to the struggle for justice and liberation, as a people who follow Jesus in the struggle for justice, and as a people who are often persecuted for belonging to the reign of God. Similarly, students will be taught that the celebration of Eucharist and commitment to solidarity and justice are indissolubly bound. In the Eucharist we express a profound communion with those who suffer through poverty and express with joy our hope for the creation of a more just and equal communion of people through the Spirit of the Risen Christ.[44]

Special Education

The religious education of people with learning disabilities, both physical and intellectual, is a very important contemporary issue for Catholic religious educators. Teachers are particularly concerned about the lack of suitable resources and materials for religious education of children with special needs. Recent research undertaken by Martina Ní Cheallaigh concluded that within current religious education practice in Ireland there is 'a serious neglect of the area of special religious education'. Furthermore, Ní Cheallaigh uncovered 'a high level of frustration' among teachers in the teaching of this subject. This frustration cannot be ignored.[45]

When we consider the gifts and capacities of children with learning disabilities we receive a new perspective on the question of what constitutes Catholic identity. One fruitful avenue of exploration lies in the symbol of Jesus' resurrection. Nancy Eiesland, author of *The Disabled God*, draws attention to the fact that the resurrected Jesus still bears his wounds even as he reveals the new life of salvation to his apostles. This, says Eiesland, calls all to 'recognise in the marks of Jesus' impairment' our own connection with God, and our own salvation. The resurrected Jesus reminds us that 'full personhood is fully compatible with the experience of disability'. The challenge for Catholics is to embrace those with disabilities who symbolise the possibility of a new humanity connected to God.[46]

Religious education and special education

To take this challenge seriously means that we seek real inclusivity in religious education. As Ní Cheallaigh argues, 'Religious educators, particularly, have a duty, to promote genuine inclusiveness within schools and to inculcate an attitude based on the acceptance and celebration of difference rather than simply on tolerance alone'.[47] While the Catholic Church has been to the forefront in providing educational services for people with learning disabilities, it seems that this caring service was undertaken not in a spirit of equality but merely in a spirit of charity. Ní Cheallaigh explains:

> The focus lay on what could be done for those with learning disabilities, rather than on seeing people with learning disabilities as equals within the Christian community and who, themselves, have something of value to offer... If it is accepted that all are made in the image and likeness of God (Genesis 1: 27) then the invitation to belong fully in Christ's Body, the Church, ought to be made to all equally. All should be viewed not merely as recipients of what the community has to offer, but as participators and contributors who themselves

have something of importance and value to offer
the community.[48]

From a practical point of view, the kind of inclusion advocated
by Ní Cheallaigh requires that the gifts of all children be
recognised and given expression in the religious education
class. *The General Directory for Catechesis* recommends
'personalised and adequate programmes' for children with
special needs.[49] Children with intellectual learning disabilities
have particular educational strengths which should be fostered:
tactile-based strengths, sensory-based strengths, and a love of
music and drama. Appropriate programmes must be developed
which build on these specific strengths. Such programmes
would provide concrete materials, with emphasis on visual,
musical, and kinaesthetic elements rather than on language. In
the absence of specialised programmes, religious education
programmes such as *Alive-O* can be used by teachers to create
individualised curricula for children with intellectual learning
disabilities. There is need, however, for guidelines for teachers
wishing to adapt such programmes. These guidelines would
suggest appropriate methods and provide age- and need-
appropriate resources for children with special needs.

The educational needs of children with learning disabilities
challenge Catholic religious educators to a renewed
understanding of the meaning of catholicity for this time. The
Christian impetus to care for and educate these children will be
further deepened as we learn from them what the Christian
vision of inclusivity really entails.

CONCLUSION

This chapter presents education for Catholic identity as a
creative process of nurturing people in a distinctive faith
identity that embraces 'difference' and welcomes 'the other'.

Catholic religious education enables students to absorb the richness of the tradition to which they belong, to engage in its practices, and to share in the process whereby those practices are adapted, altered and transformed for the present generation. Ideally, the kind of 'Catholic Identity' students develop through this educational process will manifest itself in action which will contribute to combating the suffering of the poor, particularly the socio-economic poor and the socially marginalized of this world. As people engage in the struggle for transformation and for fullness of life for all humankind, Catholic identity will become a source of empowerment and grace. In this way Catholicism will continue to contribute to human participation in the fullness of God's gift in Christ and God's reign on earth – the goal of Catholic religious education.

NOTES

1   Richard R. Osmer and Friedrich Schweitzer, *Religious Education between Modernization and Globalization*, GrandRapids, Michigan/ Cambridge, U.K.: William B. Eerdmans Publishing Company, 2003, pp. 263-5. Important questions that potentially have a religious answer include those relating to death and dying, the reason for being moral, and the basis of self-identity.

2   The challenge of teaching for religious diversity is examined in detail in chapter seven and so is not commented upon in this essay.

3   At baptism Christians are baptized into the death and new life of Jesus Christ, and are anointed with God's life-giving Spirit. The Holy Spirit draws the person into the fullness of God's life. This turning to God through Christ in the Spirit, is the central Christian experience and hence constitutes the heart of Christian identity.

4   Thomas H. Groome, 'What Makes a School Catholic?' in McLaughlin, O' Keefe S. J. and O' Keeffe (eds), *The Contemporary Catholic School*, Washington, D. C.: The Falmer Press 1996, p.123.

5   This definition of catholicity recognises:

a) that catholicity is fullness of life in Christ.

b) that catholicity is both a divine gift (*free*) and a human task (we must respond) and so it has profound social implications. It's source is in the triune God's self-communication. Consequently, we should not overestimate the value of human effort for achieving the fullness of catholicity.

c) that liturgy (*celebration*) is the central process through which the Catholic Church actualises and preserves its catholicity.

d) that catholicity is an *open* invitation so that non-Christian groups can enter into a saving relationship with the Church (see *LG*). Catholicity is sharing in 'the universal community, rooted in cosmic nature, that transcends the barriers of time and place.' Avery Dulles, *The Catholicity of the Church*, Oxford: Clarendon Press, 1985, p.185.

e) that catholicity has the character of 'already now' and 'not yet'. It won't reach its consummation until Christ returns in glory.

f) that catholicity is not a static absolute but an ongoing process of invitation such that the reign of God continually expands in the world.

6   The 'good news' is expressed in the doctrine of the Incarnation and constitutes the heart of the Catholic tradition. This news is that God chose to become one of us thus revealing what it means to be a human being; the dignity and goodness of being human; and that it is our humanity that unites us with God.

7   Monika K. Hellwig, 'Catholicism' in Mary Collins, Joseph A. Komonchak and Dermot A. Lane (eds), *The New Dictionary of Theology*, Collegeville, Minn: The Liturgical Press, 1987, p. 168.

8   Dulles, *Catholicity*, p.83.

9   Thomas H. Groome, *Educating for Life*, Allen,Texas: Thomas More, 1998, p.394.

10   This approach to Catholic education assumes a dialectical relationship between education and identity. See Fayette Veverka, 'Re-imagining Catholic Identity: Toward an Analogical Paradigm of Religious Education', *Religious Education*, 88: 2 (1993), p. 241.

11   Roger Haight, *Jesus Symbol of God*. New York: Orbis Books, 1999, p. 334.

12   For the idea that relations with the wider culture are the crucial determinant of Christian identity rather than something one

considers *after* one has established what that identity is see Kathryn Tanner, *Theories of Culture*, Minneapolis: Fortress Press, 1997, p. 116.

13   The idea that the educational strategies we employ should be shaped by the particular identity we seek to nurture and sustain is that of Veverka, 'Re-Imagining Catholic Identity', p. 242.

14   Robert J. Schreiter, *The New Catholicity: theology between the Global and the Local*, Maryknoll, New York: Orbis Books, 1997, p.8.

15   Lucien Richard, 'Theology and Belonging: Christian Identity and the doing of Theology', *Religious Education*, 79:3 (1984), pp. 392-413.

16   Marianne Sawicki, 'Historical Methods and Religious Education', *Religious Education*, 82: 3 (1987), pp.375-376. Emphasis mine.

17   Dulles, *Catholicity*, p. 7.

18   Tanner, *Theories*, p. 112.

19   Veverka, 'Re-Imagining Catholic Identity', p.247.

20   Jaan Valsiner, *Culture and the Development of Children's Action*. New York: John Wiley & Sons, Inc. 2nd ed. 1997, p.170.

21   CA, no. 24.

22   Mass Media culture is the term for 'a culture that is permeated by images, artefacts, music, and other elements available for the creation of meaning, which are produced by commercial industries that also, for the most part, control their distribution. Such mass distribution is made possible primarily through mechanisms such as radio, film, television, supermarket magazines and so on.' Mary E. Hess, 'From Trucks Carrying Messages to Ritualized Identities: Implications for Religious Educators of the Postmodern Paradigm Shift in Media Studies', *Religious Education*, 94:3 (1999), p.274. Popular culture describes that which has become 'popular' from the mass culture, for example, Harry Potter, the Lord of the Rings, McDonalds.

23   Michael Paul Gallagher, *Clashing Symbols*, New York: Paulist Press, 1998, p.114.

24   Pope John Paul II has noted that the synthesis between faith and culture 'is not just a demand of culture, but also of faith. A faith which does not become culture is a faith which has not become fully received, not thoroughly thought through, not fully lived out.' Letter from John Paul II to Cardinal Casaroli appointing him as president of the Pontifical Council for Culture; quoted in *L'osservatore Romano*, 28 June 1982, pp. 1-8.

25   For this approach to inculturation see Thomas H. Groome, 'Inculturation: How to Proceed in a Pastoral Context', *Concilium* 2 (1994), pp. 120-133.

26   Kathy Gallo, 'Communicating the Word in the World of Computers', *The Living Light* 33: 4 (1997), p. 7. Note also that the *General Directory for Catechesis* defines evangelization and catechesis as forms of ministry of the Word (no. 50).

27   Andrew McGrady, 'Cultural Ecology and Media Ethics: a Perspective From a Christian Philosophy of Communication' in Eoin G. Cassidy and Andrew G. McGrady (eds), *Media and the Marketplace: Ethical Perspectives*, Dublin: Institute of Public Administration, 2001, p. 122.

28   John Shea, 'Catholic Identity and its Carriers,' in John Roberto (ed.), *Faith Maturing: A Personal and Communal Task*, Washington, D. C.: National Federation for Catholic Youth Ministry, 1985, p.61.

29   Hess, 'From Trucks Carrying Messages', p. 279.

30   Gregor Goethals, 'Ritual dimensions of Popular Culture' in S. Hoover and K. Lundby (eds), *Rethinking Media, Religion and Culture*, Thousand Oaks, California: Sage Publications, 1997, pp. 117-32.

31   Rolv Nøvtvik Jakobsen, 'The Impact of the Media on the Religious Formation of Boys and Girls', *Concilium* no. 4, London: SCM Press, 2002, p. 40.

32   McGrady, 'Cultural Ecology', pp. 127, 129.

33   Katherine E. Zappone, *Achieving Equality in Children's Education*, Dublin: St Patrick's College, Drumcondra, 2002, p. 20.

34   This is the definition of educational disadvantage used by the Educational Disadvantage Centre of St. Patrick's College, Drumcondra, Dublin, Ireland. For more information see the website: http://www.spd.dcu.ie/main/academic/edc The European Social Fund Programme Evaluation Unit (1997) identified educational disadvantage as a phenomenon which arises 'if a person's experience of, access to, participation in and benefits from education are not characterised as equitable.' Cited in Aine Hyland, 'Looking to the Future – Ending Disadvantage' in *Primary Education: Ending Disadvantage, Proceedings and Action Plan of National Forum*, St Patrick's College Drumcondra, 2002, p. 47.

35   Irish National Teachers' Organisation, *Poverty and Educational Disadvantage: Breaking the Cycle*, Dublin: INTO, 1994. p. 29.

36   Gustavo Gutiérrez, 'Option for the Poor' in Jon Sobrino and
      Ignacio Ellacuría (eds), *Systematic Theology: Perspectives From
      Liberation Theology*, Maryknoll, New York: Orbis Books, 1996, p.
      105.

37   Jon Sobrino, *Jesus the Liberator*, Maryknoll, New York: Orbis
      Books, 1993, p.82.

38   Gutiérrez, 'Option for the Poor', p. 27.

39   Sobrino, *Jesus the Liberator*, pp.71, 79-84.

40   James B. Nickoloff (ed.), *Gustavo Gutiérrez: Essential Writings*, New
      York: Orbis, 1996, p. 292.

41   Gutiérrez, 'Option for the Poor,' p. 26.

42   Nickoloff (ed.), *Gustavo Gutiérrez*, p. 120.

43   The imperative of recognizing home-culture strengths in helping
      children to be successful in school is emphasized by Louise
      Derman-Sparks in 'Disadvantage and Diversity: Untangling Their
      Roles in Children's Development and in Education', *Primary
      Education: Ending Disadvantage*, p. 59.

44   Nickoloff (ed.), *Gustavo Gutiérrez*, pp.248, 258.

45   Martina Maria Ní Cheallaigh, 'The Irish Primary Religious
      Education Programme: An Investigation into its Inclusivity for
      Children with Learning Disabilities.' Unpublished M. Ed thesis, St
      Patrick's College, Dublin, 2002, p. i.

46   Nancy L. Eiesland, *The Disabled God: toward a Liberatory Theology
      of Disability*, Nashville: Abingdon Press, 1994, p. 100.

47   Martina Ní Cheallaigh, 'Towards Inclusivity in Religious
      Education' in Raymond Topley and Gareth Byrne (eds), *Nurturing
      Children's Religious Imagination*, Dublin: Veritas, 2004, p. 75.

48   Ibid, p. 67.

49   GDC, no. 189.

CHAPTER SEVEN

Teaching in a religiously diverse context

• •

John Henry Newman's dictum 'To live is to change, to be perfect is to have changed often' might give some solace to those involved in Ireland's fast changing Catholic primary religious education sector. Recent changes in primary religious education have been propelled by factors including: the 1998 Education Act; The 1999 Primary School Curriculum; the second representation of the National Catechetical Programme (1996-2004); the emergence of new religious education syllabi at primary and post-primary levels; developments in the field of theology and education; as well as the social and religious changes brought about by a rapidly growing post-millennium Irish economy.[1] In the midst of this change primary Religious Educators must engage with key issues in primary education. The 1999 primary curriculum has identified 'pluralism, a respect for diversity and the importance of tolerance' as one such key issue.[2]

Diversity is an umbrella category incorporating areas such as religious diversity, diversity of school types and ethnic and cultural diversity.[3] It also includes linguistic diversity as well as diversity of ability and teaching methodologies and gender issues.[4] While all of these aspects of diversity influence the context and manner in which religious education is taught in the primary classroom, this chapter focuses primarily on religious diversity, that is on the reality that primary teachers are not teaching religious education in a homogeneous mono-faith context and consequently their teaching must address the needs of different participants in the contemporary primary educational process. This chapter argues that effective teachers understand the issue of diversity and address it positively. This chapter also states that Catholic schools are themselves religiously diverse communities with a mandate to acknowledge, respect and support diversity. Chapter six stressed that the word Catholic comes from the word 'kata holos' meaning 'including everything and everyone' so that the ethos of Catholic schools should be inclusive and welcoming of diverse cultures, ethnic groups, abilities and religious beliefs. Furthermore this chapter argues that every classroom contains teachers and children with a diverse range of religious abilities and attitudes towards religion. Catholic Religious Educators should assess the needs of teachers and pupils honestly so that Catholic schools can provide effective, appropriate, supportive and inclusive learning environments.

It is beyond the remit of this chapter to explore the highly significant issues of linguistic diversity or diversity of ability in religious education. The *Beo Go Deo* series attempts to address the Irish language needs of teachers and pupils and while there are no catechetical guidelines or materials to support English as a Second Language (ESL) pupils, the *Alive-0* programme shows an awareness of the need to communicate to children by translating the gospel message into appropriate language without diminishing its content. It is also important to acknowledge that the Catholic Church places great emphasis on the inclusion of people with special needs in the educational enterprise[5] through initiatives such as SPRED catechesis and the *Sacramental Programme for Children with Special Educational Needs.*[6] This chapter will explore the issue of diversity under the following three headings: (1) religious diversity, (2) diversity of school types and (3) ethnic and cultural diversity.

Ireland as a culturally diverse country.

Diversity has become a major issue within the primary school sector because the primary school is a microcosm of an increasingly diverse Irish society. Ireland is attracting foreign nationals to its shores and the growing number of individuals seeking asylum in Ireland has risen quite dramatically in the last decade, from just thirty-nine applications in 1992 to 11,598 in 2002. This figure fell to 7,483 in 2003[7] and was just under five thousand in 2004. The six countries of origin from which most people seeking asylum in the Republic of Ireland originated in 2004 were: Nigeria; Romania; Somalia; China; Sudan and the Democratic Republic of the Congo.[8] It is important to note that any statistics on immigration and asylum must be placed in the context of Irish people's own history of migration and emigration. It is estimated that since the seventeenth century 'around seven million people have emigrated from Ireland',[9] most of them to Britain, America, Australia, Canada, Africa and Asia so that their descendants number in the region of 70 million today.

It would be a gross misrepresentation to suggest that Ireland has only become culturally and religiously diverse in the last decade of the twentieth century. Many commentators argue that Ireland has been culturally and ethnically diverse for centuries although this diversity has only recently been acknowledged.[10] The NCCA's guidelines on intercultural education show 'how migration and immigration, conquest and plantation, emigration and return have all featured in Ireland's history as a nation and have shaped the richness that is

"Irishness"'.[11] Ireland's long history of cultural and religious diversity challenges the myth that, until recent decades, Ireland was a country populated by a discrete, pure race of essentially similar people. This myth denies the complex nature of a hybrid, diverse and inter-related Irish national identity. Throughout the nineteenth and early twentieth centuries many Irish nationalists adopted what could be termed a 'nativist' position as the most effective means of achieving their ultimate goal of Irish independence. Nativism is 'the belief in an authentic ethnic identity, and the desire to return after the catastrophe of colonialism, to an unsullied indigenous cultural tradition' as in the various forms of cultural nationalism.[12] Douglas Hyde's (1860-1947) lecture of November 1892, on 'The Necessity of De-Anglicising the Irish People' is often cited as the quintessential example of the Irish nativist position. Hyde states:

> We must strive to cultivate everything that is most racial, most smacking of the soil, most Gaelic, most Irish, because in spite of the little admixture of Saxon blood in the north-east corner, this island is and will ever remain Celtic at the core.[13]

The history of the island of Ireland and the composition of its people is far more complex and heterogeneous than Hyde's reference to a Gaelic nation with a 'little admixture of Saxon blood' suggests. There is evidence that foreign invasions and settlements were a feature of Irish life from at least as early as 200 BCE.[14] If one goes further back one discovers that the expansion of Mesolithic farmers from Scandinavia through Scotland and into the north of Ireland was well under way by 6,000 BCE. Indeed excavations at Lough Gur in Co. Limerick point to a relatively sophisticated Stone Age farming society who, it is thought, were descendants of earlier settlers from around 3,000 BCE.[15] This cycle of invasion and assimilation has given Ireland a complex, diverse and often contradictory political, cultural, religious and social history that makes even generic statements concerning national identity all the more difficult.[16]

It is impossible to identify and classify what may be termed the 'indigenous people' of the island of Ireland as they are most likely themselves composed of the social and cultural legacies of previous invaders and settlers who have assimilated into the indigenous culture over differing periods of time.[17] George Bernard Shaw (1856-1950) recognised this when in *John Bull's Other Island* (1904) he said:

> I am a genuine typical Irishman of the Danish, Norman, Cromwellian and (of course) Scotch invasions. I am violently and arrogantly Protestant by family tradition; but let no English government therefore count on my allegiance. I am English enough to be an inveterate Republican and Home Ruler. It is true that my grandfather was an Orangeman; but then his sister was an abbess; and his uncle, I am proud to say, was hanged as a rebel.[18]

The complex history of the peoples of Ireland illustrates that a series of successive invasions, migrations and assimilations were punctuated by landmark events, such as the plantation of English and Scottish settlers in Ulster by 1610, which had huge implications for a religiously plural society. Roy Foster, in an essay entitled 'Varieties of Irishness – Cultures and Anarchy in Ireland',[19] suggests that in the nineteenth century, the differing religious groups in Ireland were not necessarily confrontational and in fact their mutual interests often overlapped in a variety of social, cultural and political organisations and movements.

Foster argues that far from being polarised at opposite ends of a national identity, the two dominant cultures, what he refers to as the 'Irish-Gaelic identity'[20] and the 'Protestant Unionist' (both northern and southern)[21] tradition, co-existed in an environment in which both traditions contributed to a notion of cultural diversity. Foster argues for inclusive rather than exclusive definitions of nationalism and his preference for 'the discovery of an outward-looking and inclusive cultural nationalism, not predicated upon political and religious differences'[22] is a central concept underpinning contemporary perceptions of Irish identity. This inclusive cultural nationalism is epitomised by major reformists such as Edmund Burke and nationalists such as Wolfe Tone, Henry Grattan, Thomas Davis and Charles Stuart Parnell, all of whom were members of the Protestant ascendancy class, who nonetheless promoted the notion of Ireland as a nation. Irish educators need to be sensitive to the cultural and religious complexity which preceded them and continues to surround them. Teachers can help to shatter the 'nativist' myth of a pure Irish race unsullied by cultural, ethnic and religious diversity by putting children in touch with story traditions which celebrate diversity. The story of Eiriu from the twelfth century book, *An Leabhar Gabhala*, presents the founding mothers and fathers of Ireland as a series of immigrants, who travelled to Ireland from across the sea.[23] Children could be reminded that Patrick, Ireland's patron saint, was an immigrant who contributed to the diversity of Irish culture and religious belief by bringing the Christian tradition to Ireland and by building upon elements of the pre-existing Celtic tradition.[24] Teachers could also use Crosscare's (Catholic Social Services Conference) high quality programme for intercultural education in the senior primary classroom entitled *Celebrating Difference*. [25]

1 IRELAND AS A RELIGIOUSLY DIVERSE COUNTRY.

An analysis of the religious affiliation of the Irish population in the twenty-first century further substantiates the argument that Ireland is not a homogenous, mono-cultural or mono-faith society. Indeed, the 2002 census figures reveal that while almost 90 per cent of the population cite Catholicism as their religion, Ireland is home to more than twenty different religious traditions.[26] Caution should also be exercised when exploring Catholicism, the majority religion in Ireland. Recent research points to the fact that even societies and religious groups which initially appear to be culturally homogeneous provide evidence of regional variations of practice and local interpretations of religious symbols.[27] Irish Catholicism is a complex, diverse cultural and religious phenomenon. In the post-modern context it is necessary to challenge not only the myth of a pure 'Irish' nation but also the myth of a pure 'Catholic' Irish nation. There is a broad spectrum of Catholic belief and practice which ranges from non-practising, traditional and conservative on the one hand to practising, liberal and radical on the other with a series of possible inter-relationships in between.

Religious diversity in Ireland is no recent phenomenon. The ancient religious practices of the Celts have been the focus of much recent academic research.[28] There is documented evidence that Jews arrived in Ireland in the year 1079, and while the number of Jewish immigrants in the twelfth and thirteenth century was small, more substantial communities of Jews settled in Ireland during the sixteenth and seventeenth centuries.[29] The 1881 census shows that while Catholicism was overwhelmingly the religion of the majority of the population, (3,465,332 identified adherents) the society of the time was undoubtedly religiously diverse. Other religions mentioned in the 1881 census are: Church of Ireland (317,576); Presbyterian (56,498); Methodist (17,660); Jewish (394) and other stated religions (12,560). No breakdown of the constituent groupings of these other stated religions is given in 1881, nonetheless their presence is significant. The most recent 2002 census figures for the Republic[30] show that in the intervening years an increasingly religiously complex and diverse Irish society has developed. The causes for this religious diversity are manifold.

> Irish citizens leaving the faith or choosing a different denomination for their children are two factors...but they are merely minor ones. The main factor is immigration. Non-nationals – whether from Britain, continental Europe, America, Africa or Asia – account for 5.8% of the population, and the majority of the immigrants have brought their faith with them.[31]

It is evident that factors such as immigration (people of different faiths and cultures coming to Ireland), emigration (Irish people travelling to all parts of the globe and developing relationships with people of different faiths and cultures and subsequently returning to Ireland), secularisation, the postmodern emphasis on pluralism and the increasing importance of choice in all areas of Irish society, are creating a religiously diverse topography. The 2002 Census figures[32] revealed that:

> The number of Muslim and Orthodox adherents increased significantly between the censuses of 1991 and 2002 - the former more than quadrupling to 19,000 and the latter increasing from less than 400 adherents in 1991 to over 10,000 in 2002. Immigration had a major impact on the increases observed, with non-Irish nationals making up 70 per cent of the Muslims and over 85 per cent of

those of the Orthodox faith who were usually resident and present in the State on Census night.[33]

In the year 2002 the fastest growing religions in Ireland were Islam and Orthodox Christianity. The 'No Religion' or '(Religion) Not Stated' categories are some of the most interesting categories to examine in the 2002 census. These categories first appeared on census forms in 1961 when only 1,107 people stated that they had no religion while 5,625 were listed under 'Not Stated'. In the intervening four decades these figures have increased dramatically in so that in 2002, 138,264 stated that they had no religion while 79,094 were listed under 'not stated'. Contemporary research provides some insight into why many people may find themselves uncomfortable with the notion of adhering exclusively to any one faith tradition or why they may be hesitant to state their religious affiliation. Robert Jackson describes plural societies as those characterised by a growing individualism where eclectic beliefs, competing rationalities and the perception of all truth claims as tentative, cause people to suspiciously resist absolute commitment to any one religious tradition.[34] Oliver Brennan attributes this reticence to commit oneself exclusively to any one faith tradition to the post-modern condition.

> One of the features of post-modernity is its challenge to any one grand explanation of human existence, be it Christian, Jewish, Muslim, Hindu, or Buddhist.[35]

Post-modern society rejects the notion that there is some absolute, knowable, universally valid truth upon which all life and reasoning can be based. It rejects uniformity and absoluteness in the face of diversity and relativity. It sees that there is no one worldview, religious, political or economic system which can be regarded as universally true. Human beings are left with fragmentary, diverse and competing understandings of the world. The post-modern world is a world saturated with uncertainty and the need to constantly re-evaluate the known. In religious terms this translates into a world where the post-modern subject is faced with a variety of faith traditions, each making conflicting truth claims about their own unique capacity to reveal the true nature of God and the ultimate meaning and destiny of human beings. In a world of competing truth claims many people experience difficulty in selecting one religious tradition over others. This may result in a crisis of religious belief and a rejection of religion, as in atheism (reasoned rejection of God) or agnosticism (the belief that it is impossible to know what is true in religion), or indeed in a type of religious relativism where all religions are seen as being equally valid or invalid. People may reject organised institutional religious systems and still see themselves as people of 'personal belief' with their own individual spirituality and value system.[36] In a post-modern context even the terms 'religious' and 'non-religious' are subject to revision and qualification. People may describe themselves as 'Catholic atheists' or 'agnostic Christians'. One primary teacher articulates the uncertainty and confusion surrounding religion in post-modern Ireland when she stated 'Nobody believes it (religion) anymore. The problem is the children question it, the parents have no interest in it and very few of us believe half of what we're teaching'.[37]

However religious diversity and religious pluralism is not necessarily a negative category. Indeed post-modernism's acceptance of diversity, its resistance to closed categories and definite meanings involves a possible openness to the transcendent and the spiritual.[38] God eludes arid, neat, quantifiable categorisations and post-modernity invites the restless individual to a spiritual search for meaning. Post-modernity is less sure about everything than modernism, atheism included.[39] It has also been argued that an acceptance of religious diversity leads to religious tolerance. Brennan notes that the young Irish people he interviewed 'prized diversity and tolerance for various points of view and ways of life, and they had little regard for those who judged others for being different'.[40] Evidently religious diversity is not necessarily an impediment to religious belief, and can in fact help nurture and deepen faith. Keith Ward puts it succinctly when he states:

> ...it is a small step to see that religious diversity actually helps us in our search for spiritual truth. For even though we are committed to our religious path to truth, we can see that there are other paths from which we might learn. Other paths that are critical of ours can help us to see undesirable consequences of our beliefs that we might not have noticed. Other paths that put things very differently can help us to see aspects of reality that we have missed.[41]

According to Ward's reading, a religiously diverse society is a potentially religiously and theologically enriched society. Celebrating religious diversity within Irish society could enable believers of different religious traditions to appreciate the spiritual and theological wealth, not alone of other traditions, but also of their own. Dermot Lane comments on the intimate inter-dependence of different religious traditions when he states 'When one religion is diminished all religions are diminished'.[42] One could argue that the opposite is equally true and that when one respects one religious tradition all religious traditions are enriched.

It is important to celebrate Ireland's religious diversity by documenting the history, beliefs, practices and inter-faith initiatives of among others, the Baha'i, Buddhist, Chinese, Christian, Hindu, Jewish, Muslim and Sikh communities in the thirty-two counties. The pioneering work of academics like Maurice Ryan makes it evident that 'Another Ireland'…is beginning to emerge: an Ireland of more than 'two cultures', a multi-religious, multi-cultural, multi-ethnic Ireland, north and south.'[43] The real challenge for contemporary religious educators is to understand and contribute positively to Ireland's religiously complex society. This means recognising the plurality of theological perspectives and religious positions not only within Irish Christian traditions, including Catholicism, but also within different Irish World Faith communities, as well as people of personal faith. In order to do this, religious educators should research the belief systems and practices of different faith traditions and engage in open, creative and critical dialogue with members of different faith groups. In the classroom, religious educators must develop religiously and educationally appropriate methodologies so they can educate children about diverse religious and secular traditions thus enabling children to participate knowledgeably and respectfully in a religiously plural society.

Religious diversity in the Primary School.

Primary religious education should address the needs of a religiously diverse population. Research shows that the overwhelming majority of Irish primary teachers support teaching children about 'Other Religions'.[44] While little research has been carried out into the teaching of world faiths in Ireland, teachers implicitly believe that this is a worthwhile area. One teacher recently commented: 'I would think that you have to teach children about other religions, because if you didn't then it would create ignorance, racism and discrimination.' Current research suggests that children who inhabit a world of diverse beliefs already 'discuss' the theology underlying those beliefs at an informal level even if they do not study them at a formal level in school.[45] Obviously it is preferable if school provides children with a formal opportunity to learn accurately and respectfully about the different rituals, belief systems, festivals, dress and food customs which are embodied in a religiously diverse society.

The Catholic primary school does address the issue of religious, ethnic and cultural diversity, through a variety of curricular areas including religious education.[46] However, to date, the National Catechetical Programme has not sufficiently emphasised the importance of acknowledging, exploring and supporting religious diversity. Indeed it is ironic that in many Catholic primary schools it is in the area of SESE that the issue of the rituals and cultures of diverse human communities are formally explored. For instance in the History curriculum, the Strand unit for Third and Fourth classes on 'Feasts and festivals in the past' explicitly mentions 'feasts and festivals celebrated by various members of the school and local community, including Christian, Hindu, Jewish, Muslim and other celebrations...'[47] Numerous examples abound where the revised curriculum provides children with the opportunity to explore important aspects of religious education through the culture and beliefs of diverse religious communities,[48] through people's 'myths, stories, art,... clothes'.[49] The opportunities for integration with religious education are enormous and yet one may legitimately question whether this occurs in many Catholic schools since the vast majority of formal primary religious education appears to occur from within a largely mono-faith perspective. This is a huge oversight since the Catholic school sector is committed to a culturally inclusive ethos.[50] Chapter three has argued that Catholic schools are based on a Catholic vision of education involving at least seven principles which emphasise the importance of social justice, human rights and an anti-racist and anti-discrimination approach to education. Vatican II calls all Catholics to inclusivity when it states that 'We cannot truly call on God, the Father of all, if we refuse to treat in a brotherly way any man *(sic.)*, created as he is in the image of God.' In the same document the Church condemns 'any discrimination against men *(sic.)* or harassment of them because of their race, color, condition of life, or religion.'[51] Contemporary practice in Catholic primary schools raises the question of the efficacy of the *Alive-O* programme in teaching children about diverse faiths. To suggest that there is no awareness of diversity in the *Alive-O* programme is incorrect. Mícheál Kilcrann enthusiastically argues that *Alive-O* is 'all-embracing' and can be used to promote the three R's of inter-cultural education (Recognition, Respect, Response).[52] In terms of inter-religious education, *Alive-O* is acutely aware of the Judeo-Christian rootedness of the Catholic tradition. However this awareness does not always translate into an appreciation of the importance of Judaism as a religion *in its own right.*

In the *Alive-O* programme there are occasions where world faiths make a brief appearance,[53] but if the teacher does not feel secure in her or his knowledge of these faith traditions the temptation to avoid the subject area, as well as the children's questions, may be acute. Michael Barnes notes that the temptation 'to retreat to somewhere more safe, to a place which – we feel – is ours to command, a place which is at all costs to be defended against the darkness of an unknown threat', is always a part of inter-religious dialogue and indeed education about diverse faiths.[54]

If the National Catechetical Programme does not integrate an inter-religious awareness into the subject of religious education, linking it to other subjects within the revised curriculum, then it becomes very difficult for teachers to respond to Vatican II's exhortation that Catholics 'acknowledge, preserve, and promote the spiritual and moral goods found among these men (*sic*), as well as the values in their society and culture.'[55] How can a teacher or a pupil acknowledge, preserve and promote something about which they know nothing? And if the National Catechetical Programme remains silent on the issue of religious diversity what information is being communicated by its silence? Perhaps in the absence of direct guidance it could be surmised that it is appropriate for Catholics to be unconcerned or embarrassed by religiously diverse communities?[56] It is interesting to note that these questions are not unique to Irish Catholic religious education. Catholic schools in Britain and in Northern Ireland are encountering similar difficulties and debate. One Catholic primary Head teacher in Britain said 'we don't touch other religions. It's a bit odd really... we seem to be saying that other races and faiths are irrelevant.'[57]

The suggestion that Catholic schools should acknowledge, promote and respect the truths found within different world faiths is not equivalent to saying that Catholics should deny the distinctiveness of their own tradition or cease believing in it. It is not to suggest that a type of religious relativism permeate the school where all religious traditions are accorded equivalent status. Catholic teaching makes this abundantly clear. *Dominus Iesus* sees that the Church's missionary proclamation is 'endangered today by relativistic theories which seek to justify religious pluralism.'[58] In other words the Catholic Church does not teach that all religions are equally valid. The Church rejects 'the theory of the limited, incomplete, or imperfect character of the revelation of Jesus Christ, which would be complementary to that found in other religions'.[59] While the

Catholic Church holds a sincere respect for the religions of the world it simultaneously rules out 'the belief that "one religion is as good as another."' [60] Teachers should be aware that the Catholic Church acknowledges that world faiths contain 'deeply religious texts' and are 'living expressions of the soul of vast groups of people' whose quest for God is 'made with great sincerity and righteousness of heart'[61]. However the Church does not teach that they are equivalent, identical or a supplementary complement to the Catholic faith. Primary teachers in Catholic schools might be guided by Oliver Brennan's emphasis on the principle of 'unity-in-diversity', which helps to accord value to diverse viewpoints (diverse faiths) while simultaneously allowing believers of a specific religious tradition to maintain their own particular beliefs and practices in the post-modern context.

> If religious education and pastoral ministry are to be effective in the contemporary cultural situation, they need to be based on a fundamental principle centring on unity-in-diversity. This principle embraces diversity, allowing all viewpoints to be accorded value, while at the same time preserving the essential parameters of belief, structure and practice within the Catholic tradition.[62]

This principle of unity without uniformity and diversity without divisiveness could enable Catholics to be enriched by exploring diverse religious traditions while simultaneously developing their understanding and appreciation of their own. This may well necessitate a conversion from the viewpoint that diverse faiths are in competitive conflict with the Catholic faith to one of collaborative inter-religious dialogue where the beliefs and practices of world faiths enable Catholics to develop a renewed appreciation of both the Catholic and world faiths traditions. Indeed as Brennan remarks many 'people are crossing over to other religious traditions and returning to their own greatly enriched.'[63]

Catholic teaching does not state that Catholic children should learn exclusively about the Catholic faith; Catholic schools, in order to be true to Catholic teaching and to operate on the principles of respect for cultural and religious diversity, should build a knowledge of, and respect for, diverse cultures and faiths into all areas of the curriculum, most especially in the area of religious education. The 1999 primary curriculum gives Catholic schools an opportunity to bear witness to their Catholic faith by promoting tolerance and respect for all human beings regardless of religious, cultural or ethnic origin. Archbishop Diarmuid Martin, Primate of Ireland, has emphasised that 'celebrating difference' is central to the mission of Catholic schools.

> This desire to be welcoming and to recognise the talents and difference of each person should be a special hallmark of the Catholic schools in this diocese (*Dublin*). They are already showing that in the manner in which children from over a hundred countries are welcomed into our Catholic schools. I have initiated a dialogue with leaders of other faiths in Dublin to ensure that where children of other faiths are present in Catholic schools their needs are attended to and are never the object of discrimination or marginalization. We have the possibility of leading the way, rather than waiting to react to tensions should they occur. What happens in the schools will help other initiatives also within Irish society.[64]

In 2005 the NCCA launched a set of guidelines for Inter-Cultural Education in Primary Schools. There is an equivalent need for the Catholic Church to develop guidelines governing inter-religious education in Catholic primary schools. Certain basic principles could be applied to such inter-religious education. The first principle is that all children in all Catholic schools have a right to learn about the diverse faiths precisely because they are in a Catholic school that respectfully acknowledges, promotes and preserves the truths of those traditions. Teaching about world faiths should not be based on the number of pupils who come from diverse faith traditions in a class or school. Children have the right to be educated as citizens who can participate respectfully and knowledgeably in a religiously and culturally plural world. In the primary school each faith tradition should be taught in its own right and not as an appendix to the Catholic tradition. Introducing children to two or more faiths simultaneously or consecutively causes confusion and children should be given accurate, clear, age and ability appropriate information concerning the faith. The positive aspects of the faith should be explored and the teacher should always attempt to shatter crude stereotypes and superficial understandings. The teacher should avoid focusing excessively on what children may perceive as bizarre or unusual details of a faith tradition (for example slaughter rituals; sacred undergarments) which may give children an unbalanced view of the faith tradition. Teachers in Catholic schools should show children that there are many living faiths practised by ordinary people in contemporary Ireland. Where possible nuanced understandings of faith traditions, which incorporate variations of practices and beliefs, should be presented. Ideally local members of faith traditions should be invited into the Catholic school to inform the children about their religious beliefs and practices.

A recent positive initiative by the Irish Catholic bishops saw the introduction of guidelines for developing a policy on religious education for post-primary schools.[65] If every Catholic primary school developed a policy on religious education they could ensure that the major faith traditions were given a basic, respectful coverage in the primary school. Whole school planning in primary schools could operate to ensure that every academic year, each class (in many countries it occurs in the Junior as well as the Senior classes)[66] could be allocated a sizeable block of time, to explore one world faith in religious education class. Obviously integration could occur with other cross-curricular areas and ongoing inter-cultural initiatives so that this inter-religious education is not seen as an artificial, one-off, injection to immunise against an otherwise mono-faith educational programme. The children might start with the monotheistic, prophetic religions (Judaism/Christianity/Islam) before exploring the Eastern religious traditions (Hinduism/Buddhism/Sikhism). However the needs of the local school, the religious abilities of the children, the expertise of teachers, as well as the availability of school and community based resources mandates a diversity of approaches to inter-religious education in Catholic schools. Inter-religious education would provide Catholic primary schools with an opportunity to teach children respect and tolerance for Ireland's religiously diverse society. It would also integrate the Catholic primary religious education programme with the newly established, state examined, post-primary religion programme which provides ordinary and higher level sections on the major world faiths.[67] Finally it would provide children in Catholic schools with a deeper realisation that inclusivity, tolerance and respect are at the heart of the Catholic faith.

Catholic schools must welcome, respect and support their own pupils and parents of minority faith. A passive or silent toleration of minority faith children which never engages in consultative and supportive discussion with their parents or guardians can not be counted as inclusive. Schools should respect the wishes of minority faith children and their parents and offer every educational and institutional support necessary for their educational and personal development. Inevitably there are resource and in-service implications if inter-religious education is to become an important aspect of the Catholic primary religious education programme. However a greater range of inter-cultural[68] and inter-religious multi-media[69] resources are currently being designed for Irish schools.[70] Where diverse faiths, including the Catholic religion, are being taught in state schools the Catholic Church argues for accuracy, lack of prejudice and education for mutual understanding as guiding principles.

> State schools sometimes provide their pupils with books that for cultural reasons (history, morals or literature) present the various religions, including the Catholic religion. An objective presentation of historical events, of the different religions and of the various Christian confessions can make a contribution here to better mutual understanding. Care will then be taken that every effort is made to ensure that the presentation is truly objective and free from the distorting influence of ideological and political systems or of prejudices with claims to be scientific. [71]

Such principles could also be used in Catholic schools where the teaching of diverse faiths is concerned. Catholic primary schools must develop a religious education programme which addresses the issue of religious diversity in a religiously and educationally defensible systematic and sustained manner.[72]

2 DIVERSITY OF SCHOOL TYPES

Chapter IV of the 1971 Curriculum dealt with what it termed 'Religious Instruction' without ever referring to the issue of religious diversity. In 1971 the curriculum simply maintained the Department of Education's policy of providing no syllabus or examination for religious instruction, which it ironically described as 'by far the most important' part of the school's curriculum. It succinctly reiterated Rule 68 of the Department's Rules for National Schools by stating that 'Religious Instruction is, therefore a fundamental part of the school course, and a religious spirit should inform and vivify the whole work of the school'.[73] The 1971 curriculum gave very little space to religious instruction as it 'felt that this statement needs no further elaboration'. One suspects that in the politically sensitive and religiously conservative atmosphere of the time this indicated a reticence to comment inappropriately rather than a belief in the futility of further comment. Religious diversity was not mentioned in the 1971 curriculum for a whole host of reasons including the rise of religious sectarianism in the island of Ireland in the late sixties and early seventies with what Victor Griffin refers to as Nationalist and Unionist 'tribal religion masquerading as Christianity'.[74] Diversity is a key post-modern concept and in the early seventies it was not seen as pertinent to religious instruction in Ireland. A huge change occurred between 1971 and the Education Act of 1998 which was based on the principles of partnership, pluralism, equality, accountability and quality.[75]

The 1999 revised primary curriculum marks a considerable departure from the prescriptive language of 'religious instruction' to what it terms 'religious education'.[76] It places religious education in the context of the holistic development of the child as well as the 'inextricable' relationship of 'the spiritual dimension' to Irish culture and history. Using a liberal education argument for religious education,[77] the curriculum states that religious education is significant as a subject area because it contributes to the child's capacity to understand its culture and history as well as developing the individual's 'full potential'.[78] The rights of the individual to religious expression and freedom are emphasised and a far more pluralist, inclusivist understanding of religion and the individual prevails. The 1999 curriculum manifests its respect for diversity and tolerance[79] by stating that the school should be 'flexible in making alternative organisational arrangements for those who do not wish to avail of the particular religious education it offers'.[80] Diversity, tolerance and pluralism have become crucial issues within primary religious education because as Irish society becomes increasingly pluralist, multi-faith and post-religious,[81] the primary school sector has become increasingly diverse in an attempt to answer the educational needs of that society.

In the twenty-first century it is evident that the Catholic sector, which presently accounts for just over 92 per cent of Irish primary schools,[82] cannot be complacent by assuming that confessional religious education is non-problematic for the teachers, parents and pupils. The results of the 2002 INTO survey shows that just over 10 per cent of surveyed primary teachers do not wish to teach religion or have opted out of teaching it.[83] Parents are increasingly exercising their right to withdraw children from religious education classes and the growth of the multi-denominational Educate Together movement, the fastest growing sector in Irish primary education,[84] suggests that parents and teachers are looking for what they perceive to be a more democratic, multi-denominational, transparent and inclusive school system. Educate Together predict that by 2010, ten thousand children will be educated in multi-denominational schools and their aim is that no family will have to travel an unreasonable distance each day to access an Educate Together school.[85] Paul Rowe, Chief Executive of Educate Together states that:

> Successive Government statistics underline a rapid increase in the diversification of society, but the State is not taking proactive action to provide facilities for this increase.[86]

As chapter two has shown, at its inception in 1831 the Irish primary school system was originally inter-denominational (Anglican, Presbyterian and Catholic) and subsequently, in the latter half of the nineteenth century, became denominational. In the twenty-first century there are eight categories of Irish primary schools (Catholic; Church of Ireland; Inter-denominational; Jewish; Methodist; Multi-denominational; Muslim; Presbyterian) included under the umbrella of the denominational primary school system in Ireland.[87] Even the term 'denominational'[88] used to describe these schools is problematic as it fails to describe the present multi-faith educational sector which includes schools of separate Jewish and Muslim religions as opposed to denominations or subgroups of another religious tradition. Different school systems have developed to respond to the needs of different target groups and since its inception in 1978 the Educate Together movement has challenged the denominational nature of Irish primary education for a variety of reasons. Educate Together schools have developed a culturally inclusive and democratic ethos which is committed to multi-denominational education where:

> The schools typically use a variety of faith festivals in the school year to promote understanding of different religious views. At the same time, the

school is committed to making facilities available
to any group of parents who so wish, to organise
Religious Instruction or doctrinal classes outside
school hours.[89]

Educate Together schools are: (1) multi-denominational; (2) co-
educational; (3) child-centred and (4) democratic. In an attempt
to be truly inclusive of people of religious and personal belief
as well as those with secular backgrounds the Educate Together
schools no longer use the language of 'religious education' to
describe one of their seven curricular areas. In 2005 Educate
Together launched an Ethical Education curriculum called
Learn Together. This cyclical, evolving curriculum contains four
strands (Moral and Spiritual, Equality and Justice, Belief
Systems, Ethics and the Environment) which must be
interpreted, delivered, assessed and resourced, in the local
school context, in a collaborative partnership between teachers,
children and parents. *Learn Together* encourages children to
'explore their own spiritual identities in a secure setting while
also being aware of and respecting the notion that other people
may think differently to them.'[90] The curriculum provides a
series of guidelines, exemplars and resource suggestions for
each of the four strands which facilitate an integrated and
developmental approach to ethical education. These
curriculum documents are beautifully designed and illustrated
with children's artwork, and are clearly written and logically
organised. The Learn Together documents are a welcome
contribution to the whole area of religious education and
Ethical Education in the primary curriculum. They have
broadened the concept of 'religious' education as one of the
seven curricular areas by renaming it 'Ethical Education' and
have placed diversity, tolerance and anti-racist education at the
heart of the school and at the heart of the curriculum.

Furthermore the emphasis on an integrated cross-curricular approach, with creative forms of assessment, strands and strand units, is consistent with the overall approach in the 1999 Primary School Curriculum. The Ethical Education curriculum cycle developed as a consequence of a curriculum needs analysis based on consultation with children, teachers and parents in the Educate Together community. The curriculum cycle involves an inbuilt process of future consultation, evaluation and updating.

However there is a larger issue at stake brought to light by the rapid expansion of the Educate Together sector. Educate Together suggests that its expansion:

> is a strong indication of the growing demand from the general public for schools that respect and cherish the identity of children from all religious, social and cultural backgrounds. It is a powerful call for the end of the monopoly of denominational education and for the state to act to bring the system of primary education into conformity with its obligation to uphold the human rights of its citizens.[91]

In January 2005 Educate Together submitted a Shadow Report to the United Nations Committee on the Convention on the Elimination of all Forms of Racial Discrimination in Geneva. In the report Educate Together argued that the Irish Government fails to fund and provide an adequate choice of non-denominational or multi-denominational schools for Irish parents, teachers and children. The report reasons that the state's failure to provide a network of primary schools which ensure 'equality of access and esteem irrespective of...social, racial, ethnic, cultural or religious backgrounds' is inherently discriminatory. To support its case the report cites: the 1971 curriculum's requirement that 'the religious ethos of the school permeate the whole programme'; the 1998 Act's placing of an obligation on 'the Board of Management of a National school to promote the religious ethos of its patron'; the 2000 Equal Status Act's acknowledgement that schools may 'discriminate on religious grounds to maintain their characteristic or religious spirit' as well as the prevalence of enrolment policies which only give places to non-Catholic children if there are 'vacancies unfulfilled by Catholics'.[92]

Educate Together is not unique in claiming that the Irish primary system of education is problematic. In the mid-eighties Desmond Clarke argued that a religious monopoly of state schooling was unconstitutional.[93] More recently Fintan O'Toole suggested that Ireland's primary education system was 'a system funded by a secular state and run to an overwhelming extent by lay people....according to the ethos of one Church'.[94] The Irish Humanist Association view the religious-based, state funded, Irish denominational primary school system as discriminatory. Their concern is that a denominational primary school system unjustly excludes those of no religious affiliation or of a religious affiliation that differs from that of the school. This is a major bone of contention for 'non-religious, tax-paying parents who feel strongly the injustice of a national school system which discriminates against their children'... Allied with this is 'the issue of discrimination against teachers who may be barred from employment because of their religious or non-religious position.'[95]

Anne Lodge argues that Ireland's denominational and confessional primary school system 'does not allow for equal recognition or respect for difference'.[96] Lodge conducted interviews with people of minority belief including members of the Baháʼí and Buddhist communities, people of personal belief,[97] and a member of a minority Christian faith, about how they and their children experienced the denominational, confessional Irish system of primary education. Key issues emerging from this research are: children sometimes feel alienated because of their different religious or personal beliefs; sacramental preparation heightens this sense of exclusion and alienation; bullying and teasing can be based on the perception of the child as religiously different;[98] and that both participation in and withdrawal from religious education can be problematic. In denominational schools teachers' attitudes to minority belief children and parents varied from positive and supportive to negative and exclusive. Lodge concludes that 'differences in belief are denied in the denominational primary system and those whose beliefs are different are rendered invisible and subordinate.'[99]

These are serious charges that denominational schools must address. Lodge's research highlights the need for urgent action. The Catholic sector is far from perfect and while it embodies examples of excellent practice it also shows signs of serious deficiency. Her work also highlights the fact that while denominational schools may have wonderfully inclusive aspirational mission statements these can be effectively contradicted by their school practice. Indeed some commentators argue that the very denominational structure of Irish primary education denies the principles of diversity of values and beliefs that are central to recent government legislation on Education. In 2005 the UN found in favour of the Educate Together submission and 'recommended that the State promote multi-denominational education'. Educate Together states that:

> Unless the option of free, inclusive, multi-denominational education is made available to parents all over the country, the State is open to

the accusation that it is compelling families to send their children to schools that conflict with their conscience. We believe that it is only by creating primary educational spaces of equality and respect that we can hope to build a society that mirrors such values.[100]

In a recent address Colm O Cuanacháin, Secretary General of Amnesty International Ireland, argued that 'it is only in a multi-denominational school, where a multi-denominational religious education curriculum can be taught, that we can truly educate in and for human rights.' Only in a context where 'all religious belief systems and none are seen as equal' can one cultivate 'a democratic human rights school'.[101] Now there is a huge difference between stating that a lack of *choice* in the Irish primary school system is discriminatory and stating that Catholic primary schools and indeed all confessional schools *per se*, Christian, Jewish, Muslim, and so on, are discriminatory because of the religious ethos which they endorse. There is a big difference between one school sector saying 'We are an inclusive sector catering for diversity' and saying 'we are the *only* truly inclusive sector which caters for diversity and human rights'.

The Catholic school sector should welcome the advent and growth of the Educate Together sector as the diversification of the Irish primary school system with the consequent positive development of the increased choice for parents, teachers and children. Chapter Two has identified that, for historical reasons, the Irish national school system was originally inter-denominational and subsequently, in order to address the needs of the parents and children in the nineteenth and twentieth century, became denominational. In the late twentieth and early twenty-first century these needs have changed. The sector must change again to accommodate these needs.

However there is a huge difference between saying that the Catholic sector is the *majority sector*, a statement of historical and numerical fact, to making a value judgment that it is a *monopoly sector* with a positive desire to exclude and inhibit all other participants in the provision of primary education. Under current legislation any group of parents can come together and establish a primary school to service their needs.[102] Now Lodge and Lynch rightly stress that 'newer and less-established belief groups and groups of nonbelievers do not have the same authority or influence in establishing schools or in framing the kind of education they want for their children in religious matters.'[103] If the Catholic primary sector is genuinely desirous of not monopolising the educational system it should *actively* welcome and support new initiatives in primary education that service the educational needs of minority belief parents, teachers and children. However Catholic schools must also *actively* promote the fact that they are inclusive and welcoming of diversity. Otherwise a popular misconception will develop which views Catholic education as exclusive, bigoted and unwelcoming of religiously diverse communities.

The position that denominational schools are ultimately incompatible with human rights schools is a serious attack on the integrity of denominational institutions. It promotes the view that human rights education is incompatible with institutions founded on religious commitment and belief. It suggests that faith-based institutions are inherently discriminatory and intolerant of difference and indeed incapable of upholding the human rights of all. The logic that an institution's religious ethos disables it from being genuinely concerned with universal human rights and that only institutions which do not endow any one faith tradition are egalitarian and genuinely inclusive must be questioned. One observes that many commentators writing about diversity are acutely and rightly aware of the need for subtlety, sensitivity and an awareness of hybridity when dealing with minority faiths. Sometimes when it comes to majority faith traditions that same subtlety and sensitivity is not always evident. In one sense this is understandable in view of the huge power and privilege imbalance which the majority faith can exercise. There is an undoubted need for openness and inclusivity in the Catholic faith and in Catholic schools. However there is also a need for tolerance and subtlety on behalf of commentators who tend to see Catholicism as an oppressive majority religion. Post-modern Catholics are not homogeneous, unthinking, monolithic adherents of a religious tradition or its institutions. That O'Cuanacháin's viewpoint itself could be termed intolerant of difference is ironic. Catholic schools have a mission and a duty to serve the needs of the Catholic and wider religious and secular community. The fact that Catholic schools are denominational and provide Catholic religious education does not inhibit them from welcoming all, from upholding the dignity and freedom of all and from accommodating their diverse religious, secular, ethnic and cultural needs.

In Ireland the majority faith is not above and beyond critique. The Irish Catholic tradition has made a huge contribution to human rights and it has also been disgracefully involved in human rights abuses. What is important is that adherents and commentators neither automatically divinise or demonise the Catholic sector so that exclusively defensive or offensive debate is avoided. The Catholic Church must honestly acknowledge the difficulties resulting from its majority control of the present primary education system. It must move beyond a rhetoric of inclusivity and show a willingness to actively address the urgent issue of religious diversity within its schools as well as diversity of school types. Finally it must work in partnership with the Department of Education and Science, religious leaders and members of minority communities as well as other types of schools in the primary sector, so that it can be an inclusive part of an evolving primary school system which serves the needs of a religiously and culturally diverse Irish society.

3   ETHNIC AND CULTURAL DIVERSITY

In recent years there has been an increasing awareness of the importance of listening to, learning from and valuing different minority ethnic groups in Irish society. An ethnic group is generally classified as a social group that forms a subgroup of a society who share in common a language, history, religion or culture. Culture is notoriously difficult to define yet one can say that it is a set of ideas and forms of behaviour that a group of people share in common. There are many ethnic and cultural groups within contemporary Ireland and the largest of Ireland's minority ethnic groups is the Travelling people. The final section of this chapter will take a test case by examining the spirituality and distinctive religious practices of the Travelling people, in order to appreciate how religious belief and practice is shaped by ethnicity and culture and to see how religious education in Irish primary schools can support and celebrate ethnic and cultural diversity. President Mary Mc Aleese, in her introduction to *Travellers Citizens of Ireland*, stressed that:

> It is important that each one of us embrace and promote understanding and respect for group diversity and that we all cherish rather than shun differences in culture, creed and tradition. Such an understanding helps to avoid the pitfall of focusing negatively on minorities as somehow not conforming to our personal or group norms – and

to recognise instead that all groups within society have their own unique characteristics, each adding its own colour, richness and distinctiveness to the mosaic that is the complex landscape of society. The Traveller Community have an especially rich cultural heritage which can only enhance and enrich our society.[104]

Indeed the rich cultural heritage of the Traveller Community has not always been appreciated in Ireland and Travellers have experienced a history of marginalisation[105] and discrimination.[106] This has lead to the 'social, cultural and economic exclusion' of Travellers from Irish society resulting in a type of 'secondary citizenship on the fringes of Irish society in an environment of both direct and indirect hostility'.[107] Michael McDonagh, a noted historian of the Travelling people, points to the many common misconceptions about the origin of the Traveller community in Irish society that result in a gross misunderstanding of their culture and distinctive ethnicity. For instance the notion that Travellers were previously settled people who became dispossessed of their land at the time of Cromwell or of the famine may hold currency in the popular Irish imagination, but it is erroneous on two counts. Firstly it involves a denial of the complex and ancient history of the Traveller people and secondly it involves an erroneous desire to resettle and re-house what is assumed to be this once displaced people called Travellers.

Around the time of the Poor Law Commission (1834), statistics show that there were more than three million people on the roadside in Ireland. Within that three million Travellers were easily identified because, unlike the people living on the

> roadside who were one generation and would
> move back to the land once they got the chance,
> Travellers on the roadside were more than one
> generation, (they were great-grannies and
> grandchildren) and would not, if given the choice,
> decide to live on the land.[108]

Mc Donagh traces the origin of the Traveller community, as a distinctive ethnic group, back to the 'tinkers' of the twelfth century where 'tinceard' meant 'tin craft', and further back into Celtic and pre-Celtic times. The origins of the Traveller community are complex and largely unknown, mainly because the history of the Travelling people has been handed on through an undocumented oral tradition, yet there is ample evidence to suggest that they form a distinct, ancient ethnic group in Irish society.[109] Travellers are a largely nomadic ethnic group with a distinct means of communication and language (Gammon, Cant or Shelta) and a shared sense of values (the importance of the family and of the community). Travellers also have a spirituality and set of religious practices which are individual to them.

> For Travellers, belonging to a distinct social group
> means that they (a) have a common ancestry, (b)
> share fundamental cultural values and traditions,
> (c) have a language of their own, and (d) are seen
> by themselves and others as distinct and
> different.[110]

Diversity of spiritual and religious practices can be found among Traveller groups in Ireland and not all Travellers are Catholic or nomadic.[111] Some Travellers have settled, and consider themselves to be Travellers even when not travelling.

Other Travellers have married into the settled community. The distinctive religious culture of the Traveller people, their religious ideas and practices, is particularly pertinent to all involved in primary religious education.

An innovative piece of qualitative research was recently undertaken by a research team which included four Traveller researchers who interviewed a group of second class primary school Traveller children about their attitudes to school. While the sample group upon which the research is based is small (three girls and six boys), and the research explicitly disavows any intention of representing the views of *all* Traveller children, the findings are nonetheless stark. The findings suggest that Traveller children have little or no confidence in their education, they perceive themselves as different to settled children and some feel marginalised by their seating arrangement (at the back or side) in the classroom. Children expressed the view that they would like to have more friends at school, that the school day was long and boring, and that their preference was for activity-based subjects.[112] The research unveiled that some Traveller parents were unhappy about what they perceived as the automatic withdrawal of Traveller children for learning support.[113] Children's attitudes to teachers are complex and this study revealed that while some of the children's attitudes were positive, many of their responses reflected 'a negative pupil-teacher relationship'. 'When talking negatively about the teachers the children tend to use rather uncompromising language "I hates them", "they hates me", "they're mongrels".'[114]

No one who reads the research could doubt the degree of alienation that some of the Traveller children experience in the learning environment. Interestingly, children appear to like 'religion' better than some other subject areas especially when it involves pupil-centred activities.[115] The overarching findings are that the school world is disconnected from the Traveller child's world. Therefore it is vital that religious educators know something of this world so that they can bridge this alienation by respecting and promoting Traveller culture and spirituality in the primary school classroom.[116] Winnie McDonagh reflects on her own childhood experience of being educated in a school where 'everyone knew you were a Traveller, but it was unspoken, something best left unsaid'.[117] In order to acknowledge and positively promote Traveller culture in religious education it is necessary to profile the religious beliefs and practices of the Traveller community in some detail.

The sacraments play a pivotal role in the birth, growth and development of Traveller spirituality and life.

> As with baptism, core to this sacrament (First Eucharist) is the belief that as we enter into a closer relationship with God, the relationship deepens from our perspective, we draw closer to God but we don't presume to know where God stands in relation to us. We believe that we are ever present to God and that the sacraments are means of our delving deeper into the grace of God already present in our human existence. Within the sacraments we acknowledge the presence of the grace of God in our lives. We believe that this is a very active and connected presence within all that human existence holds.[118]

The sacraments of Baptism, Eucharist and Confirmation are particularly significant in the lives of Traveller children. Baptism is celebrated as an occasion where the child receives divine strength and protection. 'It is unheard of not to have a child baptised.'[119] The baptismal shawl holds a particular significance in some Traveller families so that 'when the child is not well, you wrap up the baby in the shawl to give it strength'.[120] Eucharist is 'a huge family occasion with great preparation' with 'children becoming more aware of God's presence in their lives'.[121] Confirmation in particular is viewed as a landmark sacrament for children, 'an important transition in faith and life, a rite of passage and the beginning of a shift from childhood to adulthood.'[122] Its importance is reflected in the fact that in the past young boys often left primary school once they had received their confirmation but this practice is becoming less common today. The sacrament of marriage is greatly esteemed in the Traveller community and it is seen as the joining of two families, not just of two individuals.

> 'Getting married is an important step in our lives. Mostly we marry young, the age varies in different families. The custom of matchmaking has changed over the years. Now there are different ways the marriage can come about. Some families agree that match making is a good custom while others feel it is a custom of the past and do not agree with it.[123]

It is interesting to note that no ordained priest or nun in the Republic of Ireland comes from the Travelling community. This could be attributed to the fact that marriage, bearing children and family life in general are held in such sacred esteem by the Traveller people.[124]

Cathleen McDonagh states that the spirituality of the Traveller people incorporates a strong sense of the sinfulness of the individual as well as God's abiding presence in the 'experience of darkness'. The God of the Traveller people is a God of justice and she notes that 'at times in our experience the only place Travellers believe that they are sure of receiving justice is with God.'[125] Pilgrimage also plays a pivotal role in Traveller spirituality and culture and pilgrimage is usually undertaken for the benefit of others. The physical process of journeying to the place of pilgrimage, be it Croagh Patrick, Knock, Lourdes, or one of the many holy wells and shrines that punctuate the Irish landscape, is an outward physical manifestation of the inward prayer and faith journey of the believer. The concrete, physical, elemental aspect of prayer through contact with holy water, wells, relics or sacred places is a very visible and significant manifestation of a deep spirituality. The world is not by-passed in this spirituality but is embraced as a vital and tangible aspect of the person's relationship with God. The environment, the earth, the cycle of nature, become living manifestations of God's tangible and intimate presence. Very often a person will go on pilgrimage to the same place three times. There is a sense of sacredness and completeness in the number three which is a living embodiment of the relevance of the trinity, God as father, son and spirit, in Traveller spirituality.

God is not remote, inaccessible and indifferent. Travellers have an acute sense of the significance of blessings as manifestations of the presence of God in the ordinary and extraordinary events of life. The arrival of a new baby, the greeting of another person, the purchase of a new van, caravan or home are all, along with countless others unnamed here, occasions for blessings. One person stated 'A blessing for us is like the hand of Jesus caressing us.'[126] God's presence is also made manifest through special individuals who are gifted with the power of healing and who serve the community through effecting cures. Often a priest or holy person will gain a reputation for their capacity to heal and families will visit this person to receive the gift of healing.[127] Traditionally on 1 May,

Irish Travellers decorate a May bush with coloured ribbons to honour Jesus' mother.[128] Mary, the mother of God, holds a treasured and esteemed place in the heart of the Traveller people while individuals or families tend to develop a particular devotion to a favoured saint.

Travellers are not a homogenous group any more than settled people (who Travellers sometime refer to as 'Country people' or 'Buffers'[129]) can be defined as a uniform group and difference of belief as well as devotional practices can vary from family to family. Some Traveller families have great loyalty to Padre Pio while others pray to St Anthony or St Teresa. The image of Our Lady is very popular and many Travellers have her image or a picture or statue of the Sacred Heart in their caravans or homes.

Pivotal to the spirituality of the Traveller community is a sense of the universal and intimate presence of God in the concrete world. Cathleen McDonagh succinctly summarises the spirituality of the Traveller community by stating that 'God is father and mother, creator and judge, all is connected and nothing stands alone from God.'[130] This impacts on the death rituals of the Traveller people who view the dead as being perennially close so that 'there is a continuation between the living and the dead that survives the passing of time'.[131] In the film *Into the West* (1993) the death of a Traveller woman is ritualised by burning the trailer in which she lived.[132] While this practice is found among some families in the Traveller community, it would be untrue to say that it is widely practised. The religious rationale behind the burning of the trailer or caravan is unclear and may be manifold. The burning of some possessions and the trailer or caravan of the deceased person could be linked to the nomadic lifestyle where the death of a family member meant the existence of a vehicle surplus to requirements. It could also be interpreted as an outward ritualised social expression of grief and bereavement which resonates with the Hindu funeral pyre.[133] The burning of some possessions or trailers is not as common today as it was in the past although 'most families will sell the caravan because it brings back too many painful memories'.[134] Funerals, including the ninth day, a gathering at the grave nine days after burial to show respect, the month's mind or the blessing of the headstone one year after the person has died, are occasions where the family gather. It is important that the deceased person is buried in the traditional family place of burial. The extended family will often travel great distances to gather for the funeral of a family member. While graveyards are significant places for the Traveller community, Travellers do not want a site to be built next to the graveyard and they would not choose to settle next to one.

As a backdrop to these reflections on the death rituals of the Traveller people it is important to bear in mind the statistics relating to health and the life expectancy of Irish Travellers. Travellers have more than double the average rate of stillbirths, treble the average rate of infant mortality and Traveller women live, on average, twelve years less than settled women while Traveller men live, on average, ten years less than settled men.[135] Issues of discrimination, social justice and exclusion rise to the fore in any reflection upon the place of the Traveller community in Irish society.

Cultural and ethnic diversity in the primary school.

It is vital that teachers in Irish primary schools are aware of the religious beliefs and practices of minority religious and diverse cultural and ethnic groups so that children do not feel culturally dispossessed and alienated in school. The Traveller community has emphasised that:

> Our education has been and continues to be exclusive, reflecting mostly settled people's culture. It needs to be inclusive of other cultures like that of the Traveller community and those of other ethnic backgrounds.[136]

Racism arises from the twin evils of ignorance and prejudice. Just as it is important to appreciate the religious practices and beliefs of Traveller children, so too is it important to understand and appreciate the beliefs and practices of majority and minority religions and to appreciate diversity with regard to people of personal faith and to those who identify themselves as non-believers. If classrooms are not inclusive places where diversity of religion, ethnicity, culture and ability are celebrated then there will be huge casualties in the form of children who feel dispossessed by the educational system, disenfranchised by the society and discarded by the world.[137]

> As a Traveller, prejudice has walked with me on my path of life, as a child and into my adult life. Forced into my life has been the experience of fear and hurt and pain because of the ignorance of others. As a child I could not understand why this was so. As I grew, I discovered fear was at its core, a fear that in most cases comes from ignorance of my reality.[138]

Racism is a malignant cancer which contaminates the educational environment and destroys the individuals and communities it comes into contact with.

CONCLUDING REMARKS

Teachers occupy an influential and privileged position and have the capacity to bring about real change in the Irish educational system. Just as it behoves the primary teacher to educate children about religious diversity the teacher should also be open to acknowledging and promoting the spirituality and beliefs of diverse cultural and ethnic groups. Intercultural education challenges racism and discrimination and celebrates cultural diversity in a context where children learn to cherish their own culture while simultaneously valuing and respecting that of others.

This chapter has argued that diversity is not a peripheral issue in primary education and an appreciation of religious, cultural and ethnic diversity should be integrated into all subject areas, especially religious education. Effective teachers and learning environments are inclusive and egalitarian. Teachers in Catholic schools should be concerned with the central issue of respect for difference, they must challenge racism and discrimination and create an environment which cherishes each human person. Catholic schools have a duty to acknowledge, support and promote religious, cultural and ethnic diversity as well as diversity of school types.

NOTES

1   'I say to parents, teachers, school management and all involved in education that changes are inevitable and we must meet them, indeed lead them, or we will see our education system slide into mediocrity.' Minister Noel Dempsey TD, Minister for Education in *The Nation*, Winter 2003, p.43.

2   *Primary School Curriculum Introduction,* Dublin: Government Publications, 1999, p.9.

3   Equality legislation in Ireland deals with: Gender; Marital Status & Family Status; Sexual Orientation; Religious Belief; Age; Race; Disability; Traveller Community. Cf. Lodge, A. & Lynch, K. Eds., *Diversity at School*, Dublin: The Institute of Public Administration, 2004.

4   See Chapter 8 Gender and Religious Education.

5   cf. Irish Catholic Bishops Conference, *Life in all its fullness,* June 2003; also *It's my Church too! The inclusion of people with a disability in the life of the Church*, Dublin: Jubilee-AD 2000; *People with a Learning Disability: Bereavement & Loss,* Dublin: St John of God Hospitaller Services, 1999.

6   *Sacramental Preparation for Children with Special Educational Needs*, Glasgow City Council Educational Services, 2002. This series of lessons was created by staff from Kelbourne school, Kelvin school and Glasgow Archdiocesan R.E. Center. See also Diane Phillips RSJ, & Patricia Murdoch, *Old and New, A Time for Everything, Gifts Galore, R.E. Programme for School Aged Young People 6-18 Who Have An Intellectual Disability*, Brisbane Catholic Educational Service, 1994. Also Liz O'Brien, *Connecting with R.E.: R.E. and Faith Development for children with Autism and / or Severe and Complex Learning Disabilities*, London: Church House Publishing, 2002. See Martina Ní Cheallaigh's essay 'Towards inclusivity in Religious Education' in Raymond Topley & Gareth Byrne, *Nurturing Children's Religious Imagination*, Dublin: Veritas, 2004, pp.66-76.

7   See lion & lamb: Issue 36: Asylum Statistics also cf. Roland Tormey, *Teaching Social Justice*, Limerick CEDR, 2003, p.26.

8   Cf. Annual Statistics Office of the Office of Refugee Applications, Department of Justice Equality and Law Reform.

9   *Refugees and Asylum Seekers – A challenge to Solidarity*, Trócaire / The Irish Commission for Justice & Peace, 2002, p.10.

10   Tormey, *Teaching Social Justice*, p.26-7.

11   *Intercultural Education in the Primary School*, NCCA, 2005. Cf. *Sunday Tribune*, June 19, 2005.

12   Ed. Laura Chrisman & Patrick Williams, *Post-Colonial Discourse and Post-Colonial Theory*, Hemel Hempstead: Harvester Wheatsheaf, 1993, p.14.

13   Ed. Mark Storey, *Poetry and Ireland since 1800 – A Source Book*, London: Routledge, 1988, p.82.

14   Eds. Moody, Martin and Byrne, *The Course of Irish History*, Cork: Mercier Press, 1967, p.43.

15   Moody, Martin and Byrne, *The Course*, p.35.

16   See John McDonagh, *Narrating the Nation? Post-Colonial Perspectives on Patrick Kavanagh's The Great Hunger (1942) and Brendan Kennelly's Cromwell (1983)*, Unpublished Ph.D., Warwick University, 1998, p.49.

17   Mícheál Kilcrann does refer to the 'indigenous Irish' and the 'new Irish' in an essay 'Welcoming the 'New Irish', Celebrating Diversity in the Irish Catholic Primary School', Topley & Byrne, *Nurturing*, p.77. The categories of new, old and indigenous are value-laden and problematic. The category of 'New Irish' arose

from a series of articles (May 9-19, 2004) on newcomers to Ireland in *The Irish Times*.

18   George Bernard Shaw, *John Bull's Other Island*, London: Constable, 1911.

19   R.F. Foster, *Paddy and Mr Punch*, Allen Lane, 1993, pp.21-39.

20   Foster, *Paddy and Mr Punch*, p.26.

21   ibid.

22   ibid., p.38.

23   Roland Tormey et al., *Stories from Eiriu's Island*, Limerick: Curriculum Development Unit, Mary Immaculate College, 2003, pp.3-10.

24   Cf. Patrick M. Devitt, *That You May Believe*, Dublin: Dominican Publications, 1992, p.89. For a selection of bilingual and beautifully illustrated intercultural children's books cf. Jill Paton Walsh, *Babylon*, London: Beaver Books, 1985. Bilingual books cf. Brian Wildsmith, *The Tunnel*, Oxford University Press, 1999 (English-French book). For an English Urdu book see *Topiwalo The Hat Maker*, London: David Brin Ltd, 1986. For a celebration of difference see Ann Grifalconi, *The Village of Round and Square Houses*, London: Macmillan, 1995. Kristina Rodanas, *Dance of the Sacred Circle A Native American Tale*, MA: Little, Brown & Co., 1994. Eric Maddern, *The Fire Children – A West African Folk Tale*, London: Frances Lincoln, 1993.

25   Michael O'Reilly, Sheila Nunan, Pat Brady, Brendan Hyland, *Celebrating difference: an intercultural programme for Senior Primary Classes*, Crosscare: the Catholic Social Service Conference, 1995. For a 2005 revised and online version of the entire programme cf. www.crosscare.ie/celebratingdifference/poster1.htm accessed 26/6/05.

26   Catholicism's percentage share of the Irish population was 88.4% in 2002.

27   Robert Jackson, *Rethinking Religious Education and Plurality Issues in diversity and pedagogy*, USA: Routledge Falmer, 2004, p.8.

28   See Maura Boyle Mc Nally, 'What Can the Spirituality of the Celts Contribute to Spirituality Today?' in Topley, *Nurturing*, p.216-233. Also D. Ó hÓgáin, *The Sacred Isle: Belief and Religion in Pre-Christian Ireland*, Cork: Collins Press, 1999, p.2.

29   Maurice Ryan, *Another Ireland*, Stranmillis College: The Learning Resources Unit, 1996, p.1.

30   It must be remembered that the 1881 census figures are for the 32
        counties.

31   Paul O'Brien *Irish Examiner*, Friday, April 9, 2004.

32   This information is contained in *Census 2002, Volume 12 – Religion*,
        which gives further detailed results of the census conducted on 28
        April 2002.

33   Press Statement, Central Statistics Office, April 8th, 2004.

34   Jackson, *Rethinking Religious Education*, p.12f.

35   Oliver Brennan, *Cultures Apart? The Catholic Church and
        Contemporary Irish Youth*, Dublin: Veritas, 2001, p.163.

36   cf. Anne Lodge 'Denial, tolerance or recognition of difference?
        The experiences of minority belief parents in the
        denominational primary system' in Jim Deegan, Dympna
        Devine & Anne Lodge Eds., *Primary Voices Equality, Diversity and
        Childhood in Irish Primary Schools*, Dublin: Institute of Public
        Administration, 2004, p.22, fn.8. Lodge finds the term non-
        believer disrespectful of the personal spirituality and values
        system of those who do not adhere to an institutionalized belief
        system.

37   *Teaching Religion in the Primary School Issues and Challenges*, Dublin:
        INTO, 2003, p.47.

38   Jackson, *Rethinking Religious Education*, p.12.

39   Michael Paul Gallagher, *Clashing Symbols An Introduction to Faith
        and Culture*, Darton Longman & Todd, 1999, p.92.

40   Brennan, *Cultures Apart?*, p.163.

41   Keith Ward, 'The search for truth and respect for diversity',
        REtoday, Vol.21, No.3, Summer 2004, p.26.

42   Dermot Lane, *The Irish Times*, 22 January, 2002.

43   Ryan, *Another Ireland*, p.ix.

44   86.1% of teachers surveyed support teaching children in primary
        schools about other religions.

45   See Kevin O'Grady 'Dialogue in Secondary Religious Education'
        in *Resource The Journal of the Professional Council for Religious
        Education*, Vol. 27:2, Spring, 2005, p.11. O'Grady provides a brief
        account of the work of Julia Ipgrave.

46   Cf. A Note on Cultural Background *Alive-O 7 Teacher's Book*,
        Dublin: Veritas, 2003, p.6.

47   *Primary School Curriculum History*, Dublin: Government
        Publications, 1999, p.44.

48   *Primary School Curriculum Geography,* Dublin: Government Publications, *1999,* p.54.

49   *Primary School Curriculum Geography,* p.56.

50   cf. *Alive-O 5 Teacher's Book,* Dublin: Veritas, 2001, p.7.

51   The *Documents of Vatican II, Nostra Aetate* , Par. 5. Henceforth N.A.

52   Mícheál Kilcrann, Welcoming the 'New Irish', Topley & Byrne, *Nurturing,* p.86ff.

53   *Alive-O 5,* Video, Unit 6: We relate to God, segment 1 & 2. The leaflet which accompanies the video includes a series of questions which the teacher might ask but these are by no means comprehensive. The wisdom of simultaneously introducing children to two world Faiths without giving teachers any detailed guidelines must also be questioned.

54   Michael Barnes, *Walking the City,* SPCK, 1999, p.xiff.

55   N.A.,Par. 2.

56   See Patricia Kieran, 'Promoting Truth? Inter-faith education in Irish Catholic Primary Schools', in *Teaching Religion,* 2003, pp.119-130.

57   Elizabeth Hughes, *Religious Education in the Primary School Managing Diversity,* Cassell, 1994, p.93. cf. James Nelson, Uniformity and diversity in religious education in Northern Ireland, *British Journal of Religious Education,* Vol. 26, No. 3, September 2004, p.249-258. Nelson's work looks mainly at the post-primary school context.

58   *Dominus Iesus,* 6 August 2000, par. 4.

59   ibid. par. 6.

60   Ibid. par. 22.

61   *Evangelii Nuntiandi,* pars 52, 53. Henceforth EN.

62   Brennan, *Cultures Apart?,* p.163. cf. p.50f.

63   Brennan, *Cultures Apart?,* p.164.

64   Archbishop Diarmuid Martin, Inauguration of Crosscare Website and Celebrating Difference, St. Patrick's College, 17 June 2005.

65   The Irish Catholic Bishops' Conference, *Towards a Policy on RE in Post-Primary Schools,* Veritas, 2003.

66   In the UK children learn thematically and experientially about Christianity and one of the following religions: Buddhism, Hinduism, Islam, Judaism and Sikhism at Reception and Key Stage 1. cf. *Living Faiths: Today's Model Syllabuses for religious education, Key Stages 1-4,* School Curriculum and Assessment Authority, London, 1994.

67 *Junior Certificate Religious Education Syllabus* (Ordinary and Higher level) 2000 Department of Education and Science, Section C Foundations of Religion – Major World Faiths, pp. 20-25.

68 Intercultural Education in the Primary School, NCCA, 2005.

69 To see an example of children's work on Sikhism in a Dublin (Educate Together) primary school visit the website http://www.iol.ie/~ndnsp/beliefs/sikh2.htm. One must always be mindful of taking extreme care when using the internet with children (see the FBI guidelines www.familyfriendlysites.com /FamilyFriendly/viewcat_ws.asp?ID=241). Also use a children's search engine such as Yahooligans.

70 For instance the Intercultural Calendar 2005 which is provided by Access Ireland, The Refugee Social Integration Project, or Rafiki Trocaire's interactive CD-Rom for Irish children.

71 John Paul II, *Catechesi Tradendae*, 1979, par. 34. Henceforth C.T.

72 Maruice Ryan and Patricia Malone *Exploring the Religion Classroom*, Australia: Social Science Press, 2000, p.119f. shows how Edward De Bono's six thinking hats can be used to cater for children's multiple intelligneces in religious education.

73 *Primary School Curriculum Teacher's Handbook,* Part 1, p.23.

74 cf. Vitcor Griffin *Enough Religion to make us hate*, The Columba Press, 2002, p.21, 37, 48-9.

75 Padraig Hogan, Religion in Education and the Integrity of Teaching as a Practice, *Teaching Religion*, p.67.

76 *Primary School Curriculum Introduction*, p.58.

77 See Ralph Gower, *R.E. at the Primary Stage,* Lion, 1990, pp.34-41.

78 *Primary School Curriculum Introduction*, p.58.

79 ibid. p.9.

80 ibid.

81 Cf,. Desmond O'Donnell, 'Young Educated Adults: A Survey' *Doctrine and Life*, January 2002. O'Donnell quotes a special edition of *Newsweek*, Issues 2001 which says that 'Modern Europe is a post-religious society. More accurately, what was once the heartland of Christendom is a post-Christian society.', p.4.

82 Latest figures from the DES show that in 2003-4 the breakdown of schools was: Catholic 2,912; Church of Ireland 182; Presbyterian 14; Methodist 1; Jewish 1; Inter-denominational 4; Muslim 2; Multi-denominational 33; Other 1.

83   *Teaching Religion in the Primary School*, p.47. cf. p.51. In reality only 0.3% of survey respondents actually opted out of teaching religion whereas 5.7% would prefer if they didn't have to give religious instruction/education; 3.0% would like to have the option of opting out of teaching religion and 2.0% would like to opt out of teaching religion. It must be noted that 61.2% of respondents teach RE willingly.

84   In 2001-2 the Multi-denominational sector accounted for 24 schools. In 2002-3 it had risen to 30 schools. In 2003-4 this figure rose to 33. Source: DES.

85   *Irish Examiner*, April 9 2004, quoted from Juno Mc Enroe's article 'Educate Together slam State's stance on schools'.

86   ibid.

87   No new Catholic or Church of Ireland Schools opened in the 2002-3 academic year as multi-denominational schools and gaelscoileanna become more popular. Cf. Emmet Oliver, *The Irish Times* August 24 2002.

88   A confessional approach has predominated in Irish primary schools where historically primary education has been denominationally arranged. The DES "in the context of the Education Act (1998), recognises the rights of the different church authorities to design curricula in religious education at primary level and to supervise their teaching and implementation." Thus, the responsibility of curriculum in the primary school lies with the various Church authorities.

89   Educate Together Email Newsletter, Vol.2 No. 4 - September 2 2002. Henceforth ETEN.

90   *Learn Together*, Educate Together, 2004, p.9.

91   ETEN Vol. 2. No. 4., September 2 2002.

92   *Shadow Report by Educate Together on The First National Report to the United Nations Committee on the Convention on the Elimination of all Forms of Racial Discrimination by Ireland*, January 2005, p. 3-4.

93   Desmond M. Clarke, *Church and State: Essays in Political Philosophy*, Cork University Press, 1984.

94   *The Irish Times*, October 12 2004.

95   Dick Spicer & Ellen Sides, *The Humanist Philosophy*, Humanist Publishers, 1996, p.58.

96   Deegan, *Primary Voices*, p.32.

97   Lodge in Deegan, *Primary Voices*, p.22, fn. 8.

98   See Chapter 6 on Religious Belief especially section 6.4 on 'Harassment' in Lodge, A & Lynch, K., *Diversity at School*, Dublin: Institute of Public Administration, 2004.

99   Lodge, Primary Voices, p.32.

100   ETEN. Vol. 5 No. 9 – June 8 2005.

101   Speech by Colm O Cuanacháin, Secretary General Amnesty International Ireland, Launch of *What is an Educate Together School?*, April 20 2005.

102   cf. Education Act, 1998. The objects of the act are Section 6 (c) 'to promote equality of access to and participation in education..' and Section 6 (e) 'to promote the right of parents to send their children to a school of the parents' choice'... The Minister must Section 7 (a) 'ensure that ... there is made available to each person resident in the State, including a person with a disability or who has other special educational needs, support services and a level and quality of education appropriate to meeting the needs and abilities of that person.'

103   Lodge, A & Lynch, K., *Diversity at School*, p.52.

104   Ed. Erica Sheehan, *Travellers Citizens of Ireland*, The Parish of the Travelling People, 2000, p. 8f.

105   Eleanor Gormally, *Whiddin to the Gauras – Talking to Our Own*, Veritas, 2005, p.24ff.

106   Sheehan, *Travellers Citizens*, p.27.

107   *different ... but equal A study of the unmet needs of Travellers in Limerick city and environs*, Limerick Travellers Development Group, Treaty Press, 1997, p.11.

108   Sheehan, *Travellers Citizens*, p.23.

109   McDonagh points to the similarity between pre-13th century old Irish and Shelta or Gammon or Cant, the Traveller language as well as the 'landless people' mentioned in the *Tain Bo Cooley* as examples of the ancient origins of the Traveller people. Cf. Sheehan, *Travellers Citizens*, p.24-5.

110   *Guidelines on Traveller Education in Primary Schools*, Department of Education and Science, 2002, p.7.

111   Winnie Mc Donagh states that 'most young Travellers today haven't traveled, they haven't lived as nomadic a life as their parents or grandparents have.' Cf. 'Travellers and education: a personal perspective' in Deegan, *Primary Voices*, p.98.

112   Gormally, *Whiddin*, p.86, p.103.

113   Gormally, *Whiddin*, p.104, p.93.

114   Gormally, *Whiddin*, p.106. Winnie McDonagh recounts an incident which highlights the impact of negative teacher attitudes on Traveller children. 'I know of a teacher who during Confirmation preparations handed back a Traveller girl her baptismal certificate, with the words that 'you will be needing this soon as you will be getting married soon.' This particular girl liked school and was a good student who intended to go on to secondary school. In this instance she was challenged by the prejudice she had experienced.' Winnie McDonagh, in Deegan, *Primary Voices*, p.104.

115   ibid. p.89f., p. 104.

116   See Crosscare's website http://www.crosscare.ie/celebratingdifference/poster1.htm accessed 26/6/05.

117   Winnie McDonagh, Deegan, *Primary Voices*, p.95.

118   Cathleen McDonagh, Sheehan, *Travellers Citizens*, p.73.

119   cf. *Wrapped in the Mantle of God*, Teamworkers Project 92, Christenings.

120   Frank Murphy & Dan O'Connell, *The Light Within*, The Parish of the Travelling People, Dublin, 2000, p.8.

121   Murphy & O'Connell, *The Light Within*, p.9.

122   ibid. cf. Winnie Mc Donagh, Deegan, *Primary Voices*, p.100.

123   ibid., p.10.

124   Gormally, *Whiddin*, p.72f., p.125.

125   Sheehan, *Travellers Citizens*, p.74.

126   cf. *Wrapped in the Mantle*, Blessings.

127   One such instance was Fr McDonagh, a Salesian Priest at Warrenstown College, Co. Meath, who had a special ministry of healing. After his death in 1975 many Travellers went on pilgrimage to his grave and attributed cures to his healing ministry.

128   cf. Intercultural Calender 2005, Access Ireland Refugee Social Integration Project.

129   Gormally, *Whiddin*, p.112f.

130   Sheehan, *Travellers Citizens*, p.79.

131   ibid. p.77.

132   The Parish of the Travelling People in Dublin has produced a 35 minute video on the religious rituals and spirituality of the Travelling People called *The Light Within*.

133   In the sacred Hindu creation pyre, the ritual burning liberates the soul (Atman) from the body.

134   Murphy & O'Connell, *The Light Within*, p.23.
135   *Guidelines on Traveller Education*, p.10. cf. Murphy & O'Connell *The Light Within*, p.22.
136   ibid., p.21.
137   See Henry Michael Canning, *A Critical Investigation into whether Information and Communication Technology can improve Traveller' self-esteem and promote fuller participation in learning and education*, M.Ed. Dissertation, MIC, 2000.
138   Murphy & O'Connell, *The Light Within*, p.20.

CHAPTER EIGHT

Gender and Religious Education in the Primary Classroom

• •

INTRODUCTION

In an environment where issues of equality and gender are acutely important[1] the Catholic Church has been accused not alone of legitimising gender inequality, but of sacramentalising it by saying that it is divinely ordained. If this is true, then it is hugely problematic for religious educators committed to educating children in an inclusive, egalitarian understanding of the Catholic faith. Factors which mitigate against gender equity in the Catholic tradition include: a male-centred religious and theological tradition where women are largely invisible and silent; a sacramental system with six sacraments potentially available for females and seven sacraments potentially available for males, and an almost exclusive dependence on male or what is known as 'God-he' religious language and imagery. However, issues of religious language (whether we refer to God as she or he) and ordination (ordained female/male priesthood) may capture the popular imagination, but they only represent a tiny fraction of the debate surrounding gender and religion.

Every area within the Christian religious tradition, its scriptures, doctrines, philosophy, sacraments, morality, liturgy, spirituality and pedagogy, has been critiqued and challenged by

16

feminist theorists. Religious educators should not simply note these debates; they must actively ensure that religious education does not contribute to marginalisation or domination on the basis of gender. Susan Ross sees that 'the process of faith formation in children is complicated by a tradition in which girls and boys see themselves differently in relation to their tradition and in relation to God'.[2] Religious educators must appreciate how gender impacts on children's self perceptions and their view of God for 'there can be no doubt that current difficulties with bringing up boys and girls in the Christian faith calls for a careful analysis of the situation and for new approaches.'[3]

Gender Theory and Religion.

Gender is a social construct that is related to but separable from sex. All human experience is influenced by gender. Whereas biology determines sex, culture determines gender. Gender theorists argue that traits associated with femininity and masculinity are learned and not inborn. While one's sex is biologically based (human beings are born as females or males[4]) one's gender is socially constructed. Gender refers to social expectations, power relationships, and cultural-linguistic constructions associated with the female and male sex. In many Western societies once the sex of the child is established in the labour ward, gender comes into immediate effect through the provision of pink clothes for a girl, blue clothes for a boy, with the accompanying expectation that the child will behave appropriately as a 'girl' or a 'boy'.[5] A trip to a toyshop provides immediate visual evidence of the exaggerated stereotypical gender conditioning exercised by toys such as 'Tiny Tears' and 'Action Man'. While these toys are almost bi-polar caricatures of female and male gender it is interesting to note that they co-exist in a complex modern Western society that simultaneously emphasises an inclusive 'unisex' culture.

Gender theory deconstructs and questions all assumptions and stereotypes concerning gender and sex. It argues that the bi-polar categorisation of male or female, masculine or feminine, heterosexual or homosexual are subject to radical questioning. Michael Ryan has argued that 'normatively heterosexual men are masculine and normatively heterosexual women feminine because the reigning cultural discourses instruct them in behaviour appropriate to the dominant gender representations and norms, while stigmatising non-normative behaviour'.[6] Gender theory questions the assumption that the female baby will grow up to be a heterosexual feminine adult, and the male baby will grow up to be a heterosexual masculine adult. A host of cultural enforcement procedures privilege certain traits while denigrating others. Popular gender role stereotypes present the man as 'the one who enjoys sex, is ambitious in his career, knows how to use a drill, can read a map, and has difficulty expressing his emotion. The woman is the one who wears cosmetics, loves shopping, wants to get married, has a very loudly ticking biological clock and works just to get out of the house'.[7] The cultural assumptions that females will generally have good interpersonal skills, be unafraid to express their emotions, and that males are generally more independent and less able to express emotion in public, is perceived by gender theorists as a self-fulfilling social construction.[8] If females are rewarded for exhibiting emotion they will tend to replicate that action. If men who cry in public are seen as wimps, they will tend to eliminate that action. Recent research tends to posit the opinion that males and females share huge areas of commonality.[9] Gender theorists challenge interpretations of the innate emotional nature of femininity and of masculinity's innate emotional retentiveness.

To date, Gender studies has mainly focused on women because women's experience of acute marginalisation and discrimination has caused them to acknowledge and challenge gender discrimination. More recently Men's Studies, which explores male genderedness, has contributed to the debate by focusing on men's experience and simultaneously on a more inclusive analysis of gender relations between men and women. Gay and Lesbian as well as Queer Theory questions the notion that one is either male or female, masculine or feminine, heterosexual or homosexual and that there are appropriate ways for males or females to behave. Theorists see a continuum of possibilities between these fluid categories including male-feminine-heterosexual or female-masculine-homosexual. Some gender theorists look to biology or neurology to provide an understanding of gender while others look to sociology and psychology to explain why women and men behave, think and act in particular ways. For example, neurological research has emphasised that women have stronger left hemisphere brains than males while males have stronger right hemisphere brains. While it is blatantly obvious that female and male biology differs,[10] it would be ironic if Gender studies, which challenges gender based stereotyping, used biology or neurology to simply exchange new stereotypes for old. Sandra Lipsitz Bem in a book called *Toward Utopia* imagines a society 'wherein the biology of sex might be considered as one of minimal presence in human social life, important only in the narrowly biological context of reproduction.'[11]

Contemporary research emphasises the changing nature of genderised roles. A recent study shows that men do more cooking than women, are doing almost twice as much housework as they did in 1961, and their 'unpaid chores include taking children to school, cleaning, household repairs and administration'. Professor Jonathan Gershuny speaks of women and men 'converging' in the way they spend their time.[12] In the Western world, changing gender roles for males has resulted in masculinity undergoing an identity crisis and Men's Studies explores the causes, contours and consequences of this crisis. While feminism empowered women to speak of their marginalisation and to work to eradicate it, it simultaneously critiqued masculinity as oppressive and abusive. The consequent impact of this critique has left many attempting to liberate maleness from an understanding that sees it as automatically oppressive and discriminatory.

Once one perceives gender as a fluid social construct which is historically and culturally conditioned, one begins to appreciate the importance of socialisation in all areas of life, and especially in religion. Socialisation is a process whereby role models provide women and men with acceptable versions of the 'feminine' or 'masculine' as well as legitimate female or male aspirations. Religion is a powerful tool of socialisation and has the capacity to allocate fixed, value laden, non-transferrable and separate roles to females and males. Within the official Catholic Church a female is socialised into desiring not to become an ordained priest. One could argue that falling numbers for male ordination illustrates that males are now similarly socialised. The difference is that for men who choose it, ordination is generally considered an acceptable and legitimate option. Gender theory sees that while theological reasons are given for the exclusion of women from the priesthood (e.g., Jesus was male, Jesus' disciples were male, no basis in scripture and tradition),[13] what is operative here is a gender construction which should be critiqued and challenged.

It must be noted that gender does not exist in isolation from other factors that shape social and personal identity including class, race, sexual preference, ethnicity, and culture. Any analysis of gender must also take into consideration these powerful and all pervasive categories. Neo-Marxist and post-colonial critics such as Gayatri Chakravorty Spivak[14] have argued that perhaps the greatest form of discrimination occurs on the grounds of class and not gender. Spivak points to the collusion between the native male and female upper middle classes and the colonising forces to the exclusion of indigenous lower class male and female groupings. One of the unexpected consequences of this collusion resulted in the empowerment of relatively small groups of women within a largely patriarchal system. In the colonial system some white Western middle-class women were also involved in the oppression of black colonised men and women. Therefore, the nomenclature of oppressor becomes increasingly problematic and ambivalent when applied exclusively to men.

Men and Patriarchy

Anthony Clare, a psychiatrist broadcaster and writer, explores the causes and consequences of the contemporary crisis of male identity in the Western world. Clare reveals that in his own life although nobody ever explicitly addressed what it meant to be a man, a son, a brother, a lover, a father, he nonetheless learned by a kind of 'osmotic' process that his work as a man was more important than who he was. In contemporary society, Clare argues, a man is defined in terms of doing, not being. If male identity is dependent on occupation then any change of employment pattern results in a potential identity crisis. In the nineteen nineties Clare observed lonely, confused middle aged male clients increasingly requesting his services as a psychiatrist because they were in crisis as a consequence of retirement or their children growing up or their wives being busily occupied with their own careers. Clare states 'it is the women who now play the golf, who have jobs and friends at work. It is the men who cower in the empty nest, nervously facing what an eloquent Irish businessman friend has termed 'the forgotten future'.[15] The real impact of Clare's intimate writing comes from the fact that he is not just describing a crisis he observes in his patients. He simultaneously explores his own identity crisis as a male. He confesses that 'as a young father, I shouted at my children in order to feel powerful, and covertly and sometimes overtly declared that manly boys didn't complain but had to be strong and responsible and suppress vulnerability, particularly if they were to avoid being bullied by other boys.'[16] Now Clare questions his own adequacy as a father and as a man and sees that his own questioning and uncertainty is part of a much larger cultural crisis for masculinity, which he describes as the dying phallus:

> Now, the whole issue of men – the point of them, their purpose, and their value, their justification – is a matter for public debate. Serious commentators declare that men are redundant, that women do not need them and children would be better off without them. At the beginning of the twenty-first century it is difficult to avoid the conclusion that men are in serious trouble. Throughout the world, developed and developing, antisocial behaviour is essentially male. Violence, sexual abuse of children, illicit drug use, alcohol misuse, gambling all are overwhelmingly male activities. The courts and prisons bulge with men. When it comes to aggression, delinquent behaviour, risk taking and social mayhem, men win gold.[17]

Clare provides chilling statistics of the male suicide rate outnumbers female suicides by a factor of between three and four to one in North America, Europe and Australia. He identifies the fact that, throughout Europe, girls are outperforming boys in schools, at college and at Universities and notes that many men are afraid to put a foot wrong for fear of being charged with being sexist. Of course Clare's thesis needs to be critiqued and contextualised. While he is not writing a 'decline and fall' history which laments the passing of patriarchy he does raise the question of the impact which patriarchy has upon masculinity. Furthermore he raises the question of the impact of the empowerment of women as well as changing gender roles upon men. Clare avoids the facile conclusion that women are responsible for men's crisis. However he hints at the interrelationship between women's confidence in taking up new gender roles and men's fears of relinquishing old ones. There is no doubt that he writes movingly and sensitively about masculinity and provides much data to support the premise that, whatever the causes, contemporary men are indeed undergoing a multi-faceted crisis.

Feminism

Sandra Cullen notes that Men's Studies has not 'yet begun to critically examine the influence of religion on masculine gender construction'.[18] The same cannot be said of feminism, which has generated a large body of research on the relationship between religion and gender. Feminism is an umbrella term that describes a complex movement that seeks to critique and confront the devaluation of women in all aspects of life, to eliminate sexism, and to generate an egalitarian society. The systematic devaluation of women on the basis of their perceived inferiority is termed misogyny. The word misogyny is a composite word that comes from the Greek term *'misein'* to hate and *'gyne'* meaning woman.[19] Misogyny portrays women as intellectually inferior (icon of dumb blond), emotionally unstable (the word hysterical comes from the Greek word for womb '*hystera*')[20] and physically weak (fit for *Kuche, Kinder, Kirche*).[21] Feminism challenges all forms of misogyny and advocates women's rights to full citizenship and equality in all spheres.[22] There are many different types of feminism and it is important to note that while all women are not feminists, not all feminists are women.

Feminism has made a huge impact on the discipline of theology. Alistair McGrath notes that feminist theology is a 'major movement in western theology since the 1960s which lays particular emphasis upon the importance of women's experience and has directed criticism against the patriarchalism of Christianity.'[23] McGrath's definition could be refined on two counts. Firstly, feminist theology is by no means an exclusively Western phenomenon. Black Womanist theology, Asian feminist theology and Hispanic and Latino feminist theology are just some of the feminist theologies that can be found in the world's continents. Secondly, feminist theology has a long history that pre-exists McGrath's nineteen sixty date. The roots of feminist theology go back hundreds of years. Mary Wollstonecraft's *A Vindication of the Rights of Women* (1792) is generally seen as one of the founding texts of modern feminism. Less well known is the work of one of her American contemporaries, the Black American evangelical preacher Sojourner Truth (1797-1883), who argued for freedom from the twin evils of slavery and gender oppression. In the nineteenth century Elizabeth Cady Stanton's (1815-1902) pioneering work in advocating women's civil and religious rights culminated in her edition of *The Woman's Bible* (1895).[24] Stanton argued that the degrading ideas about women in the bible were not divinely inspired and that the bible must be analysed and assessed in terms of its male bias. More recently feminist writers have looked beyond the bible and reclaimed women's invisibility by documenting their role in the early Church, as well as their contribution to theological thought in the medieval, reformation, modern and post-modern periods.

There are different stages and types of Christian feminism and it is important to take note of these before engaging in any exploration of important themes to emerge from feminist scholarship on religion and gender. In the first half of the twentieth century much mainstream theological thinking was carried on from a pre-feminist perspective (unaware of its male-centred bias) or a soft feminist perspective (suggested that women have divinely ordained distinct roles as wife or mother). Critical feminist research which acknowledges, challenges and works to eradicate patriarchy, began to enter mainstream theological discourse from the late nineteen sixties onwards. While feminist theology was originally seen as a marginal area of specialist research of relevance only to women, it is now widely accepted as relevant to all aspects of theology. Radical feminist theologians emphasise the Christian tradition's marginalisation and abuse of women, while Post-Christian feminists reject Christianity as irretrievably sexist. Post-modern feminists acknowledge that 'woman' is not a universal, unitary, unproblematic term. They argue that concern about equality is not simply the preserve of feminists but of mainstream culture and so they see feminism as being superseded by less oppositional and more inclusive understandings of male and female. In this sense, one can speak of a Post-feminist movement where feminism has been overtaken by a more inclusive and universal concern with male and female genderness and the use and abuse of power by males and females. Post-modern feminism, neo-Marxist and post-colonial theorists all explore how women themselves are not necessarily exempt from the abusive use of power as a consequence of their privileged race, class, age, sexual orientation and geographical location.

Religious Tradition and Patriarchy

Patriarchy can be defined as the view that the male perspective is normative (use of term mankind/ God-he language), legitimate (Freud's notion that women suffer from penis envy)[25] and superior (male-only priesthood). The exclusive use of male imagery for God or the view that women are incapable of representing God in the way that males can, are seen as typical manifestations of patriarchy. Even the word for theology, derived as it is from the Greek masculine word for god *'theos'*, as opposed to the feminine word for god *'theas'*, marks theological activity as male-centred.[26] Traditionally, theology involved males reflecting upon a male God. The history of theology bears witness to this fact and so we speak of the 'Patristics' or 'Fathers of the Church' whose work is the bedrock upon which subsequent theological reflection was built. Medieval theological reflection took place in the 'school' (university) and involved 'schoolmen' or scholars like Thomas Aquinas (1225-1274) or Duns Scotus (1270-1308) seeking to understand faith in a way that did not take account of women's experiences and ideas.[27] Up until the late twentieth century the vast majority of theological thinking was done by men and while most people might have heard of male theologians like Augustine, Aquinas, Karl Barth, Karl Rahner and Hans Kung, relatively few know of any female theologians such as Frances Young, Mary Grey and Rosemary Radford Ruether. In a patriarchal society one did not even begin to question the possibility of women doing *thealogy*. This situation is not unique to theology and prior to the twentieth century other academic disciplines witnessed the systematic exclusion of women from most areas of scholarship.[28] One has only to look at the preponderance of female writers using male pseudonyms, or female artists and composers having their work presented by male artists and composers to realise how women were obliterated from formal participation in a myriad of cultural, academic and social activities.[29] Patriarchy did not result in the exclusive abuse of females; it also had a negative impact upon men. The German philosopher G.W. Hegel's (1770-1831) reflections on the 'Master-Slave' relationship may help to analyse the impact which patriarchy had on men as well as women.[30] Hegel recognised that the master's exploitative, illegitimate use of power over the slave did not only result in the dehumanisation and diminishment of the slave but also in the concomitant dehumanisation and diminishment of himself. The struggle for domination and suppression is internalised by the master who is not untouched by his own abuse of another. Treating the slave as less simultaneously involves self-abuse by treating the self as more. Patriarchy not only diminished females by treating them as less, it also diminished the male who was incorrectly perceived as a dominant superior.

Scriptures

Many feminist scripture scholars acknowledge the prevalence of patriarchal texts in the bible yet they also emphasise that the bible is a complex, potentially empowering and liberative text. Elisabeth Schussler-Fiorenza sees the bible as 'a cacophony of interested historical voices and a field of rhetorical struggles in which questions of truth and meaning are being negotiated.'[31] The bible is neither totally patriarchal nor totally egalitarian. It is simultaneously a source of suffering and empowerment for women and men. Many feminist scripture scholars investigate biblical texts critically, acknowledge the presence of patriarchy, but also find in the scriptures a source of nourishment for those who are oppressed and seeking liberation. Schüssler-Fiorenza investigates scripture texts critically before re-visioning the scriptures for an ethic that nurtures the oppressed. For Schüssler-Fiorenza the scriptures, which contain patriarchal texts, are also a source of liberative nourishment for women and other marginalised groups. As part of this re-visioning of scripture texts, feminist scholars have focused on powerful biblical women (Mk.14:3, a woman anoints Jesus), who shatter domestic stereotypes (Lk.10:38, Mary), who recognise Jesus' messiahship (Jn. 4:11), witness the resurrection (Lk.24:49, 55, 25:10) and teach in the Church (Acts 16:4, Llydia).

Phyllis Trible speaks of a three-stage approach to biblical texts. Stage one involves documenting discriminatory texts. Stage two involves discovering and recovering women who counter patriarchal culture. Stage three involves retelling the biblical stories of abused women sympathetically and creatively in order to lead to liberation. Trible's first stage is embodied by feminist scholarship which concentrates on emphasising the abuses which Christianity and other patriarchal religious traditions perpetuated against women.[32] She explores some of the issues which feminists first focused on when they began to study the bible:

> Less desirable in the eyes of her parents than a male child, a girl stayed close to her mother, but her father controlled her life until he relinquished her to another man for marriage. If either of these male authorities permitted her to be mistreated, even abused, she had to submit without recourse. Thus, Lot offered his daughters to the men of Sodom to protect a male guest (Gen.19:8); Jephthah sacrificed his daughter to remain faithful to a foolish vow (Judg. 11.29-40); Amnon raped his half-sister Tamar (2 Sam. 13); and the Levite from

> the hill country of Ephraim participated with other males to bring about the betrayal, rape, murder and dismemberment of his own concubine (Judg. 19).[33]

Trible rightly names these narratives 'texts of terror'.[34] These terrifying accounts create a consciousness of the radical inequality between biblical men and women. Feminist scholarship focuses on the fact that in the Hebrew Scriptures women were defined as the male's property (Ex. 20. 17; Deut. 5:21), a female slave was worth half the monetary value of a male slave (Lev.27.1-7) and a woman was far more unclean than a male (Lev. 15).

In the creation accounts of Genesis, the first account (Genesis 1) is relatively egalitarian and tells of God's simultaneous creation of the male and female (Gn.1:28) who share joint stewardship over the earth. However, the second creation account (Genesis 2) portrays the creation of the male as prior to that of the female. The female is given helper and partner status only because of the male's dissatisfaction with the animal kingdom. The female is named by Adam who, in an inversion of the actual birthing order, painlessly gives birth to her. Genesis tells us 'woman is her name because she was taken out of man' (Gn.2:23). In Genesis 3 woman is vulnerable to the temptation of the serpent. She disobeys God and eats the fruit of the tree and also offers it to Adam. Adam is punished 'because you have listened to the voice of your wife'. Adam's painless birthing of Eve contrasts with God's condemnation of all woman to suffer labour pains as a consequence of Eve's transgression. Eve's foolish disobedience is responsible for the downfall of the human race and her own biological ability for reproduction, a source of power in matriarchal culture[35], is seen as an occasion for divine punishment: 'in pain you shall bring forth children, yet your desire shall be for your husband, and he shall rule over you' (Gn.3:16).

The post-Christian feminist Daphne Hampson can be interpreted in the context of Trible's first wave of feminist scholarship. Hampson, who documents Christianity's patriarchal texts and traditions, has abandoned the Christian tradition because she judges it to be irredeemably patriarchal and sexist.

> That the bible reflects a patriarchal world is clear. The majority of biblical figures, whether patriarchs, prophets, priests, disciples or Church leaders, are male. The scriptures largely concern the interaction of men with one another and with their God. The central figure of the tradition for Christians, Jesus Christ, is of course male. A handful of women who play a part on the stage form the exception. Likewise the parables and ethical sayings are largely directed to the world of men. But it is not simply that women are noticeable by their absence. When they are present they are present for the most part performing female roles as defined by that society.[36]

Feminists have understood the word 'history' as a literal testament to the predominance of 'his' 'story' and the exclusion and invisibility of her story, 'the forgotten history of over half of the Christian community'.[37] An example of the male-centred (andro-centric) history and concomitant exclusion of 'herstory' is found in the bible, in Luke's presentation of Jesus' ancestors (Lk.3: 23-28.)[38]. Luke's genealogy begins with Jesus[39] and through a filiation formula 'was the son of', lists and names all of the fathers and sons leading right back to Adam, the son of God, the original male progenitor. The genealogy is totally silent with regard to the women in this lineage. This is consistent with a patriarchal culture where females are largely marginalised and invisible so that one can speak of a 'sexism by omission'.[40]

Patriarchy generally means that women are defined in relation to the primal male (traditionally the Ní or Uí in Irish culture) and are circumscribed according to their role as the daughters, wives and mothers of men.[41] One of the main consequences of patriarchy has been the inappropriate elevation of males as superior, legitimate and normative, and the consequent denigration of woman as inferior, illegitimate and non-normative. The Judeo-Christian tradition provides numerous examples of patriarchy.

Sandra Cullen hints at the disproportionate emphasis on males in the Hebrew scriptures by providing some salient statistics. 'A total of 1,426 names are mentioned in the Hebrew Scriptures, 1,315 are men and 111 are women.'[42]

Trible's second stage of feminist biblical interpretation involves the rediscovery and recovery of women who had been marginalised by patriarchal culture. Anne Thurston emphasises that 'the feminist interpreter is suspicious of controlled readings of texts, of readings which mask the dominance of the interpreter under an apparent cloak of objectivity'.[43] Feminist interpreters acknowledge their own contextual situation and its impact on their interpretative lens as they approach the biblical text. The texts do not contain objective meaning and the reader plays an important role in framing the text, interpreting it in a particular way and creating meaning though encountering it. Thurston states 'the text is not a container into which meaning, divine or otherwise, was poured centuries before and which is waiting to be drawn out'. The interpreter interacts with the text and in the process both are transformed so that the 'context alters the text'. The manner in which a feminist interpreter views and understands the biblical text actually has the power to change not just the feminist interpreter but the text as well: 'for me this has been one of the most fascinating aspects of this whole endeavour: watching how familiar texts oddly comforting, if slightly boring, have shaped themselves so differently as I have attempted to read them 'against the grain'. They have compelled my attention again'.[44]

Trible's second stage of interpretation involves a feminist reading of familiar texts 'against the grain' which results in revisioning and reclaiming biblical women. For example Trible reinterprets Eve's 'helper' status in Genesis 2. She sees the use of the Hebrew word *ezer* for 'helper' as a mark of powerful status since it connotes superiority in several other biblical texts.[45] Trible views the serpent talking to the woman as evidence that she is recognised as the spokesperson for the couple. The woman shows theological skill in arguing with the serpent; she interprets God's word and makes an independent ethical decision. In this manner a classic patriarchal text becomes a locus for reclaiming Eve as 'theologian, ethicist, hermeneut and rabbi. Defying the stereotypes of patriarchy, she reverses what the Church, synagogue and academy have preached about women.'[46] Trible's reinterpretation of a familiar text illustrates how the creation stories can be interpreted in a variety of ways. For instance one could argue that the creation stories in Genesis reflect the culture of their place of origin and their focus is not on gender relationships but on human life having its origin in God.[47] For the Hebrew word '*Adam*' has two meanings and it can be translated as the general word for a human as well as the specific name of a man 'Adam'. If the word 'Adam' is interpreted as 'human' and not as an exclusively male name the emphasis in Genesis 2 shifts from gender relationships between a man and a woman and God to more inclusive divine-human relationships.

Trible's third stage involves retelling the biblical stories of abused women sympathetically and creatively leading to liberation. Trible interprets the story of the rape of the concubine from the concubine's perspective, and uses her suffering and death as a powerful witness and challenge to sexual violence. In this way the interpretation of these biblical texts is not circumscribed by patriarchy and it becomes a catalyst for a critique of patriarchal society and an impetus for change. The interpretation of these terrifying texts challenges the very patriarchal system of which they are a product.

Images of God and Language about God

All human beings, including religious believers, are influenced by gender constructions. It would appear that in the Christian religious tradition, religious believers project these gender constructions onto God so that God is generally imagined as male. The French theologian, Alfred Loisy (1857-1940) spoke of God's transcendental masculinity and also of his transcendental heterosexuality.[48] It is entirely possible to see the God the father, Mary the mother and Jesus the son as a heterosexual family unit reinforcing heterosexuality. Ludwig Feuerbach (1804-1872) argued that humans project whatever they value onto God.[49] Feuerbach concluded that since humans have traditionally valued masculinity they project that quality onto God so that God is father, son and (male) spirit.[50] In the nineteenth century, Feuerbach was not engaging in a feminist critique of male imagery for God. He was using his theory of projection to reinterpret the maleness of God.[51] Contemporary gender theorists do not simply accept gender constructions as Feuerbach did, rather they question them. One must question whether it is theologically appropriate and educationally desirable to attribute exclusively male gender to God. The feminist theologian Mary Daly succinctly states that 'when God is male, the male is God', for if 'God in 'his' heaven is a father ruling 'his' people, then it is in the 'nature' of things and according to divine plan and the order of the universe that society be male-dominated'.[52] Daly sees God the father as the divine male who reinforces a hierarchical patriarchal system based on power and domination where men rule over women. However, the maleness of God has not always been universally or automatically accepted. Julian of Norwich (c.1342-c.1416), a late medieval mystic, perceived God as a nurturing protective parent. In *Revelations of Divine Love* she states 'In this way I saw that God was rejoicing to be our Father; rejoicing too to be our Mother; and rejoicing yet again to be our true Husband, with our soul his beloved wife. And Christ rejoices to be our Brother, and our Saviour too'.[53] Elsewhere Julian states that the 'deep wisdom of the Trinity is our Mother'.[54] Julian uses genderised language to speak of God as father, mother, spouse and parent. She realises that God is greater than any human linguistic construct or set of gender relations and so she simultaneously and paradoxically applies what may appear to be contradictory gender categories to God. Rosemary Radford Ruether explores 'androgynous Christologies' and locates Julian of Norwich's writings in the context of a broader (early Church, medieval, nineteenth century Shaker and Pietist) emphasis on Christ unifying male and female characteristics.[55] This tradition reflects St Paul's statement that 'there is no difference between Jews and Gentiles, between slaves and free people, between men and women; you are all one in union with Christ Jesus' (Gal. 3:28). Both women and men are represented by Christ and both are redeemed by Christ. Ruether's reading of the androgynous Christ means that 'his ability to be liberator does not reside in his maleness but, on the contrary, in the fact that he has renounced this system of domination and seeks to embody in his person the new humanity of service and mutual empowerment.'[56]

Mary Grey explores the 'fairly clear, if modest, strand within Jewish tradition where God is imaged as female, as mother or midwife'. She explores Isaiah's images of God as a mother in labour crying out in pain as well as Hosea's image of God never forgetting the child in her womb.[57] Many other writers have reflected on God as mother. An autobiographical and experiential account of *Motherhood and God* is given by Margaret Hebblethwaite whose own theological understanding of God as mother developed as a consequence of her experience of conceiving, carrying, delivering and nurturing her own children.[58] Hebblewaite's captivating account of her own spiritual journey as a mother of three young children was inspired by her experience of finding God in motherhood and motherhood in God. She recounts how, as she was in labour delivering her child, she used the stages of labour as a spiritual meditation on the passion of Christ and the crucifixion.[59]

Unfortunately, when it comes to God, most children as well as many adults tend to interpret exclusively male or God-he religious language literally and so assume that God is male or indeed 'a male'. Gail Ramshaw examines religious language and explores the variety of options with which people who wish to speak of God are faced. Ramshaw repeatedly emphasises that human language is inadequate when it comes to describing human events and experiences. It is unsurprising then that language is incapable of adequately describing human encounter with God.[60] Ramshaw explores the varieties of metaphors, similes and analogies that are applied to God. Metaphoric or non-literal language is often ascribed to God to show the similarity between some aspect of God's being and another reality i.e., God is a rock.

However metaphors are always open to interpretation and are contradictable, as they are not meant to be taken literally. God is not literally a rock although God has the qualities of strength and endurance that are associated with a rock. The power of the metaphor lies in its non-literal and paradoxical ability to draw attention to an aspect of God's nature without literally reducing God to it. Likewise anthropomorphic language describes God in human terms and so God 'walks' and 'talks' in the Garden of Eden (Genesis 3). Again this linguistic device is used to emphasise God's communication with human beings without literally ascribing human physiology to God. Human personal characteristics of love, joy, anger are attributed to God as the divine is personified in the scriptures. This is unsurprising because the Judeo-Christian tradition is based on a personal God who engages in personal relationship with human beings. However as with metaphor these personifications of God are not meant to be taken literally because God is greater than any human linguistic construction or reality.

Catholic Religious Education

In an age of equality legislation contemporary teachers and children may assume that issues of patriarchy and misogyny are only of historical relevance to their lives. They may identify that in the past, people held anachronistic sexist views that are of no contemporary significance. Jean-Jacque Rousseau's (1712-1778) ideas about the education of women may provide an example of one such patriarchal attitude in the history of ideas.

> The whole education of women ought to be relative to men. To please them, to be useful to them, to make themselves loved and honoured by them, to educate them when young, to care for

336

them when grown, to counsel them, to console
them and to make life sweet and agreeable to them
– these are the duties of women at all times and
what should be taught them from their infancy'.[61]

Teachers may be unsurprised to locate sexist ideas about
education in previous centuries but may fail to see the relevance
of gender to religious education in the present Irish primary
classroom. It must be emphasised that issues of gender are not
only of historical concern to believers who see the Judeo-
Christian tradition as providing numerous examples of
negative, oppressive and sexist attitudes to women in the past.
Post-Christian feminists view the Christian tradition itself as a
contemporary vehicle of sexism and gender inequality, which
not only perpetuates this inequality but also legitimates it and
presents it as the divine will. In the United Kingdom Pat
Hughes's research on gender issues in the primary classroom
led him to comment that religious assemblies, which refer to all
men as Jesus' brothers and prayers for all mankind, provide
some of the most striking examples of the lack of inclusive
language in the primary school.[62]

It behoves those who take Catholic religious education
seriously to explore the issue of gender in religion, to assess
whether or not Christianity has a case to answer before they
advocate nurturing children in the Christian faith. It would be
extremely irresponsible for parents and teachers to promote a
religious tradition which denigrated females and allocated
illegitimate superiority to males, promoted sexist language and
institutions and disabled children and adults from critiquing
and challenging exploitative and unjust gender relations. In
Catholic schools religious educators face the difficult task of
'passing on a tradition which already has within it certain
unquestioned assumptions about gender roles and a liturgical

tradition that reinforces these roles in significant symbolic ways. Children see the (male) priest celebrating Mass, hear references to God the Father, and thus grow up with a set of unquestioned assumptions about gender and faith that may come under scrutiny only later in life, if at all.'[63]

Gender in the Classroom

Contemporary Gender theory has moved beyond the opposition of females versus males, girls versus boys, women versus men. In the classroom this means that teachers can emphasise the importance of the child having a healthy, positive sense of who they are as a girl or a boy. Teachers should emphasise non-hierarchical co-operative relationships between girls and boys (for example, in groupwork, seating arrangements, task allocation, assessment) where one sex is never seen as better than the other.[64] Teachers need to be aware that a positive sense of what it means to be a girl simultaneously contributes to a positive sense of what it means to be a boy. The elevation of one sex and the denigration of another is unhealthy for both sexes. It is important to acknowledge gender difference by recognising that while girls and boys are not bi-polar, neither are they identical. However the recognition of difference must be uncompromising in its simultaneous emphasis on equality. Educators should not make generalised assumptions about girls' or boys' preferences or performance in any area of the curriculum, including religious education. Furthermore educators should model good practice by using inclusive language as well as culturally, ethnically and gender inclusive imagery in the classroom. References to man or mankind as generic are no longer acceptable in children's literature or in the classroom. For almost thirty years the guidelines of reputable publishing houses specify that occupational titles which are sex-specific e.g. actress, poetess, should be abandoned as there are only a few occupations which are dependent on sex e.g. wet nurse, surrogate mother, egg donor, sperm donor.[65]

Practical exercises can enable children in the senior primary classes to address the issue of gender in religion in a supportive yet critical manner. For instance the biblical story of the feeding of the five thousand, which is found in all four gospels,[66] tells the story of Jesus' miraculous feeding of 5,000 people with five loaves and two fish. Now while John, Mark and Luke's accounts stress that there were 5,000 'men', Matthew's account states that 'the number of men who ate was about 5,000, not counting the women and children' (Mt. 14:21). Matthew's observation about the absence of numerical data for women and children enables religious educators to critique gender constructs and to support children in asking evaluative and inferential questions concerning the text. For instance children can initially conjecture why the number of children might have been excluded from Matthew's account and they can subsequently discuss how the knowledge that children were excluded makes them feel. Then they can further discuss why the number of men present is recorded whereas the number of women is not. Once more they can explore what it feels like to be invisible in the gospel record. The teacher can lead them to appreciate that while boys are excluded on the basis of age (children) girls are excluded on the basis of age and gender (children and women). Furthermore the children can imagine the story from a child's or a woman's perspective and can revision and reclaim a story from which they where initially excluded. The aim of this exercise is not to create tension between girls and boys but rather to enable the children to explore how in certain cultural and religious traditions, at certain historical epochs, people have been allocated different status according to age and gender.

Children can also use their religious imaginations to conjecture about females who may have been present at certain events (e.g. Last Supper) but whose presence is not recorded in the biblical account. Since the Christian scriptures largely document the faith testimonies of men, children could imagine what the women would have written about Jesus' birth (Mary Jesus' mother/ Elizabeth Mt.1-2, Lk.1-2.), his ministry (Martha & Mary / Suzanna/Joanna/Mary Magdalene, Jn. 11, Lk.8) his death (the two Marys, Mk.15.) and resurrection (Mary Magdalene/ Joanna/Mary the mother of James, Lk. 23). One strategy for reclaiming these largely invisible women involves focusing on women and men who are mentioned in the text but whose characters are largely unexplored. When dealing with the scriptures children can use their fertile religious imaginations to repopulate the stories with characters who, although they do not figure in the text (e.g. the prodigal son's mother, sister, uncle, nephew), can enable the children to penetrate the story from a variety of dramatic and gender perspectives. This enables them to break open the story and give it a new transgender relevance. It is important to state that this interpretative device does not involve rewriting the text but involves interpreting it within a larger imaginative framework. The children's religious imaginations bring the story to light in a new manner.

Language

The classroom should never become a locus for gender warfare between a God-she and a God-he tradition. The view that all God-he religious language is patriarchal and oppressive of females denies the complexity of the Hebrew and Christian scriptures, the power of God-he language to mediate spiritual meaning, as well as the impact which exclusive language has on males as well as females. Many teachers resist using God-she language for fear of confusing children. However it must be noted that the Hebrew and Christian scriptures and the Christian tradition are authoritative sources of positive female and male imagery and language for God. Teachers may wish to use non-gendered references to the God who is beyond gender and address God directly in prayer as 'You' or alternatively with older children speak of God as 'the divine' or 'God-self'.

While children generally know that Jesus taught us to call God 'Our Father' (Mt.6:9) they may be less aware that in the bible the parable of the woman looking for the lost coin comes in between the parable of the lost sheep and the parable of the Prodigal son.[67] Now many Catholics have little difficulty in imaging God as a Good Shepherd minding his sheep[68], or as a loving father welcoming his son home, yet they have considerable difficulty in imaging God as a woman searching for them ceaselessly in the way that she searches for a lost coin. While one can empathise with people who experience cultural or social discomfort when using female imagery for God, this in itself is insufficient reason for excluding all feminine imagery and language for God in the classroom.

To speak of God in the feminine is not to engage in a new departure from the Catholic religious tradition but to reclaim and revision an existing rich scriptural and theological tradition. However the success of introducing female imagery and language for God in the classroom depends on how it is done. There is no point in suggesting a simple substitution of one set of gendered language for another and of substituting the pronoun 'she' for 'he' whenever it comes to speaking of God. A total and exclusive replacement of God-she language for God-he language would not be any more inclusive than God-he language. In the same way that Gender studies has moved beyond an antithetical bi-polar understanding of female and male, a contemporary theological tradition influenced by gender studies appreciates the need to move beyond either exclusive matriarchal or exclusive patriarchal imagery and language for God. Neither is adequate taken in isolation. Taken together and complimented with other non-gendered ways of imaging and speaking of God they give a fuller image of who we are, as females and males created in God's image, as well as a glimpse of God's incomprehensible otherness. At the end of his life Thomas Aquinas experienced what some have interpreted as a mystical vision and thereafter was unable to complete his theological masterpiece *Summa Theologiae*. Aquinas declared that he could no longer write 'because all that I have written now seems like straw'.[69] Aquinas was aware that God eludes all human attempts at defining divine nature. There is always more to experience, more to know, more to say. The more religious educators present children with a sense of God's transcendence, with a sense that while we can speak about God, there is always a beyond, an otherness to God that we can try to talk about but that we can not fully describe, the truer they are to the Judeo-Christian tradition. Teachers can lead children to appreciate the unknowability of the God made known through revelation, the paradoxical otherness of God who is experienced as intimately present in the world, by using inclusive and non-gendered religious language. Julian of Norwich's simultaneous use of male, female and non-gendered images of God provides a powerful medieval model which explodes the boundaries of gendered language and appreciates that God is beyond all linguistic and cultural categories.

Images

Teachers have a very significant role to play in developing children's religious imaginations so that children can image God and speak positively of God in a way that is comfortable with female and male gender and that does not reduce God to any one gender. While religious educators can of course use male imagery for speaking of God they should not depend on it exclusively any more than they should depend entirely on conventional Western images of God as white, elderly and male. Children's religious imaginations need to be nurtured with a variety of inter-cultural and gender inclusive images of God, so that children can begin to appreciate that there are many ways of speaking of and imaging God. Jesus was not culturally constrained by gender-based stereotypes and he challenged the gender, ethnic and class conventions of his society. His acknowledgement of his messiahship to the Samaritan woman at the well provides evidence of this (Jn.4:26). Margaret Cooling and Jane Taylor's presentation of the way in which Aboriginal, African, Asian, South American, European and North American artists have depicted biblical stories and themes is a wonderfully refreshing classroom resource.[67] It enables children to perceive Christ and many other biblical characters through the eyes of diverse artists from different cultures and epochs and it broadens their capacity to understand them. If religious educators rely exclusively on conventional Western religious art they miss an opportunity to engage with diverse theologies and aesthetic and cultural perceptions of God.

Just as Phyllis Trible's second stage of feminist interpretation led to the reclamation and revision of the forgotten women in scripture, contemporary Irish religious education needs to reclaim and revision female imagery for God and female language about God in the classroom. The Jewish and Christian scriptures and tradition contain inclusive imagery and language for God and use of this in a classroom context enables children to appreciate God's nature more deeply, to view themselves more positively as girls and boys made in God's image, and to develop their own self-transcendent spirituality. Gender studies helps to establish a counter-canon of women and men in scripture, of women theologians, of women reformers and writers within the Irish tradition. Children can benefit from learning about powerful female and male religious educators in the past like St Brigid and St Patrick, Nano Nagle and Edmund Rice, and more recently Frank Duff and Edel Quinn. If religious educators use inclusive language, culturally diverse imagery as well as teaching methodologies which reclaim and celebrate invisible women in the Christian tradition then religious education will offer a counter narrative and a powerful voice to contemporary girls and boys in Irish primary schools.

NOTES

1   See The Employment Equality Acts 1998 & 2004; The Equal Status Acts 2000 to 2004.

2   Susan A. Ross, 'Gender, Culture, and Christian Faith Formation', in Werner G. Jeanrond & Lisa Sowle Cahill, Eds. *Religious Education of Boys and Girls, Concilium,* Canterbury: SCM 2002/4, p. 17.

3   Jeanrond & Sowle Cahill, *Concilium,* p.7.

4   Anthony Clare writes 'The one biological difference between the sexes on which everybody is agreed is that whereas women possess two X-shaped sex chromosomes, men possess one X and a little Y-shaped chromosome. The Y chromosome accounts for superior male strength, stature, mass of muscle, sleight of hand, speed of foot.' Anthony Clare, *On Men: Masculinity in Crisis The Dying Phallus,* London: Chatto and Windus, 2000, p.6. Inter-sex babies are those who have traces of male and female sex organs and are of indeterminate sex. This condition is sometimes referred to as *Hermaphroditism.* Of course modern medicine means that people can avail of artificial sex changes so that even the biological category of female and male is fluid and open to change.

5   Adjectives teachers used to describe typical behaviour from boys include 'non-compliant, demanding, excitable, talkative, attention-seeking and active. Girls tend to be described as gentler, more caring, sensible, obedient, hardworking, co-operative,

quiet, dependent and passive'. Pat Hughes, *Gender Issues in the Primary Classroom*, Scholastic Publications Ltd., 1991, p.131.

6   Michael Ryan, *Literary Theory: A Practical Introduction*, Oxford: Blackwell, 2002, p.116.

7   Sandra Cullen, *Religion and Gender*, Dublin: Veritas, 2005, p.33.

8   See Terry L Martin, Kenneth J. Doka, *Men don't cry....women do: transcending gender stereotyping of grief,* London: Brunner/Mazel, 2000.

9   See Cathy Gunn, Dominant or Different? Gender issues in Computer Supported Learning in *Journal of Asynchronous Learning Networks*, Vol. 7, Issue 1, Feb. 2003. Also Kelly Rathje, Male Versus Female Earnings – Is the gender wage gap converging?, in *Economica Ltd*, Spring 2002, Vol.7, No.1.

10   'Science demonstrates that there are at least six differentials in establishing the sexual differentiation process: genes and chromosomes, sex glands, sex hormones, differentiation of internal reproductive tract, differentiation of external genitalia and the differentiation of some brain areas.' Cullen, *Religion and Gender*, p.23.

11   Ursula King, *Religion and Gender*, p.9.

12   *The Sunday Times*, June 19, 2005. The study was carried out in 2001 by Professor Jonathan Gershuny, and was published by the Institute of Social and Economic Research at Essex University, 2005.

13   *Declaration on the Question of the Admission of Women to the Ministerial Priesthood*, 15 October, 1976. This declaration states that there must be a 'physical resemblance' between the priest and Christ. For a commentary see Ruether, *To Change*, p.47. The Vatican strenuously emphasises that its teaching is scripturally and theologically based and resists the notion that its teaching is influenced by gender.

14   Gayatri Chakravorty Spivak, *The post-colonial Critic: interviews, strategies, dialogues*, London: Routledge, 1990. Donna Landry, Gerald MacLean, *The Spivak reader: selected works of Gayatri Chakravorty Spivak*, London: Routledge, 1996. Cf. essay Can the Subaltern Speak?

15   Anthony Clare, *On Men: Masculinity in Crisis*, Chatto and Windus, London: 2000, p.2.

16   Ibid

17   Clare, *On Men*, p.3.

18   Sandra Cullen, *Religion and Gender*, p.37. See King, *Religion and Gender*, p.12.

19   While misogyny is usually associated with men, women can also harbour a hatred of their own sex. The antonym of misogyny is misandry.

20   The word hysterical originates from '*hystericus*' which means 'of the womb'. Hysteria was a female specific neurotic condition which medics thought developed as a consequence of a uterine dysfunction.

21   '*Kuche, Kinder, Kirche*' refers to women's suitability for three roles: their domestic role as cook (*Kuche*); maternal role with children (*Kinder*) and religious role praying in church (*Kirche*).

22   Feminism is the advocacy of women's rights to full citizenship i.e. political, economic and social equality with men. cf. L. J. Nicholson Ed., *Feminism/Postmodernism*, London: Routledge, 1990, p.26.

23   Alister McGrath, *Christian Theology: An introduction*, Oxford: Blackwell, 1994, p.497.

24   Cady Stanton wrote the woman's bible with other women members of a Revising Committee. It was produced in two volumes in 1892 and 1895. cf. Elizabeth Griffith, *In her own right*, OUP, 1985.

25   Freud believed that at around four years of age young girls first realised that they had no penis. The girl child blames her mother for her sense of loss and focuses on her father as a love object. Anthony Clare reflects on the huge change which has occurred since Freud. 'A century ago, a peevish Sigmund Freud, perplexed by a seeming epidemic of hysterical, depressed, lethargic and dissatisfied women, asked, "What do women want?" He asked it at a time when to be a woman was to be pathological, to be male was to be health personified. A century later it is not women who are seen to be pathological, but men; it is not women's wants, but men's, that mystify us.' Clare, *Men in Crisis*, p.8.

26   One could argue that the word theology is an English construction and that it is the consonants of 'ology' and not the masculine or feminine of the the Greek word for God '*theo/a*' which forms the word the/ology. According to this reading there is nothing inherently male or female about the activity.

27   Faith seeking understanding was St Anslem's (1033-1109) definition of theology.

28   Cf. B.Smith, & Ursula Appelt, *Write or be written: early modern women poets and cultural constraints*, VT: Ashgate, 2001. Mary

Cullen, ed. *Girls don't do honours: Irish women in education in the 19th and 20th centuries*, Dublin: Women's Education Bureau, 1987.

29   In a 2005 BBC Radio 4 'In Our Time' vote on the world's greatest philosopher, listeners compiled an all male shortlist for the top twenty greatest philosophers ever. No woman was included.

30   Patricia Kieran, *A Study in the Roots of Modern Atheism*, Unpublished M.Th. Thesis, University of London, 1985, p.11.

31   Elisabeth Schussler-Fiorenza, *Searching the Scriptures Vol. 1*, Canterbury: SCM Press, 1994, p.7f.

32   cf. Rosemary Radford Ruether, *Sexism and God Talk Toward a Feminist Theology*, Boston: Beacon Press, 1983, p.228, for an account of Radical Feminism. 'For many, the logic of this position leads to lesbian separatism. Women can't be liberated from patriarchy until they are liberated from men'.

33   Phyllis Trible, Biblical Tradition and Interpretation in Ann Loades, *Feminist Theology A Reader*, London: SPCK, 1990, p.24.

34   Phyllis Trible, *Texts of Terror: literary-feminist readings of biblical narratives*, Philadelphia: Fortress Press, 1984.

35   Síle na Gig (sometimes spelled Sheela na Gig or Sheila Na Gig) is a powerful female, perhaps Goddess image, found on medieval buildings and churches. It is a powerful reminder of women's sexuality and capacity for reproduction.

36   Daphne Hampson, *Theology and Feminism*, Oxford: Blackwell, 1990, p. 86.

37   Barbara J. Mac Haffie, *Her Story Women in Christian Tradition*, Philadelphia: Fortress Press, 1986.

38   Matthew also presents a genealogy of Jesus in Mt.1:1-17. Matthew's account emphasises Jesus' male lineage but unlike Luke's account his does make three references to the names of important biblical women eg. Tamar, Rahab, Ruth, yet only in the context of describing them as the mother of a male. Matthew also makes reference to Uriah's wife without mentioning her by name.

39   He was the son (Jesus), so people thought, of Joseph, who was the son of Heli, the son of...etc. Lk.3.23f.

40   Ursula King Ed., *Religion & Gender*, Oxford: Blackwell, 1995, p.2.

41   Only three of the books of the bible bear the names of women: Ruth, Judith and Esther.

42   Cullen, *Religion and Gender*, p.70.

43   Anne Thurston, *Knowing Her Place Gender and the Gospels*, Dublin: Gill & Macmillan, 1998, p.xiv.

44   Thurston, *Knowing Her Place*, p. xv.

45   Ps. 121.2; Ps.124.8; Ps.146.5; Exod. 18.4; Deut. 33.7, 26, 29. Cf. Trible in Loades, *Feminist Theology*, p.26.

46   Trible in Loades, *Feminist Theology*, p.27.

47   Both creation stories are generally seen as non-Jewish in origin and while Genesis 1 is Egyptian in origin Genesis 2 is generally recognised as having originated in Mesopotamia.

48   Patricia Kieran, *New Light on Alfred Loisy? An exploration of his religious science in Essais d'histoire et de philosophie religieuses (1898-1899)*, Unpublished Ph.D. thesis, University of London, 1994.

49   Ludwig Feuerbach, *The Essence of Christianity*, New York: Harper Torchbooks, 1957, p.282. 'Man is the beginning, the middle and the end of religion'.

50   Feuerbach sees the spirit as male and so sees Mary as the legitimate female aspect of the Trinity of Father, Son and Mother. Many writers have written about the breath or spirit *ruah* as a feminine aspect of God.

51   Feuerbach, *The Essence*, p.30.

52   Mary Daly, *Beyond God the Father Toward a philosophy of women's liberation*, Boston: Beacon Press, 1974, p.13.

53   Julian of Norwich, *Revelations of Divine Love*, London: Penguin Books, 1984, p.151.

54   Julian, *Revelations*, p.157f. Chapter 54.

55   Rosemary Radford Ruether, *To Change the World Christology and Cultural Criticism*, SCM Press, 1981, p.49f.

56   Ruether, *To Change*, p.56.

57   Mary Grey, *Introducing Feminist Images of God*, Sheffield Academic Press, 2001, p.24. 'Texts such as Isa. 42.14, 46.3-4, 66.13, speak of the tender motherhood of God, crying out in labour who at the same time does not forget the child of her womb (Hos. 11.3-4; Isa. 49.15).'

58   Margaret Hebblethwaite, *Motherhood and God*, London: Geoffrey Chapman, 1984.

59   Hebblethwaite, *Motherhood*, p.78.

60   Gail Ramshaw, 'The Gender of God' in Loades, Ann, Ed., *Feminist Theology*, p.173.

61   Quotation from *Emile* (1762) in Pat Hughes, *Gender Issues in the Classroom*, NY: Scholastic Publications, 1991, p.21.

62   Pat Hughes, *Gender Issues*, p.57.

63   Ross, *Gender*, p.21. The word educate comes from the Latin *'educere'* meaning to lead out. Religious educators could model themselves on religious teachers or *gurus* who bring children from the darkness (*gu*) of religious stereotypes which diminish and devalue females and males to the light (*ru*) of critical, informed and egalitarian faith.

64   The work of Margaret Spear and Margaret Crossman has revealed that teachers award higher marks on average to work they think is from a boy than to identical work that they think has been produced by a girl. Hughes, *Gender Issues*, p.99.

65   Gail Ramshaw in Loades, *Feminist Theology*, p.176. Hughes, *Gender Issues*, p.58.

66   John 6:1-14; Mt.14:13-21; Mk.6:3-44; Lk.9:10-17.

67   Parable of The Lost Sheep, Lk.15: 1-8. Parable of the Lost Coin, Lk. 15:8-10. Parable of the Lost Son, Lk.15:11-32.

68   Indeed this image of the Good Shepherd has given rise to Sofia Cavalletti's Good Shepherd school of catechesis.

69   Anthony Kenny, *Aquinas*, Past Masters, Oxford University Press, 1980, p.26.

70   Margaret Cooling, Jane Taylor, Diane Walker, *The Bible Through Art*, RMEP, 2000. Margaret Cooling, Jane Taylor, *Jesus Through Art*, RMEP, 2000.

CONCLUSION

· ·

Religious educators are facing many changes and challenges at
an exciting juncture in the history of religious education in
Ireland. Change is a vital sign of life, but one that needs to be
carefully evaluated and critiqued before it is unquestioningly
embraced. In the contemporary Catholic primary school,
teachers involved in religious education are facing a difficult but
not impossible task. They must be conversant with the
discipline of religious education and the context in which they
are teaching as well as being capable of responding critically to
emerging issues in the contemporary classroom. In the primary
school the Catholic teacher needs to be grounded and literate
in the Catholic tradition yet capable of proclaiming the
Catholic faith in a post-modern context. Teachers are called to
nurture the children's religious imaginations and must be
committed to learning about the unique contours of each
child's spirituality in the contemporary world. Catholic
teachers, as disciples of Christ, must be concerned with issues
of social justice and human rights and so a strong emphasis on
valuing difference and welcoming diversity lies at the heart of
Catholic education. If teachers are to provide religious
education that caters for children's diverse learning styles,

abilities and religious needs then they cannot view themselves simply as technicians whose duty is to implement a standard pre-set classroom programme. Teaching religious education is a creative task, as the religious educator needs to interpret, adapt and supplement the religious education programme to suit the learning needs of the children. Finally religious educators need to lead children to a mature Catholic faith and support them as they question and explore that faith through critical religious education.

Post-modernity has had a huge impact on Irish Catholicism so that one can not speak of Catholic schools as if they are a homogenous reality any more than one can speak of Irish Catholicism as if it is a universally agreed standardised category. There is a broad spectrum of Catholic belief and practice within Ireland that ranges from non-practising, traditional and conservative on the one hand to practising, liberal and radical on the other, with a multiplicity of possible inter-relationships in between. The President of the National Conference of Priests of Ireland, Fr John Littleton, states that:

> For many Catholics, if they are not lapsed, an á la carte approach has become the norm. They choose what suits them from Catholic doctrine and, for whatever reasons, ignore the remainder. This makes it difficult to describe Catholicism with any degree of consistency.[1]

The complex issue of religious belief and practice in Ireland cannot be isolated from trends in other European countries. In 2005 a Eurobarometer report on *Social values, science and technology*, presented data on a range of issues, including religion and spiritual beliefs. The data was gathered from the population of EU member states and identified that 73 per cent of surveyed Irish people believe in God, while 22 per cent believe in some sort of spirit or life force with 4 per cent stating no belief in God, a spirit or life force.[2] This data is interesting, not least because it shows how Irish people, in conformity with their European counterparts, are tending to move away from traditional organised belief systems and religious groupings into the more nebulous area of a personal spirituality or a personal belief in a life form. This disenchantment with traditional religious institutions and the emergence of new spiritualities makes a significant impact on those who teach religion within a confessional context. Allied to this is the fact that the Irish Catholic school system is not monolithic, but is hegemonic and is characterised by internal differentiation and by internal ideological struggles.[3] Catholic primary schools vary from traditional and conservative to radical and human rights orientated. Religious educators need to be aware of these contemporary cultural and religious contexts for faith formation in Ireland. Furthermore clerical child-sex abuse, increasing secularisation and declining numbers of church attendance are just some of the contextual factors which impact on Catholic religious education in the primary sector. However while teachers need to be cognisant of these realities they should not be constrained by them as there are also counter-indicators which show that Irish people have a deep sense of the spiritual, an interest in diverse faiths and an openness to a religious interpretation of life.

While there is insufficient research into teachers' attitudes to teaching religion in Irish primary schools, one recent study has indicated that not all teachers are happy with the confessional and sacramental-based approach to religious education in Catholic schools. The results of the 2002 INTO survey show that just over ten per cent of surveyed primary teachers do not wish to teach religion or have opted out of teaching it.[4] The Catholic Church attempts to support all teachers in their task of faith formation but it also needs to address teachers' concerns. Chapter Three outlined Derek Bastide's 'understanding religion' approach and this may provide an educationally and religiously appropriate approach for teachers who are non-believing or non-practicing Catholics and yet who find themselves teaching in Catholic schools.[5] The Church might also support such teachers by exploring methodologies based on religious instruction that may enable teachers to nurture children's knowledge of the Catholic faith without assuming that either the teacher or the child is a believer. In some instances religious instruction can be a form of pre-evangelisation as it is always open to the possibility that faith will develop as a consequence of exploring religious beliefs and practices in a respectful and empathetic environment.[6]

This book has identified a range of emerging issues which challenge those involved in Catholic primary education. One of the most significant issues is the Catholic Church's majority control of the primary school sector. It has been argued that the Catholic Church exercises a monopoly of the Irish primary schools and that this monopoly discriminates against freedom of choice for parents, children and teachers. Some commentators argue that Catholic schools curtail freedom of choice and equality of access for minority faith and non-religious groups. These are grave allegations that merit serious discussion. In March 2005 a United Nations Committee on the Convention on the Elimination of all Forms of Racial Discrimination (CERD) formally recommended that the Irish State 'promote' multi-denominational and non-denominational schools.

'The Committee (CERD), recognising the 'intersectionality' of racial and religious discrimination, encourages the State to promote the establishment of non-denominational and multi-denominational schools and to amend the existing legislative framework so that no discrimination may take place as far as the admission of pupils (of all religions) in schools is concerned.'[7]

The CERD Committee concluded that because of the lack of choice and equality of access for all citizens in the Irish primary educational system the state should promote non-denominational and multi-denominational schools. While the United Nations Committee did not rule that Catholic schools were discriminatory *per se* it did see the Irish primary educational system, of which the Catholic school sector has the majority share, as inegalitarian and it specifically referred to admissions procedures as well as to the 'intersectionality' of racial and religious discrimination. Now one could retort defensively that that the Catholic Church's control of 92.7 per cent of primary schools only represents a marginal overshot of the 2002 census figures for the number of Catholics in Ireland (88.4 per cent). However such a line of argumentation is of no great benefit to those whose educational needs are not being met by the present educational system as well as to the Catholic school sector. Official Church teaching states that any 'kind of school monopoly … is opposed to the native rights of the human person, to the development and spread of culture, to the peaceful association of citizens and to the pluralism that exists today in ever so many societies.'[8] As a consequence of the historical evolution of the Irish primary school system the Catholic Church emerged as the majority sector in order to respond to the educational needs of the majority of citizens. However as those educational needs change the Catholic school sector, along with all other sectors, must change to better service emerging needs. The Catholic Church has no desire to monopolise the primary educational system and the last decades of the twentieth century have witnessed the establishment of diverse types of confessional, inter-denominational and multi-denominational primary schools in Ireland.

One most important issue to emerge from CERD's recommendations is the issue of diversity in Catholic schools. This book has argued that the Catholic primary sector is genuinely desirous of not monopolizing the educational system and to this end it *actively* welcomes and supports new initiatives in primary education that service the educational needs of parents, teachers and children. However Catholic schools must simultaneously *actively* promote the fact that they are inclusive and welcoming of diversity. Otherwise a misconception will develop which views Catholic education as exclusive, bigoted and unwelcoming of religiously, ethnically and culturally diverse communities. This book strongly argues that a Catholic vision of education is one in which Catholic schools are non-discriminatory, welcoming of all and committed to anti-racist, inclusive education. In the area of religious education the Catholic school sector should follow best practice and develop guidelines on inter-religious education so that it can respond to Vatican II's call to Catholics to 'acknowledge, preserve, and promote the spiritual and moral goods' found in diverse world faiths 'as well as the values in their society and culture'.[9]

It is not good enough for Catholic schools simply to adopt a policy of 'tolerating' children of minority or personal belief. These groups must be actively welcomed and supported within the Catholic school.[10] There is an urgent need for detailed research into attitudes towards minority religious groups within the Catholic majority sector. If, as one initial study suggests, children of minority faiths or of personal belief are being marginalised in Catholic schools, then this issue needs immediate attention.[11] The Catholic school has a responsibility to ensure that cultural or ethnic difference as well as difference of belief or practice, within diverse religious and non-religious traditions, does not become an occasion for the bullying or harassment of any member of the school community. Catholic schools are called to celebrate difference and to follow the example of Jesus Christ whose radical ministry of love led to an uncompromising emphasis on the uniqueness and dignity of each individual human being. Jesus was not culturally constrained by religious or gender stereotypes and he challenged the religious, gender, ethnic and class conventions of his society.[12]

The 1999 curriculum manifests its respect for diversity and tolerance[13] by stating that the school should be 'flexible in making alternative organisational arrangements for those who do not wish to avail of the particular religious education it offers'. Catholic schools should provide high quality Catholic religious education for all those children who desire it but they should also accommodate the needs of those who do not wish to avail of religious education in the Catholic school. Schools need to develop a conversation among management, staff, parents and children about how best these needs can be met at a local level. Academic freedom and concern for universal human rights are central aspects of a Catholic vision of education. This Catholic vision of education emphasises the call to evangelise and catechise yet these should never be undertaken against the wishes of the teacher, the parent or the child. Catholic education must never use coercive methods to proclaim the word of God. Indeed the mark of a Catholic school is the degree to which it responds to Christ's call to proclaim the good news freely and to invite children to respond in freedom to the call to become disciples.

One issue that merits serious attention is the issue of whether there should be a state syllabus for religious education in the primary school sector. Such a move would have the advantage of providing a standardised syllabus with common core content that would be taught to all children in all denominational, inter-denominational, and multi-denominational primary schools. Some would welcome the advent of a Department of Education and Science regulated and monitored religious education syllabus which would remove the design, implementation and monitoring of religious education from the exclusive control of individual patronal bodies. By doing this the state could ensure that each child had access to information about religious and non-religious beliefs, values and ideas from within a broad cultural context that accommodated and respected the diversity of denominational and religious belief but that was not entirely confined to any one denominational, faith or non-religious perspective. A state syllabus in religious education could be interpreted and adapted by the various patronal bodies to suit the denominational, inter-denominational or multi-denominational needs of their school. Different faith traditions, denominations and non-religious groups could work collaboratively with the Department of Education and Science in the creation of such a state syllabus so that it demonstrated a strong interfaith and ecumenical orientation but also maintained a degree of flexibility so that each patronal body could interpret it in the context of their own ethical or religious ethos. A state syllabus would have the further advantage of developing a consistent approach to religious education in the primary sector that could function as a developmentally structured preparation for the state's post-primary state syllabus in religious education.

In Catholic schools a state syllabus could mean that rather than having one nationally agreed catechetical programme, such as the *Alive-O* programme, one might have a state syllabus for religious education from which various publishing houses could design a plurality of Catholic approved programmes. One could envisage a situation where there would be different programmes in Catholic schools, all implementing the state syllabus and adapting it for a Catholic context. This could be of benefit to primary schools by leading to increased choice where schools could select the programme they felt was most appropriate to their needs. At present the lack of a published Catholic syllabus for religious education means that there is only one Catholic programme with a consequent lack of choice for schools.

In such a state syllabus inter-religious education could play an important role where all children in all Irish primary schools could learn about the beliefs and practices of diverse faith communities in a respectful, supportive environment. Commentators have noted that the development of the second-level religious education syllabus 'involved a process of consultation with the representatives of minority as well as majority religious bodies regarding curriculum development... The development of more inclusive practices of consultation marks a new and more pluralist approach to the development of religious education in Ireland.'[14] The advantages of the Department of Education and Science taking responsibility for religious education in the primary school might result in: a national religious education in-service programme for all primary teachers in RE in conformity with other curricular subject areas; the establishment of standardised strands and strand units in religious education; integration between religious education and all other areas of the primary curriculum; consistency of approach in the assessment of religious education; formal monitoring of the programme of religious education in the primary school and a consequent increase in the status of religious education.

However a state syllabus would undoubtedly have some disadvantages. A state syllabus for religious education might lead to suspicion among different patronal bodies that a non-religious or inter-religious programme was being imposed upon their schools with a resulting compromise in the school's right to engage in confessional faith formation. It could be argued that a state designed, monitored and assessed programme of religious education could compromise the school's specific denominational, inter-denominational or multi-denominational ethos and approach to religious education. Others might argue about the futility of developing a state syllabus for religious education when the present system, where each patronal body takes responsibility for the design, implementation and assessment of their own syllabus or programme, works perfectly well. Furthermore in the present system there is a healthy plurality of approaches, programmes and methodologies whereas the implementation of a standardised, uniform national syllabus might curtail this creativity and freedom. One might assert that the advent of a state syllabus for religious instruction would simply involve different patronal authorities adapting, delivering and assessing the state syllabus in the context of their own schools and in accordance with their own denominational, inter-denominational or multi-denominational perspective. One could stress that the different patronal bodies would simply represent what they are already teaching in their own schools in a manner that complied with a state syllabus so that it would be a case of *plus ça change*. In summary, without engaging in a radical change of legislation governing schools including the Rules for National Schools, one could argue that a state syllabus would not alter radically the existing system of primary religious education in Ireland.[15]

This book began as a conversation between two lecturers in religious education in two Colleges of Education in Ireland. It attempts to contribute a voice to a larger national debate on religious education and to encourage an ongoing and lively conversation among all those with an interest in primary religious education. While it is vitally important to applaud the work of teachers, parents, priests, diocesan advisors, school managers and those who contribute to the Catholic primary school sector, it is also important to acknowledge that the future holds many challenges and much change. Catholic educators should not react defensively or negatively to these challenges but should operate positively from a deep conviction of the identity and mission of the Catholic school. Catholic educators are called to respond critically, intelligently, generously and honestly to the challenges that face them so that they can embrace the changes necessary to serve the gospel of Jesus Christ, the Catholic school community and the wider Irish society.

NOTES

1   In June 2005 Fr John Littleton spoke at a conference at The Priory Institute, Tallaght, titled *Irish and Catholic? Towards An Understanding of Identity*. A synopsis of his presentation was featured in *The Irish Catholic*, Thursday June 30, 2005.

2   *Social values, Science and Technology*, Special Eurobarometer Report 225, European Commission, June 2005. For an on-line version of the report see http://europa.eu.int/comm/public_opinion/archives/ebs/ebs_225_report_en.pdf accessed July 12, 2005.

3   Gerald Grace, *Catholic Schools: Mission, Markets and Morality*, London: Routledge Falmer, 2002, p.108.

4   *Teaching Religion in the Primary School Issues and Challenges*, Dublin: INTO, 2003, p.47. cf.p.51. In reality only 0.3% of survey respondents actually opted out of teaching religion whereas 5.7% would prefer if they didn't have to give religious

instruction/education; 3.0% would like to have the option of opting out of teaching religion and 2.0% would like to opt out of teaching religion. It must be noted that 61.2% of respondents teach R.E. willingly. However this research on teachers' attitudes was carried out in all school sectors and not just in the Catholic sector.

5   Derek Bastide, *Religious Education 5-12*, The Falmer Press, 1987, p.7.

6   Pre-evangelisation refers to the stage or process of preparing the potential believer; of raising the non-believer's interest and thoughtfulness about life and so awakening in him or her a sense of the religious dimension of life. Pre-evangelisation is also understood as the initial step in evangelisation. Cf. EN, no. 71.

7   International Convention on the Elimination of all Forms of Racial Discrimination, Sixty-sixth session, 21 February – 11 March 2005, http://www.ohchr.org/english/bodies/cerd/cerds66.htm accessed 6/7/05. See the Educate Together press release issued on March 14, 2005, at http://www.educatetogether.ie /press_releases/pr050314.html accessed 2/7/05.

8   GE par. 6.

9   NA par. 2.

10 Anne Lodge uses the term 'people of personal belief in her essay 'Denial, tolerance or recognition of difference? The experiences of minority belief parents in the denominational primary system' in Jim Deegan, Dympna Devine & Anne Lodge, Eds., *Primary Voices Equality, Diversity and Childhood in Irish Primary Schools*, Dublin: Institute of Public Administration, 2004, p.22, fn.8. Lodge finds the term non-believer disrespectful of the personal spirituality and values system of those who do not adhere to an institutionalized belief system.

11 See Chapter 6 on Religious Belief especially section 6.4 on 'Harassment' in Lodge, A & Lynch, K., *Diversity at School*, Dublin: Institute of Public Administration, 2004, p.53.

12 Jesus' acknowledgement of his messiahship to the Samaritan woman at the well is one example of this (Jn.4:26).

13 *Primary School Curriculum Introduction*, Government Publications, 1999, p.9.

14 Lodge & Lynch, *Diversity*, p.54.

15 Rules 68 and 69 for national schools deal with the issue of religion.

Brief Chronology of
Religious Education in Ireland

• •

1529	Martin Luther's Small Catechism
1545–1563	The Council of Trent.
1566	*The Roman Catechism* prescribed by Trent is used in the teaching of Catholic clergy.
1608	The printing of Bonaventure O'Hussey's Irish language catechism *Teagasg Críosdaidhe.*
1614	The provincial synod of Armagh prescribes *The Roman Catechism* for Irish clergy.
1660	The Tuam Synod directs that every parish priest should have a copy of *The Roman Catechism.*
c.1775	Butler's catechism is published.
1775	Founding of schools of the Presentation sisters.
1782	The abolition of the penal laws (with certain conditions) with regard to education.
1792	The founding of *The Association for Discountenancing Vice and Promoting the Knowledge and Practice of the Christian Religion.*

1793	The Repeal Act (Penal Laws largely ended).
1798	The Irish Rebellion.
1801	The Act of Union.
1802	Founding of the Presentation Brothers' schools.
1802	Founding of the Christian Brothers' schools.
1802	Revision of Butler's catechism.
1822	Founding of the Sisters of Loretto schools.
1824–5	Establishment of the Commission on Education in Ireland to survey the work of bodies involved in Irish education. It recommends that two teachers, one Roman Catholic and one Protestant, be appointed to each school.
1827	Founding of the Sisters of Mercy schools.
1829	Catholic Emancipation.
	October 31, 1831, the Chief Secretary of Ireland, Edward G. Stanley (1799-1869) writes his famous letter to the Duke of Leinster, outlining the principles upon which a new National Education system of education should be established.
1835	Announcement that the national system of education will be spearheaded by thirty two model or flagship interdenominational schools. In reality all thirty two schools were not established.
1838	Denominational religious instruction is allowed in national schools during the official school day.

1840	A local Bishop or clergyman from each denomination can apply to become a patron of a mixed interdenominational school. The patron appoints a manager and the manager appoints the teacher.
1841	Pope Gregory XVI exhorts Catholics to support national systems of education.
1845–c.1851	The great famine.
1850	The Synod of Thurles condemns the state system of mixed education.
1860	The Catholic bishops ban all Catholic children and teachers from attending interdenominational model schools and training colleges.
1869–70	Vatican I.
1870	Education Act introduces a national system of education in England.
1875	The founding of St. Patrick's Training College for men in Dublin under the direct auspices of the Archbishop of Dublin.
1878	Intermediate Education Act prohibits examinations in religion at secondary level. It also includes a conscience clause which governs all schools and gives parents the right to withdraw children from denominational religious instruction of which they did not approve.
1882	A further revision of Butler's catechism subsequently known as the 'Maynooth Catechism'.

1883	Government recognition of Our Lady of Mercy Training College for women teachers, Baggot Street, Dublin, subsequently known as Carysfort College.
1883	Government recognition of the Church of Ireland Training College in Kildare Place, Dublin.
1883	Government recognition of denominational training colleges.
1891	Opening of the De la Salle Brother's teacher training college in Waterford.
1898	Opening of Mary Immaculate College, the Mercy Sisters' training college in Limerick.
1900	Opening of St Mary's, Dominican sister's training college in Belfast.
1900	Adoption of a new Revised Programme for National Schools.
1905	Founding by the Christian Brothers of St Mary's, Marino, a teacher training college for Christian Brothers.
1916	Easter Rising.
6 December 1921	Signing of the Treaty.
17 March 1922	Irish becomes an obligatory subject in all national schools and children are obliged to study it for at least one hour each day.
6 December 1922	The Free State comes into being.
1924	Establishment of the Department of Education to co-ordinate primary, secondary and technical education under the one Minister for Education.

1925	Department of Education recognises St Mary's, Marino which is now called Coláiste Mhuire, Marino.
1929	The introduction of a voluntary Primary Certificate examination to assess primary children's competence in a range of subject areas.
1934	Ireland's first Jewish national school, Zion national school, opens in Bloomfield Avenue, South Circular Road, Dublin under the management of the Dublin Talmud Torah.
1936	Jungmann's text *The Good News, Yesterday and Today* outlines the Kerygmatic approach to Catechesis.
1937	The Irish Constitution outlines the basic rights of all Irish citizens. Article 42 concerns education while Article 44 concerns religion.
1943	Founding of Maria Assumpta College, by the Dominican Sisters in Sion Hill, Dublin, otherwise known as Froebel College.
1943	The Primary Certificate examination, which focuses on 'the three R's', becomes compulsory for all children in sixth standard.
1949	Ireland becomes a Republic.
1953	Founding of Stratford College by members of the Dublin Jewish Community. (Now a post-primary, co-educational, multi-denominational school with a distinct Jewish ethos.)

1962–1965	Second Vatican Council.
1971	Primary School Curriculum.
1972	First lay students begin to train as teachers at Coláiste Mhuire.
1973	Development of the first National Catechetical Programme, the *Children of God* series.
1978	The founding of the Dalkey School Project marks the beginning of Ireland's multi-denominational primary school sector.
1980	Relocation of Jewish national school to the site of Stratford College, Rathgar and change of name from Zion national school to Stratford national school.
1983 to 1987	Maura Hyland engages in a *second* presentation of the original *Children of God* series.
1988	Closing of Carysfort College, Dublin.
1 September 1990	The first Muslim national school in Ireland, established by the Islamic Foundation of Ireland, opens at the Islamic Foundation's offices on the South Circular Road, Dublin.
January 1993	The Muslim national school moves to Roebuck Road, Clonskeagh, Dublin.
1993	Founding of An Foras Patrúnachta with the aim of establishing Gaelscoileanna. An Foras is patron to catholic (with a small 'c'), interdenominational and multidenominational schools.
1994	English translation of *Catechism of the Catholic Church*.

1996–2004	The *re*-presentation of the National Catechetical Programme results in the *Alive-O* series.
1998	Education Act.
1998	Founding of the National Consultative Committee on Racism and Interculturalism, known as NCCRI.
1999	Primary School Curriculum.
2000	Post-primary religious education syllabus is introduced as part of the Junior cycle programme.
2000	The Weekend Islamic School opens in Dublin to provide regular Islamic education (Arabic, Qur'an and Religious Studies) for children who do not receive Islamic education in their local schools.
2001	Opening of Ireland's second Muslim national school, North Dublin Muslim School, in the Navan Road, Cabra, Dublin.
2001	*Follow Me* Series is launched edited by Jacqui Wilkinson and developed by the Church of Ireland, Methodist and Presbyterian Boards of Education based on the *Alive O* series.
2001	Establishment of National Council for Curriculum and Assessment.
2002	Founding of the Evening Qur'anic School which teaches Qur'an for children from the age of four and up.
2002	The 'Dunboyne' controversy concerning sacramental preparation in an inter-denominational school.

2003	First examination of the Junior Cycle religious education programme and in September 2003 the introduction of the religious education syllabus for Leaving Certificate.
2004	Parish based Sacramental Programme *Do This in Memory* is launched.
2004	Launch of *Learn Together* the Ethical Education Curriculum for Educate Together schools.
2005	Launch of the Teaching Council in Ireland.
2005	United Nations Committee on the Convention on the Elimination of all Forms of Racial Discrimination (CERD) encourages the state to promote the establishment of non-denominational and multi-denominational schools.
2005	Guidelines on Intercultural Education.
2005	First examination of the Leaving Certificate religious education programme.

GL●SSARY

• •

Aesthetic: that which concerns the appreciation or criticism of things perceptible by the senses, particularly that which is beautiful or tasteful. Aesthetics is that branch of philosophy concerned with the study of such concepts as beauty, form and taste.

Affective: concerned with the emotions or affection.

Apostolic: used to describe the way in which the whole Church shares the faith of the first apostles and communicates that faith. Apostolicity includes such elements as service, witness, suffering and struggle. Apostolic succession is understood within the broader context of apostolicity and describes a relationship between the first apostles and the bishops. As successors to the first apostles, the bishops have the authority to communicate the Lord Jesus by safeguarding the teachings handed down from the apostles.

Catechesis: Catechesis describes the educational process whereby the good news of the Gospel is announced and the faith of the Church is handed on to believers in the Church community. Catechesis presumes an initial conversion and openness to ongoing conversion. Through the experience of learning about the faith, liturgy, morality and prayer, 'catechesis prepares the Christian to live in community and to participate actively in the life and mission of the Church' (GDC 86).

Catholicism: The basic meaning of the term is universality, comprehensiveness. Historically Catholicism has come to mean the traditions, practices, way of life, beliefs, institutional structures, worship and moral standards of Christian communities which maintain full communion with the church of Rome. Sometimes the term 'catholicism' is used more broadly to include Anglican and other churches whose traditions are close to the church of Rome.

Catholicity: as applied to the Church, means the universal reconciling ministry of the Church to all people in every place and time. This attribute of universality and inclusiveness is God's gift whereby the Catholic Church constantly strives to unite the whole of humanity under Christ in the unity of the Spirit.

Contemplative Prayer: This is a form of prayer where one quietens and stills the mind and body so as to communicate with God in the silence and depth of one's own heart. Contemplative prayer enables us to see and respond to God's purposes in the world.

Confessional: Confessional religious education usually indicates instruction in particular beliefs to the exclusion of all others. Some argue however that confessionalism need not imply a limited denominational objective, but merely the intentional nurturing of a particular religious commitment.

Conversion: Describes the opening of a human person to God's love. It literally means 'to turn around' or 'to change direction'. It is a turning away from sin and selfishness and a re-orientation of one's desires, thought processes and actions towards God. Conversion occurs at different levels within the person: physical, spiritual, emotional, intellectual and/ or moral.

Curriculum: describes any programme of study or training. A distinction can be made between curriculum as content (what needs to be studied) and curriculum as process (educational activities that are valued.

Denominational schools: schools that uphold a specific religious ethos. In a denominational school faith is lived and all education is carried out in the context of a distinct religious world-view. Nevertheless, denominational schools should be places where the belief and practices of other faiths are respected. While pupils in these schools are not necessarily expected to make a faith commitment, the school does offer pupils opportunities to develop spiritually and morally in the context of a distinct religious tradition.

Diversity: an umbrella category which acknowledges and values a plurality of ethnic, cultural, gender, religious and faith groups and which also recognises and supports variety of ability, as well as linguistic difference.

Doctrine: The term 'doctrine' refers to what the Church believes, teaches and confesses. Church doctrines are those aspects of Christian teaching which faithfully interpret the meaning of the words and deeds of Christ. (e.g., the doctrines of God, Christ, the Holy Spirit and Salvation).

Ecclesiology: that branch of theology which reflects on the Church as the assembly of the people of God and as a community of worshippers. The Church was often used in versions of the scriptures to translate the Greek word *ekklesia* – a convocation, or assembly.

Ecumenism: refers to the principle, aim or movement towards the unity of different Christian denominations worldwide, overcoming all differences of doctrines.

Ethos: describes the characteristic beliefs, values, spirit, and attitudes of a people or community. This ethic becomes the norm for behaviour, reactions, decisions and approaches to people and events. The way of being and acting inspired by the Catholic religious tradition can be termed a Catholic ethos.

Evangelisation: describes the entire work of the Church to proclaim the 'Good News' of Jesus Christ and the reign of God. Evangelisation is the call to conversion. The heart of evangelization is a proper grasp of the notion of salvation. A truly effective proclamation of the gospel should lead to ongoing conversion among those already committed to the reign of God.

Evangelism: is the preaching or proclamation of the gospel. It is derived from the Greek word *euaggelion*, which is translated as 'Good News'. It usually describes the proclamation of the gospel to those outside of the Church. It can however describe the creation of any educational experiences within which people can discover the gospel for themselves.

Faith education: A program aimed at developing the whole person through an integration of faith and life and culture. The religious education programme of the Catholic school is just one element of a larger faith education which includes the school's ethos and its entire educational programme.

Feminism is a term that describes a complex movement which seeks to critique and confront the devaluation of women in all aspects of life, to eliminate sexism, and to generate an egalitarian society.

Fundamentalism: A religious and social movement characterised by a conservative, traditional world-view and dogmatic cognitive style. Fundamentalists emphasise authority and orthodox belief, opposing any form of religious and cultural liberalism. They are opposed to contemporary liberal approaches in various fields (e.g. morality) and most reject contemporary scientific theories (e.g evolutionary theory is rejected as incompatible with the biblical account of creation in Genesis). Many fundamentalists reject some of the ethical and political values of modernity such as individual rights, pluralism, a democratic ethos, and a trust in public reason. Finally, fundamentalists will adopt a conservative interpretation of biblical texts. They reject much of the modern interpretative approaches to the bible such as historical, source, textual, redaction and literary criticism.

Gender: Gender is a social construct that is culturally determined. It refers to social expectations, power relationships, and cultural-linguistic constructions associated with the female and male sex.

Grace: refers to God's loving kindness and favour toward human beings. Grace is the gift of God's own self (love) outside the Trinity. The whole of creation exists because of this gift of grace and so we can say that grace is everywhere. Every person has the vocation and capacity – by God's grace—to become like God. This orientation to God is a gift beyond the proportions of human nature in that God moves human beings to be open and faithful to God-self. Finally, this gift of grace can be accepted or rejected by the person.

Holistic: attending to the whole person and to his/ her capacities for full human development. A holistic understanding of the person includes his/her physical, intellectual, affective, aesthetic, spiritual, moral and religious development. A holistic approach to religious education pays attention to the cognitive, affective and behavioural aspects of religious faith.

Humanisation: refers to the process of 'human becoming'. While every person conceived is a human being there is potential in human life to grow and develop and so become more fully human. One can also act in ways which damage one's basic humanity, thus becoming dehumanised.

Humanism: any system of thought or action which is concerned only with the concerns of the human race in general and which does not make reference to the divine.

Identity: That which defines the person at all times and in all places. Individuality, personality.

Ideology: a systematic scheme of ideas or a theory usually relating to politics or society that is used to justify actions. An educational ideology is a speculative ideal that may be found at the basis of an educational theory. All approaches to curriculum design and delivery are underpinned by an ideology, i.e., a particular set of beliefs and assumptions about learners and the goals and processes of learning. This ideology may be explicitly or implicitly adopted and maintained.

Incarnation: A doctrine that expresses the Christian belief that God became human in the person of Jesus of Nazareth. The incarnation is the revelation of what it means to be a human being and of the profound dignity of human personhood. The incarnation teaches that it is in striving to become fully human that we become like the God who created us. This is because God has chosen to become one like us in all things but sin.

Indoctrination: The concept of religious education as indoctrination has to do with instruction in a body of doctrine in an irrational way, i.e. without critical reflection, examination and evaluation. Indoctrinators attempt to conceal the controversial status of their beliefs and doctrines and want their subjects to adhere to them without question. Indoctrination has overtones of compulsion and is therefore detrimental to the freedom and dignity of the person.

Inter-denominational education: In the Irish context this refers to the 'mixed' system of education established by the Stanley letter (1831) in which Anglican, Catholic and Presbyterian children were jointly educated for secular subjects in the national school system. More recently An Foras Patrúnachta (1993) established inter-denominational schools where children from two separate religious denominations within the Christian tradition i.e. Church of Ireland and Catholic, were co-jointly educated for all curricular areas including religious education. Within this inter-denominational confessional approach Catholic children are also prepared for the sacraments by the school.

Inter-religious education: the practice of providing children with accurate, respectful, up to date information about the beliefs and practices of world faith communities so that they can deepen their understanding and appreciation of their own faith as well as the faith of others.

Liberation theology: represents a social movement and an approach to theology that emerged principally in Latin America in the late 1960's. It focuses mainly on the social agenda that comes from study of the social gospel of Jesus Christ and God's preferential option for the poor. Today it describes all theologies in which reflection about God emphasises God's desire to free people from suffering and oppression. This kind of reflection emerges from the actual involvement of Christians as they try to do God's will in the world.

Magisterium: A term associated with the teaching role and authority of the hierarchy. It often refers to the body of men who exercise this office in the Church; namely, the pope and bishops. The magisterium is endowed with authority to teach and interpret the gospel message in the name of Jesus Christ.

Mass media culture: Mass Media culture is the term for a culture that is permeated by images, artefacts, music, symbols, ideas which are produced by commercial industries and conveyed primarily through mechanisms such as radio, film, television, supermarket magazines and so on.

Misogyny: is the hatred of women as well as the systematic devaluation of women on the basis of their perceived intellectual inferiority, their emotional instability and their physical weakness.

Moral theology: is that branch of theology that reflects on the moral life in the light of revelation. Christian moral theology explores what it means to be moral as a Christian.

Multi-denominational Education: In the Irish educational context this refers to Educate Together schools which provide equal right of access to children of all social, religious, ethnic and cultural backgrounds and where no one religious tradition is endorsed above all others. Multi-denominational schools are co-educational, child-centred and democratic. In the multi-denominational sector religious education is replaced with an ethical education curriculum.

Original Sin: This is a doctrine which explains the human propensity to sin which is a constitutive dimension of the human condition. The Church has always taught that this predisposition to sin cannot be understood apart from the sin of Adam, a sin in which the whole human race is implicated. To be human is to have lost one's original holiness and so to be in need of redemption by Christ.

Paradigm: A pattern, model, exemplar, or example. Often used to describe a general conception of the nature of a research field or scientific endeavour. For example, Copernicus had a heliocentric worldview whereas Aristotle had a geocentric world view.

Parochialism: tendency to confine one's interests to a narrow sphere, with indifference to the world outside. Local narrowness of view; petty provincialism.

Patriarchy: the view that the male is legitimate, superior and normative.

Pedagogy: the art or science of teaching.

Pluralism: the proposal that there is an irreducible number of reasonable values and conceptions of what constitutes the good life. A pluralist society is one in which there is a variety of different beliefs and meaning systems (interpretations of reality), cultures, and religions.

Popular culture: Popular culture describes cultural activities or products which are enjoyed by many people in Western culture, for example, pop music, Harry Potter, The Lord of the Rings, and McDonalds.

Post-Christian feminism: is that aspect of feminism which views the Hebrew and Christian texts and the Christian theological tradition as being so patriarchal and misogynistic that they are judged to be iredeemeably sexist. Consequently leading proponents of post-Christian feminism have abandoned the Christian tradition in favour of a new spirituality and theology.

Post-modernists: those who see that no one world view, religious, political or economic system can be regarded as universally true with the consequence that there are only fragmentary, diverse, provisional and competing understandings of the world.

Post-modernism: is a wide ranging term which largely involves the rejection of all grand narratives, ideologies and belief systems that claim to explain human existence and to be universally true. It is characterised by an acceptance of diversity, pluralism, uncertainty, ambiguity and the need to constantly re-evaluate the known.

Pre-evangelisation: The stage or process of preparing the potential believer through raising the non-believer's interest and thoughtfulness about life and awakening a sense of the religious dimension of life. Pre-evangelisation is also understood as the initial step in evangelisation.

Proselytism: the deliberate attempt to convert members of one faith or religious tradition to another faith or religious tradition.

Psychology of Religion: that branch of science that uses psychological categories of thought and research methodologies to explore those human beliefs, experiences, and behaviours associated with the divine or with other systems of ultimate meaning in given cultures.

Redemption is the central category of Christian theology to explain the salvation brought about through the life, death and resurrection of Jesus as the Christ. The word 'redemption' literally means a buying back. Redemption is liberation from a state of sin, oppression, death, evil and darkness to a state of freedom, transformation, new birth, life and light. It describes the way in which the life, death and resurrection of Jesus Christ has saved the world. Redemption continues to be experienced by Christians as a liberation from sin, death, oppression, and the powers of evil.

Reign of God: The coming of the reign of God was the main focus of Jesus' mission and preaching. It is the central theological symbol for understanding his ministry. As a symbol the reign of God suggests God's saving power in history. As a metaphor it expresses God's promise of peace and justice, love and freedom, of fullness of life for all. While the ultimate consummation of the reign of God will bring about a profound transformation of all human reality, the inbreaking of that reality has already begun through the mission of Jesus. The Spirit of the risen Christ enables people to respond to God's offer of salvation and to be affected by it now, within history.

Relativism: A name given to theories or doctrines that truth, morality, and world-views are relative to situations and are not absolute. All paths to truth, goodness and beauty are affirmed as equally valuable. Relativism may also refer to the idea that there are no objective standards by which to evaluate cultures or religions as these cannot be understood except from the point of view of their own values.

Religious Education: is the educational process by which people are invited to explore the human religious traditions that protect and illuminate the religious dimension of their lives. Religious education invites people to acquire the knowledge, forms of knowing, attitudes, values, skills and sensibilities that being religious involves. It also invites people to think critically about religion: to study religion objectively from a distance, and to examine their own religion in relation to other religious and non-religious options.

Religious Instruction: A term used in Church documents to describe the academic study of the Christian religion in schools. The aim of such religious instruction is the facilitation of better understanding of the teaching of Christ and the Church. Furthermore, religious instruction helps students to relate the knowledge and values offered by other scholastic disciplines to the gospel. Religious instruction contributes to catechetical formation. However, religious instruction can be distinguished from catechesis in that it does not require a faith commitment in principle. It should promote genuine understanding of the Christian religion among baptised and non-baptised students alike.

Religious Knowing: may best be described as thinking in religious language. The person uses the forms of religious language (e.g., symbol, metaphor, poetry, prayer) to receive and construct meaning. Religious knowing is primarily an affective, behavioural mode of knowing. In other words, to 'know' religiously is to integrate religious insights into one's way of being and acting in the world. The ability to use religious language in this way is deeply rooted in the imagination.

Religious Knowledge: describes knowledge *about* religion, i.e., conceptual knowledge of religious facts, stories, beliefs, doctrine and theology. Religious knowledge is concerned with the *content* of religious knowing. This content can be quite literal or factual in the case of a small child.

Revelation: Revelation (from the Latin *revelare*, 'to remove the veil') is God's *self*-revelation to us. God has revealed and continues to reveal God-self and God's deepest desires for fullness of life to us. The central sign of Christian revelation is the life, death and resurrection of Jesus (the Paschal Mystery). Today revelation comes to us through concrete actions and symbols in history (e.g the sacraments) and in our daily lives.

Sacramental principle: The sacramental principle means that our communication with God is not direct but is mediated by the created world. God comes to us as a creative, healing, transforming power through the ordinary experiences and things of life – through our minds and bodies, through our relationships and friendships, through our experiences and activities, through nature and the whole created order. Since God holds everything in being, grace must be expressed, noticed, accepted and celebrated in *specific* times and places. Persons, things, places, events and actions that cause us to notice the presence of God are called sacraments.

Salvation: refers to the good news that God chose to become one of us so that we might recognise and respond to the goodness of creation. In action terms salvation refers to a healing, a bringing to health or a making whole and well. The salvation brought about through Jesus is healing from everything that oppresses human beings. While the primary salvation needed is from personal sin Jesus also brings about salvation from the social effects of sin in society. See redemption.

Sectarian: A narrow-minded and excessive attachment to a particular religion or religious group. Intolerance of other religious and nonreligious groups.

Secularism: The doctrine that religion has no place in morality or ethics. Human values alone are considered important and the transcendent dimension of life is not acknowledged. Secularism may also refer to the attitude that religion should have no place in the civic life of a nation.

Self-transcendence: overcoming of the limits of the individual self and its desires in a movement towards other people, the world, and some source of Ultimate Transcendence (e.g., God). True self-transcendence necessitates a proper love of self and regard for one's own unique identity, loved by God. The experience of self-transcendence supports the gospel's view that we become our true selves as we move beyond ourselves in an attempt to realize the good of others.

Sexism: Discrimination on the basis of sex, especially the oppression of women by men.

Spirituality: describes the overall meaning and direction of a human life. It is the way in which we pursue truth and goodness by relating to the reality of ourselves, other people, the universe and some source of transcendent value (e.g., God). For Christians the overall meaning and direction of one's life is lived in relationship to God, in Christ Jesus, empowered by the Spirit.

Theology: (from the Greek *theos*, "God" and *logos*, "meaning") describes the study of the experience of God, from within a community of faith, as that experience impacts the past, present and future. In its broadest sense, as an ordered body of knowledge about God, theology comprises a number of sciences: biblical theology, ecclesiology, liturgical theology, moral theology, pastoral theology, pneumatology, mariology, and eschatology. Some feminist theologians speak of *'thealogy'* derived from the feminine word for god *'theas'* to indicate a female-centred activity that involves females reflecting upon God.

Tradition: refers to the ways in which the Church community interprets the content of its faith, i.e. God's revelation in Jesus Christ. It is the living interpretation in history of the Christian scriptures which are recognised by the Church as inspired guides to the data of salvation history and the mystery that

God wishes to reveal. 'Tradition' may refer therefore to liturgies, creeds, dogmas, doctrines, and theologies, sacraments, rituals, symbols, myths, gestures, and religious language patterns, spiritualities, values, laws, ethical principles, songs, music, dance, drama, art, architecture, stories of holy people, Church structures and forms of governance, and so on. The core of this tradition is the offer of an encounter with the person of Jesus Christ and his 'good news of salvation'.

Transcendence: the attribute of being above and independent of the universe and of merely physical human experience. Transcendence describes that which cannot be grasped or fully understood by human beings, and which goes beyond the limitations of our human reality. To encounter transcendence is to be invited to explore Mystery. Christians have always stressed the transcendence of God as God is 'other than' the world. God is available to human experience but God also radically transcends the limitations of our human reality. God is not subject to the limitations of the material universe and cannot be fully grasped in human thought.

The Transcendent: refers to one who or that which is exalted and distinct from the universe. It also describes that which is altogether beyond the bounds of human cognition or thought. 'The transcendent' is sometimes used to describe whatever people understand to be eminently great or good, i.e., the source of ultimate value in peoples' lives.

Trinity: A doctrine which refers to the divine Mystery as experienced and expressed in the language of Christian worship and proclamation. Trinity refers to the Mystery of God the Father, the Son, and Holy Spirit. This Mystery is best understood as a relationship of self-giving love.

Virtue: describes a particular moral excellence. Moral virtues include honesty, tolerance, fair-mindedness, courage, persistence, consideration, and patience. The cardinal virtues are prudence, justice, fortitude, and temperance. The theological virtues are faith, hope and charity.

Worldview: One's view of life, an important aspect of which is one's view of what is of ultimate concern and of ultimate value.

INDEX